COMPUTATIONAL POWER

We delegate more and more decisions and tasks to artificial agents, machine-learning mechanisms and algorithmic procedures or, in other words, to computational systems. Not that we are driven by powerful ambitions of colonizing the Moon, replacing humans with legions of androids, creating sci-fi scenarios *à la The Matrix* or masterminding some sort of *Person of Interest*-like Machine. No, the current digital revolution based on computational power is chiefly an everyday revolution.

It is therefore that much more profound, unnoticed and widespread, for it affects our customary habits and routines and alters the very texture of our day-to-day lives. This opens a precise line of inquiry, which constitutes the basic thesis of the present text: our computational power is exercised by trying to adapt not just the world but also our representation of reality as to how computationally based ICTs work. The impact of this technology is such that it does not leave things as they are: it changes the nature of agents, habits, objects and institutions and hence it subverts the existing order, without necessarily generating a new one.

I argue that this power is often not distributed in an egalitarian manner but, on the contrary, is likely to result in concentrations of wealth, in dominant positions or in unjust competitive advantages. This opens up a struggle, with respect to which the task of reaffirming the fundamental values, the guiding principles, the priorities and the rules of the game, which can transform, or attempt to transform, a fierce confrontation between enemies in a fair competition between opponents rests on us.

Massimo Durante is Professor in Philosophy of Law and Legal Informatics at the Department of Law, University of Turin, Italy. He is coordinator of the Turin Unit of Research for the Law, Science and Technology Joint Doctorate: Rights of the Internet of Everything. His current research concerns issues of law and technology and digital governance from a legal, ethical and epistemological perspective.

ANTINOMIES
Innovations in the Humanities, Social Sciences and Creative Arts
Series Editor: Anthony Elliott
Hawke Research Institute, University of South Australia

This Series addresses the importance of innovative contemporary, comparative and conceptual research on the cultural and institutional contradictions of our times and our lives in these times. *Antinomies* publishes theoretically innovative work that critically examines the ways in which social, cultural, political and aesthetic change is rendered visible in the global age, and that is attentive to novel contradictions arising from global transformations. Books in the Series are from authors both well-established and early careers researchers. Authors will be recruited from many, diverse countries – but a particular feature of the Series will be its strong focus on research from Asia and Australasia. The Series addresses the diverse signatures of contemporary global contradictions, and as such seeks to promote novel transdisciplinary understandings in the humanities, social sciences and creative arts.

The Series Editor is especially interested in publishing books in the following areas that fit with the broad remit of the series:

- New architectures of subjectivity
- Cultural sociology
- Reinvention of cities and urban transformations
- Digital life and the post-human
- Emerging forms of global creative practice
- Culture and the aesthetic

Subverting Consumerism
Reuse in an Accelerated World
Edited by Robert Crocker and Keri Chiveralls

Understanding Tourism Mobilities in Japan
Edited by Hideki Endo

Computational Power
The impact of ICT on law, society, and knowledge
Massimo Durante

The Algorithmic Unconscious
How Psychoanalysis Helps in Understanding AI
Luca M. Possati

For a full list of titles in this series, please visit www.routledge.com/Antinomies/book-series/ANTIMN.

COMPUTATIONAL POWER

The Impact of ICT on Law, Society and Knowledge

Massimo Durante

Routledge
Taylor & Francis Group

LONDON AND NEW YORK

First published 2021
by Routledge
2 Park Square, Milton Park, Abingdon, Oxon OX14 4RN

and by Routledge
52 Vanderbilt Avenue, New York, NY 10017

Routledge is an imprint of the Taylor & Francis Group, an informa business

© 2019 - M ELTEM I PRESS SRL

Original title: Massimo Durante, Potere computazionale

British Library Cataloguing in Publication Data
A catalogue record for this book is available from the British Library

Library of Congress Cataloging-in-Publication Data
A catalog record has been requested for this book

ISBN: 978-0-367-56623-4 (hbk)
ISBN: 978-0-367-56624-1 (pbk)
ISBN: 978-1-003-09868-3 (ebk)

Typeset in Bembo
by Taylor & Francis Books

We know that no one ever seizes power with the intention of relinquishing it.

–George Orwell, 1984

CONTENTS

ACKNOWLEDGMENTS

This book is the brainchild of Maria Rosaria Taddeo, so my first warm thanks must go to her. Without her initial input and inspiration, I would never have undertaken this project. My sincere thanks also go to Giovanni Boniolo for generously welcoming the original version of the book into his series "Filosofia della scienza e dintorni" by Meltemi, as well as to Anthony Elliott for generously welcoming the present version of the book into his series "Antinomies" by Routledge. The reflections expressed within are the result of the long-standing dialogue and exchange of ideas with two dear friends, Ugo Pagallo and Luciano Floridi, whose valuable suggestions for improving the manuscript are gratefully acknowledged. Many of the examples and topics in the book were put to the test by a most exacting audience: my students. My thoughts on the subject of privacy and data protection were largely developed in the context of a series of lectures I held for the *Master in Personal Data Protection Law for DPO*. I would therefore like to thank Sergio Foà and Franco Pizzetti, who are respectively the director and the founder of this Turin-based MA program. My analysis of the impact of the Internet and digital ICT has naturally taken advantage of the valuable theoretical work carried out at the *Nexa Center on Internet & Society* in Turin, where I am honored to be a fellow, and a big thank you goes out to the co-directors and founders of the Center, Juan Carlos de Martin and Marco Ricolfi. I am also indebted to my co-fellows and friends at the Nexa Center for the many long and fruitful conversations we have had together: Eleonora Bassi, Carlo Blengino, Marco Ciurcina, Giancarlo Ruffo, Monica Senor and Massimo Travostino. Paola Aurucci and Jacopo Ciani have provided helpful ideas, advice and support. Further thanks go to Ludovica Paseri, with whom I discussed the basic thesis of the book and for her help in revising the manuscript, as well as to Laura McLean for her precious linguistic revision. The PhD program in "Law, Science and Technology", where I serve on the faculty, has provided an arena for helpful discussion of critical ideas, considerations and analysis, and I would like to thank my colleagues

Pompeu Casanovas, Mark Cole, Guido Boella, Michele Graziadei, Monica Palmirani and Giovanni Sartor. The section on the governance of algorithms arose from two different experiences: co-editing a special issue of *Philosophy & Technology* with Marcello D'agostino and holding a recent research seminar as part of the *Winter Academy on Artificial Intelligence and International Law* at the Asser Institute in The Hague. I am grateful to all of the many other people, too numerous to count, who have contributed the germs of ideas along the way. Many of those ideas have grown and taken shape and are now found scattered throughout these pages. The errors and weaknesses, however, are my own. Such flaws are part of what makes a book unique. I would like to dedicate this book to a special person who has helped and encouraged me, and whose steadfast presence and influence in my life sweeps the clouds away and brightens my horizons.

FOREWORD

Computational life, it seems, is increasingly expansive, at once everywhere and hidden. There is a widespread perception that life these days is rapidly accelerating – thanks to the intersecting forces of artificial intelligence (AI), advanced robotics, intensifying automation and the ubiquity of Big Data. We hear constant laments regarding digitalization – that the pace of life is spiraling out of control; that women and men are drowning in information overload; that lifestyle change is increasingly impacted by smart algorithms; that working life is reshaped and transformed by automated intelligent machines in industry and the service sector; and that politics and collective democratic life are increasingly overdetermined by digitized surveillance systems.

Massimo Durante, a most insightful analyst of contemporary socio-political, legal and ethical practices in the age of AI, has noticed a remarkable change of vocabulary and cognitive frame that marks our lives and our lives in these times of accelerating digitalization. Ours is the age of what Durante calls "computational power" which is "rooted in daily life" as part of an "everyday revolution", and which "refers not only to the quantitatively impressive growth and spread of data processing capabilities" but, even more fundamentally, to the very "way we interact and shape our world". Computational power lies at the core of our ever-increasing interaction with non-human agents and mobile devices; it is a form of power constitutive of both world adaptation as well as the reproduction and transformation of representations of reality. I particularly cherished the opportunity to learn from Durante regarding the likely trajectories that "machines, devices and artificial agents will continue to operate on the basis of computational systems that possess *their own* representation and model of the world". Technological programming of the vocabulary of the word's narrative in a manner that allows nothing but technological ends, actions and the "technological fix" dates back to the brilliant insights of Jacques Ellul. Technology, Ellul convincingly demonstrated, has become its own legitimation. Durante raises this insight to the second power, capturing the dynamics of computational power as a self-reinforcing system which is truly self-perpetuating and self-propagating. Durante also has politically urgent things to say regarding the redesign, recalibration, restructuring and reinvention of existing forms of life (social, cultural, political, juridical, ethical) against the backdrop of computational power.

That contemporary social theory and modern European philosophy would turn back to consider its origins in the contradictions of *technics* and pervasive technology was perhaps predictable; but little could have prepared us for Durante's remarkable confrontation with the entire philosophical and ontological sweep of the digital revolution. I regard this book as of the highest importance, and think it will be indispensable to sociologists, social theorists, philosophers and cultural analysts for years to come.

Anthony Elliott
Series Editor
Adelaide, October 2020

INTRODUCTION

Computational power

As human beings, we process data (inputs) and transform that data into results (outputs). In so doing, we exercise our *computational power*. Making decisions or acting in the world requires us first to know and represent reality. If not, our decisions and actions would be the result of blind decision-making and behavioral processes – we would be taking a stab in the dark, so to speak. This applies as much to us as to every other agent capable of decision-making and acting (or at least interacting) with the environment, including animals, plants, robots and any other computational system that processes inputs and generates outputs. Obviously, each computational system has its own way of doing things, which depends on its distinctive knowledge and representation of the world as well as on its computing capacity. For example, while human beings are passably fair syntactic engines on the one hand, we are excellent semantic engines on the other hand. In other words, we can perform calculations reasonably well, but what sets us apart is our extremely complex and sophisticated ability to endow things with meaning and to make sense of our world and of our lives. By contrast, while robots and other computational systems are superb syntactic engines (whose extraordinary capacity for calculation often exceeds our own), they have only rudimentary (if not proto-) semantic capabilities. Take a complex activity, such as playing chess. While chess normally calls on the semantic skills of its (human) players, supercomputers apply a purely syntactic strategy to the game, calculating the odds of their opponents' moves and proving virtually unbeatable. However, this should not be taken as a sign of some prodigious form of intelligence, but rather as the outcome of extraordinary computational power. What this means – and this is the most interesting point – is that when we play chess against a computer, there are actually *two different games* being played: one that is essentially syntactic on the part of the computer, and another that is essentially semantic on the part of the human.

In the world we are building, a multitude of agents is tasked with making decisions, working, acting and interacting, each according to its own unique computational power. This is not so unusual, for human beings have always tended to delegate decisions and tasks to other agents. However, vast increases in computational power have made it all the easier for us to do so. We find ourselves delegating more and more decisions and tasks to artificial agents, machine-learning mechanisms, and algorithmic procedures or, in other words, to computational systems. Not that we are driven by powerful ambitions of colonizing the Moon, replacing humans with legions of androids, creating sci-fi scenarios à *la The Matrix* or masterminding some sort of *Person of Interest*-like Machine. No, the revolution based on computational power is chiefly an *everyday revolution*. It is therefore that much more profound, unnoticed and widespread, for it affects our customary habits and routines and alters the very texture of our day-to-day lives. Like all great revolutions, it is rooted in daily life, so it is primarily at this level that its effects should be studied and evaluated. This opens a precise line of inquiry, which constitutes the basic thesis of the present text: our computational power is exercised by adapting (or trying to adapt) not just the world but also our representation of reality to how computationally based information and communication technologies (ICTs) work. This is the implicit claim — not always overt but increasingly put into practice — that we will have to come to terms with in the years to come.

Indeed, this claim raises complex issues of governance that stem from the very nature of computational power itself. The exercise of this power, implemented within a variety of computer systems, entails a progressive adaptation of the environment and transforms the world in ways that have a bearing on a number of increasingly important sectors of society. In addition, it leads to a veritable production of knowledge. This production of knowledge concerns not only the accrual of the knowledge-base that computational systems need to fulfill their tasks (their peculiar representation of reality), but also the representation that these computational systems present of ourselves (their peculiar representation of us). As they venture into city traffic, driverless cars represent reality (the route to their destination) differently from the way we do. Computer algorithms used to profile borrowers least likely to default on their loans rely on different data, and may even differ in their conclusions, from their human counterparts. Software programs designed to screen and rank CVs do not necessarily follow the same logic as a human being performing the same task. The number of representations of the world continues to multiply, thanks to the proliferation of artificial agents or computational systems.

But which representations of the world are going to prevail, and which ones are going to need to adapt? To stick with the previous example, will humans be adapting to driverless cars or vice versa? Will we adapt the environment to driverless cars, perhaps by building preferential or reserved lanes? Or will we ensure that driverless cars adapt to our environment, by providing them with increasingly sophisticated artificial intelligence systems? Will we develop a system that allows human beings to collaborate with driverless cars, letting them intervene in the driving process? Or maybe even one that allows driverless cars to collaborate with one another?

In fact, the first question to arise after delegating decisions and tasks to computational systems is that of how to govern and control the functioning of such systems. We are increasingly left wondering about our ability to truly understand and explain the working of such systems and the consequences of their decisions and actions. Things get even messier if we consider that not only are we delegating practical tasks, but epistemic decisions as well: algorithms carry out research on key terms, select the news we consume, guide our consumer choices, facilitate our memories – or help us to forget, sketch out our online profiles, contribute to telling the story of who we are, reinforce our beliefs, deliver intelligent solutions, reinforce inaccurate perceptions, or, more simply, may lead us up a garden path.

The governance of digital ICTs thus presents us with a significant challenge: How can we regulate the use of computational power that is made possible and realized by ICTs? We might consider trying to govern or maintain forms of control over the particular contexts in which this power is exercised, or over how this power is enacted in concrete practices. That would require the creation of complex institutional arrangements and the ability to forecast the potential secondary effects of our choices of governance, given the growing number of stakeholders involved. In addition to traditional governmental or supra-governmental bodies, a number of new subjects must now also be contended with, such as the private owners of online platforms and service providers. Traditional actors have also started taking on new and different roles, such as the constant production and dissemination of data and information by average Internet users. However, we should be careful not to aim at governing (or at wielding pervasive forms of control over) the production of knowledge: in any democratic state – to mention just one example – telling a lie is not a crime, unless by lying one *also* commits some other criminal offense (such as giving false testimony in court). Entrusting private entities with the task of monitoring the truthfulness of content shared on the Web, by allowing them to remove it *ex post* or even to censor it *ex ante*, is a risky business and could lead to unforeseen consequences. No public entity, let alone a private one, should have a *monopoly* on truth and falsehood, on memory and oblivion, on love and hate.

Computational power is the newest form of power. If data is the *new oil*, then computational power is the well from which it flows. It does not supplant earlier forms of economic, political or informational power, but arms them with new tools and means of expression. Technology has become embedded in our society, and the use of computational power continues to reshape our environment. Computational-based technologies allow us to adapt to this technological environment and to extract from it the energy and resources upon which the individual and collective well-being of information societies ultimately rests. Although this has the potential to lead to widespread improvements in living conditions, it could also accentuate existing inequalities, such that the rich become richer and the poor even poorer, and result in substantially undemocratic (or at least controversial) outcomes. The use of computational power produces new forms of knowledge, and knowledge, as we know, is in turn a form of power. The inherent circularity by which computational power contributes to producing the conditions of its own implementation still needs to be investigated. Technology ceaselessly alters and redesigns the distribution of powers in a society. Even the referees of a football match know that by submitting their evaluations to the *Virtual Assistant Referee* they increase their chances of garnering approval for their decisions, because those decisions are tinted with an aura of objectivity.

We have only just scratched the surface of the intertwining questions and issues that the use of computational power is likely to raise. The arguments contained in this book are by no means a veiled attempt to provide answers to these questions, but are rather intended to shed light on their uncertain boundaries, bearing in mind that the most difficult task in every theoretical undertaking consists in asking the right questions to begin with.

1

THE INFORMATION REVOLUTION

A starting thesis

Some texts are built on an *explicit* thesis and others are built on an *implicit* thesis. In the former, the authors state their thesis and use it as the starting point for their own reflections. In the latter, they let the reader ascertain the underlying thesis of the text. Sometimes, the explicit thesis of a book is nothing but the implicit thesis of another book, as is the case here.

In fact, the explicit thesis of the present book builds on the implicit thesis of another book, *The Fourth Revolution. How the infosphere is reshaping human reality*, by Luciano Floridi[1]. Of course, the responsibility for stating the implicit thesis of that text is ours alone and is subject to critique and revision. Floridi's book is a careful, profound and documented reflection on the complex impact that digital information and communication technologies (ICTs) have on "our sense of the self, how we relate to each other, and how we shape and interact with our world"[2]. More broadly, our book follows and delves into the reflections that the Oxford philosopher has devoted to the subject of the information revolution[3]. According to Floridi, we have entered an age defined as *hyperhistorical*, which is characterized by the peculiar impact of digital ICTs:

> Only very recently has human progress and welfare begun to be not just *related to*, but *mostly dependent on*, the successful and efficient management of the life cycle of information. [...] Prehistory and history work like adverbs: they tell us *how* people live, not *when* or *where* they live. From this perspective, human societies currently stretch across three ages, as a way of living. [...] The greatest majority of people today still live historically, in societies that rely on ICTs to record, transmit, and use data of all kinds. In such historical societies, ICTs have not yet over taken other technologies, especially energy-related ones, in

terms of their vital importance. Then, there are some people around the world who are already living hyperhistorically, in societies and environments where ICTs and their data-processing capabilities are not just important but essential conditions for the maintenance and any further development of societal welfare, personal well-being, and overall flourishing.[4]

The promotion of social well-being, individual growth and general development depend on digital ICTs and their ability to process data, or in other words, on their computational power. The hyperhistorical age distinguishes ICT-dependent societies, whose map of dependencies coincides with its map of opportunities and weaknesses. The impact of digital ICTs invites our attention, for it is more complex than one might imagine at first sight, and there is no immediately available and all-encompassing perspective from which to interpret it:

> The philosopher wonders what lies behind. Is there a unifying perspective from which all these phenomena may be interpreted as aspects of a single, macroscopic trend? Part of the difficulty, in answering this question, is that we are still used to looking at ICTs as tools for interacting with the world and with each other. In fact, they have become environmental, anthropological, social, and interpretative forces. They are creating and shaping our intellectual and physical realities, changing our self-understanding, modifying how we relate to each other and ourselves, and upgrading how we interpret the world, and all this pervasively, profoundly, and relentlessly.[5]

We are getting closer to the implicit thesis of Floridi's book, but are not there yet. We need to make further references to his text, and particularly to the very notion of what the *fourth revolution* actually is. Let us briefly do so. Taking a cue from Freud[6], the Oxford philosopher identifies three stages in the development of humankind's self-understanding, in which the centrality of the human role was increasingly called into question and it was realized that human beings are not the measure of all things. The first revolution, which can be attributed to Copernicus, removed the human being from the center of the universe. As a result of Darwin's theory of evolution, the second revolution removed the human being from the center of the animal kingdom. Finally, the third revolution, which is due to Freud's psychoanalysis or to neuroscience, led to the realization that human beings are not even at the center of their own rationality, or conscious lives. Floridi then presents a fourth revolution[7], which has Alan Turing as its eponymous hero:

> Turing displaced us from our privileged and unique position in the realm of logical reasoning, information processing, and smart behavior. We are no longer the undisputed masters of the infosphere. Our digital devices carry out more and more tasks that would require some thinking from us if we were in charge. We have been forced to abandon once again a position that we thought was "unique".[8]

Floridi insightfully observes that the modern period was witness to a constant and progressive transformation, according to which "thinking was reasoning, reasoning was reckoning, and reckoning could already be done by a Pascalina"[9]. Over time, the idea has emerged that making rational decisions and actions require the ability to calculate and process information, that is to say, to possess computational power. Until the advent of computers, this ability was considered to be the exclusive province of human beings[10]. Nowadays, machines have outstripped us in this regard, thanks to their immense computational power. And this power has gradually been harnessed by those who are able to make use of it and profit from it. As a result, we are delegating an increasing number of decisions and tasks to artificial agents, or more generically, to computational models. These, in turn, tend to adapt the environment in which they operate according to a representation of the world that suits their own functioning, and which is destined to become an integral part of our lives:

> We are increasingly delegating or outsourcing to artificial agents our memories, decisions, routine tasks, and other activities in ways that will be progressively integrated with us. [...] We are regularly outsmarted and outperformed by our ICTs. They "reckon" better than we do. And because of this, they are modifying or creating the environment in which we live. We have begun to understand ourselves as *inforgs* not through some biotechnological transformations in our bodies, but, more seriously and realistically, through the radical transformation of our environment and the agents operating within it.[11]

We can now formulate the implicit thesis of Luciano Floridi's book: computational power is the *engine*[12] that drives current history, which designates the perspective from which to interpret the main features of the impact of digitalization and the information revolution as "aspects of a single macroscopic trend", in Floridi's own words. Let us now take a closer look at some of the key features of this thesis, which constitutes the explicit thesis around which we will try to tie our reflections in the rest of the book.

Computational power

The term "computational power" refers not only to the quantitatively impressive growth and spread of data processing capabilities[13], although this phenomenon is in itself an important element and vehicle of history:

> [...] increasingly more power is available at decreasing costs, to ever more people, in quantities and at a pace that are mindboggling. The limits of computing power seem to be mainly physical. They concern how well our ICTs can dissipate heat and recover from unavoidable hardware faults while becoming increasingly small. This is the rocket that has made humanity travel from history to hyperhistory, to use a previous analogy. It also explains why

ICTs are still disruptive technologies that have not sedimented: new generations keep teaching the old ones how to use them, although they still learn
from previous generations how to drive or use a microwave.[14]

By computational power, we intend to refer more broadly to a qualitative aspect,
according to which the exercise of this power is likely to progressively change the
way we interact and shape our world. This change unfolds in a three-fold direction
that uniquely characterizes our epoch and that concerns: (1) human action; (2) world
adaptation; and (3) the representation of reality.

Firstly, action is no longer the exclusive prerogative of human beings but also
belongs to artificial agents that make decisions and act according to more or less
sophisticated and complex computational models. This involves the outsourcing of
decisions and tasks to artificial agents, which leads to two further consequences.
The first is our ever-increasing interaction with non-human agents and devices:

> At this point, an obvious question is where all this computational power goes.
> It is not that we are regularly putting people on the Moon with our smart-
> phones or tablets. The answer is: interactions, both machine-to-machine and
> human-computer ones, also known as HCI. [...] In human-computer inter-
> actions (HCI), ICTs are used to create, facilitate, and improve communications
> between human users and computational systems. When talking about ICTs, it
> is easy to forget that computers do not compute and telephones do not phone,
> to put it slightly paradoxically. What computers, smartphones, tablets, and all
> the other incarnations of ICTs do is to handle data. We rely on their capacities
> to manage huge quantities of MIPS [millions of instructions per second] much
> less to add numbers or call our friends than to update our Facebook status,
> order and read the latest e-books online, bill someone, buy an airline ticket,
> scan an electronic boarding pass, watch a movie, monitor the inside of a shop,
> drive to a place, or, indeed, almost anything else.[15]

The second consequence, equally relevant and significant, is that the outsourcing of
decisions and tasks to artificial agents and devices based on artificial intelligence (AI)
systems, machine-learning mechanisms, algorithmic procedures or other such
computational models[16] is not intended to take us to the Moon, replace humans
with legions of androids, create sci-fi scenarios or program a *Person of Interest*-like
Machine. The revolution, based on computational power, is above all an *everyday
revolution*. The deeper, more unnoticed and widespread it is, the more this revolution invests the web of our usual habits and practices, that is, our forms of life.
Like all great revolutions, it is rooted in everyday life and it is mainly at this level
that its effects deserve to be investigated and evaluated.

Secondly, it is precisely the pervasiveness of computational power that makes it
necessary for the world to progressively adapt to it. Adaptation of the world to the
functioning of computational models does not take place according to precisely-
made plans, but is rather an *emergent* feature of complex information societies. This

means, as will be better explained below[17], that the development of these societies is influenced primarily by the ability to adapt the environment to technological evolution and to adapt themselves to the technologically reshaped environment. The process of progressive adaptation of the environment is well captured in Floridi's metaphor of an envelope with which we are *enveloping* the world:

> Enveloping used to be either a stand-alone phenomenon (you buy the robot with the required envelope, like a dishwasher or a washing machine) or implemented within the walls of industrial buildings, carefully tailored around their artificial inhabitants. Nowadays, enveloping the environment into an ICT-friendly infosphere has started pervading all aspects of reality and is visible everywhere, on a daily basis. We have been enveloping the world around ICTs for decades without fully realizing it.[18]

After all, since we are still at the beginning of the hyperhistorical era, it makes sense that we are still mainly adapting the world to the functioning of machines, devices and artificial agents, rather than expecting these tools to adapt to the (more difficult to calculate) complexity of our unstructured world. This is somewhat akin to babyproofing one's home by covering sharp corners, installing bed rails and safety gates, and covering electric outlets, rather than expecting the baby to adapt to the existing environment. We instead wait for our babies to develop more mature cognitive faculties. It is here that the analogy ends, because there is no certainty (and actually seems improbable) that computational models will eventually be endowed with cognitive faculties similar to those of humans. It is more likely that machines, devices and artificial agents will continue to operate on the basis of computational systems that possess *their own* representation and model of the world. This brings us to the third and last point.

Thirdly, in fact, we will find ourselves interacting with machines, devices and artificial agents (and more broadly with digital ICTs) operating in an environment that is adapted not only to the way they function, but also on the basis of their peculiar representation of reality. This is one of the main features of the current information revolution based on computational power: the legal, ethical, political and social issues raised by digitization, and especially by the delegation of decisions and tasks to artificial machines, devices and agents will mainly be mediated epistemologically. This means that they will have to be examined and addressed against the backdrop of the specific form of knowledge and representation of reality that characterizes the computational models. To limit ourselves to just one consideration, which we will return to below[19], it is not by chance that an international debate on the recognition of a right to *explanation* has recently emerged, following the entry into force of the GDPR (the new European General Regulation for the Protection of Personal Data[20]). This debate concerns decisions based exclusively on the automated processing of personal data. The law, which finds itself in constant conflict with science, has always claimed to define the *extent to which* an explanation was legally relevant both in terms of causal regression (determining the chain of events of a legally relevant fact) and in terms of prediction (of the legally relevant consequences of the fact in question). An example may perhaps make this clearer.

Let us assume that a person, terrified by the threatening presence of a third party, steals a car and flees, causing an accident. How far does the explanation of law extend? Towards the past: to the threatening presence of the third party? To the fleeing subject's feelings of panic during childhood or genetic inability to cope with feelings of danger? Towards the future: to the theft of the car? To the resulting car accident? To the lost future job opportunities for the victim of the car accident? To the victim's missed holidays resulting from the loss of those opportunities? The law has always independently decided where it intends to interrupt the *legally relevant* retrospective or predictive explanation of an event, fully aware that the human (epistemological) explanation of the causes and consequences of an event do not stop where the legal one does. How can the law regulate an event if it cannot entirely govern where its origins and consequences begin or end?

Other examples are easy to find. The regulation – and associated ethical issues – of driverless cars or of military drones depend to a large extent on how the cars and the drones operate as autonomous artificial agents. This in turn depends on the way in which these agents represent reality. This epistemological aspect becomes all the more important precisely because it is not always easy or possible to adapt the world to the functioning of these agents; while we can conceive of adapting the environment to driverless cars by creating ad hoc lanes, it is much less obvious whether or how the environment could possibly be adapted to a military drone. As shall be seen in the course of the book, humans are called upon not just to compare their representation of the world with that of computational models; they are also an object of their representation. If an algorithmic procedure comes up with a profile of a "good borrower", individuals will struggle between their desire to resist the automated construction of this profile and their interest in being subsumed within it, in a return to "voluntary servitude"[21], albeit under modern guise.

These three directions of change bring to the forefront the inexhaustible issue of power[22], which is more pressing than ever before. We have already touched on the relationship between knowledge and power implied by computational power. From this initial summary examination (which we shall keep coming back to during the course of our discussion) emerges a peculiar concept of power. Here, power is conceived neither from a material standpoint (according to which power consists of a set of means or resources), nor from a relational one (according to which power consists in the ability to determine the will of others, even in the face of opposition, or to establish collective rules and to impose their respect, by virtue of general consent), nor even in metaphysical terms (as a result of privileged properties or positions). Here, computational power is conceived of as the ability to create the conditions of its own enactment. As in Foucault's *Microphysics of power*[23], power is not in principle localizable here or there, nor does it operate according to precisely made plans (through the rigid distinction between those who wield it and those who are subjected to it), but, unlike that form of power, it may be, at least in part, appropriated by all those who are able to make use of it, which has been made collectively possible[24].

A parallel with economic power may perhaps serve to clarify the point. Imagine the case of an individual with immense financial resources in two different scenarios. In the first scenario, buying and selling anything is forbidden: despite the endless possibilities for doing so, the individual cannot exercise their power (not even to circumvent the existing prohibition). In the second, no such prohibition exists: in principle, everything can be bought and sold (with some limited exceptions). In this case, not only can the individual exercise their power, but they can also use it to overcome existing limits (by trying to buy people's favor or attention, bribing them, or attempting to buy things that are not for sale). Here, power is exercised not only in its own right, but also to build (or strengthen) the conditions favoring its exercise. Contemporary art, literature and cinema best express the essence of economic power in modernity, when representing our world as a place where everything can be bought and sold. Kant had already glimpsed the problem, in conceiving that human dignity has an intrinsic worth, but not a market price, and is not an object of exchange[25]. It is not hard to foresee that as the visible effects of computational power will become apparent, arguments about human dignity will increase.

The main effect of the exercise of computational power consists, as we have already observed, in the formulation of a specific knowledge base, of a peculiar understanding and representation of the world, that both involves and confronts us. The dialectic between knowledge and power upon which modernity is built is thus brought up to date in today's complex information societies. This is the key aspect to which we shall now turn our attention. In doing so, we shall refer to a profound reflection on our time as a *time of crisis* and new opportunities: that of Michel Serres[26].

The production of knowledge

Michel Serres moves from a consideration analogous to that of Luciano Floridi, although he starts from different premises: he reconstructs the history of the relationship between human beings (subjects) and the world (object) through a periodization that emphasizes the idea of dependence[27]. He identifies three historical epochs: *Antiquity*, in which humans, cautiously and wisely, recognized and distinguished between that which depended on them and that which did not; they sought to rule over only that which depended on them, and respected things that were outside their sphere of control; *Modernity*, in which humans begin to see themselves as the center of the universe and the masters of the world, believing that everything depended on their decisions and plans; and the *Contemporary Age*, in which humans ultimately depend on things (such as the digital ICTs in Floridi's perspective) that, in turn, depend on us in many ways (in terms of their management, application, development, regulation, etc.). The Contemporary Age is therefore characterized by a circular relationship of mutual dependence between human beings and the world, to which Michel Serres attributes a particular meaning, from the privileged perspective of epistemology. This is precisely the point the French philosopher emphasizes, and what makes his reflection so interesting.

The information revolution has, according to Serres, a profoundly radical character – its authentic revolutionary aspect – precisely because it calls into question the long-standing paradigm on which modern epistemology has been built: the dichotomy between subject and object. Based on this constant representation – organized around the dialectic, or duality, between a subjective pole and an objective one – the subject has always been conceived of anthropologically in terms of a thinking and sentient human being capable of determining how objective reality is experienced and known. In contrast, the object has always been conceived as what is determined (by the subject) and hence can, to a greater or lesser extent, be manipulated, exploited, and appropriated. The object is literally (*objectum, Gegenstand, object, objet*) that which *stands before* the subject, with no ability to take any initiative towards the subject, which, in contrast, can take any initiative towards the object. According to this view, the human being has always been considered as the only source of relevant information from the political, legal, economic, moral and social points of view. Only human beings, for example, are conceived by legal epistemology as the subjects of the law, and as the holders of a complex subjective position of rights and duties. The objects of the world, instead, deserve attention and respect only to the extent that their value reflects a human interest. Modern epistemology is therefore at the base of a long-term asymmetric representation between subject and object, which has produced profound and constant repercussions on political, legal, economic, moral and social systems.

According to Serres, this view can change if we recognize that both human beings and things in the world (subjects and objects) share the same informational nature, that is to say, they are both *information systems*, capable of performing four fundamental informational and universal operations: receiving, generating, storing and processing information. To put it in the French philosopher's words:

> [...] the things of Land and of Life, codified like us, are capable of receiving, producing, storing and treating information, [...] This quadruple attitude does not design us as subjects nor design them [i.e., the things of world] as objects. In the same way that we communicate, we understand and speak, we write and read, both non-living and living things produce and receive information, store and treat it. Asymmetric and parasitic, the old division subject–object no longer holds; every subject becomes object; every object becomes subject.[28]

Serres rightly observes that human beings are constantly dealing with information they receive and exchange with non-human beings, and this is all the more true today, in the age of the Internet of things, and of autonomous artificial agents and intelligence systems that process and produce huge amounts of data. Of course, as Floridi suggests, it is necessary to carefully evaluate this *computational view*, which tends to extend in very broad terms the class of entities that count as information systems:

> Artificial intelligence and cognitive sciences study agents as information systems that receive, store, retrieve, transform, generate and transmit information. This is the concept based on the *ability to process information*. Before the development of connectionist models and dynamic systems in processing information, this conception was known as a *computational vision*. [...] The informational concepts are so powerful that, given the correct *level of abstraction*, anything can be depicted as an information system, from a building to a volcano, from a forest to a dinner, from the brain to a society.[29]

Bearing in mind the *caveat* brought to light by Floridi[30], it is worth emphasizing the profound change of perspective created by the informational approach. Humans are now considered one part of a whole (the infosphere as a new environment), where they are no longer the only source of relevant information. Human beings interact and constantly exchange information and data with computational systems. These computational systems are deeply involved, as we have already observed and shall see again later on, in the technological design of the environment in which we live and operate, and hence in the elaboration of a different representation of reality. There are three main consequences.

Firstly, human beings become the subjects of interaction: they create machines that make decisions, artificial agents that act autonomously, and programs that are endowed with ever-increasing computational power. The growth of computational power, however, should make us realize that we are gradually deciding to *depend* on something that does not depend entirely on us, with all the risks and opportunities that this brings about. It is necessary to grasp the scope of this change of perspective to limit what Serres defines as "human narcissism" or "jeu-à-deux"[31], that is to say, the notion of the world as the arena of human conflict, with humans unable to perceive the *finiteness* of the world. The philosopher observes that humans have always been involved in a struggle for the control and exploitation of the world's resources, as if it were a battle that someone could actually win, whereas instead it mainly turns into the progressive depletion of the world itself. The standpoint of a third party is lacking, as represented by the circular relationship of mutual dependence between human beings and the world that has been made even more evident by the information revolution.

Secondly and as a direct consequence of what has just been observed, both Michel Serres and Luciano Floridi perceive this relationship of circular dependence as a process of progressive decentralization of the human from its role as center of the universe and master of the world. Yet, this process of decentralization must turn into a progressive awareness and environmental responsibility for the world:

> ICTS are creating the new information environment in which future generations will live most of their time. Previous revolutions in the creation of the

wealth, especially the agricultural and the industrial ones, led to macroscopic transformations in our social and political structures and architectural environments, often without much foresight, normally with deep conceptual and ethical implications. The information revolution – whether understood as a third one, in terms of wealth creation, or as a fourth one, in terms of a reconceptualization of ourselves – is no less dramatic. We shall be in serious trouble, if we do not take seriously the fact that we are constructing the new physical and intellectual environments that will be inhabited by future generations. In view of this important change in the sort of ICT-mediated interactions that we will increasingly enjoy with other agents, whether biological or artificial, and in our self-understanding, an environmental approach seems a fruitful way of tackling the new ethical challenges posed by ICTs.[32]

This also means that we are part of an increasingly technological environment which we are less and less inclined to see as standing *before us* and as something to make use of as we please. Technologies, as we shall see more fully in Chapter 2, are no longer mere tools that can be discarded at any time. Or, to put it differently, we can undo *this* or *that* instrument, *this* or *that* technology, but we still have to deal with the dismantling of the subject/object dichotomy brought about by the digital information revolution. We are part of a whole and we constantly interact with agents and devices populating an environment[33] in which the idea of entering or exiting a bounded space has disappeared. When we refer to the analogical, the digital, or the virtual worlds, etc., we are no longer referring to regions in space, but to types of experience. The transformation is therefore mainly epistemological, that is, concerned with how we experience the world, and there is no other way to experience the world except within *this* technologically designed *world*. This leads to yet another important consequence.

The computational vision of Serres certainly has the merit of giving us a unified representation of human beings and things of the world, of human or artificial agents, in terms of information systems that perform fundamental and universal information operations. This breaks with the traditional distinction between subject and object, and potentially with the conception of the world that developed according to this dichotomy over the course of modernity and which is still in place. Examination of the legal epistemology reveals that many important debates on an international scale are waged within the confines of this division and deal precisely with the legal nature of artificial agents (Are they objects or subjects of law? Are they endowed with some form of legal personality?), the identification of criteria of legal responsibility for the consequences of their actions (Who is responsible for their actions? Under what terms?), the evaluation of their relative degree of interactivity and autonomy (Are they able to respond to external stimuli? Can they change their internal states in the absence of external stimuli? Are they able to autonomously choose between alternatives?).

This is just an example, but it helps us to understand an important point: in order to answer such questions we first need to understand how those agents operate; and, to do that, we need to understand how those agents represent reality. This means that the overcoming of the traditional subject/object division is likely to create a proliferation of points of view, a multiplicity of representations of reality. This is not something new under the sun. Gods and humans have different points of view about the world and diverse representations of reality, as do humans and animals, and so on. But it is an idea that needs revisiting: computational systems operate on the basis of representations of reality that may differ completely from our own. Different computational systems operate on the basis of different representations of reality and produce different representations of reality.

Nonetheless, it is not just a question of continuing to repeat, like a mantra, that computational models may produce a given representation of reality that reifies humans and represents them as an object, as a set of data, because this is precisely what the analysis assumes from the start. When Floridi suggests that *we* are our information[34], he is not affirming an ontological thesis of human nature but an epistemological thesis of how we experience our current condition at a given level of abstraction (the *informational* one). This is extremely important because, today as in the past, epistemology establishes the grounds upon which the political, legal, and moral recognition of our claims and prerogatives, rights and duties, and, ultimately, of our values is built.

Rather, we need to be aware that the information revolution not only contributes to conforming the world technologically, but also to redesigning our *forms of life*. Even without making recourse to Wittgenstein, we can say that forms of life are particular pragmatic situations formed by a set of syntactic and semantic rules, or in other words, the rules by which we organize and give meaning to our lives. Computational power produces a form of knowledge that rearticulates this set of rules and forces us to completely rethink the way we organize and give meaning to our lives.

When we post and tag a photo on Instagram, we are expressing and communicating something about ourselves, or are supplying content that helps to reveal who we are. The set of photos and comments tends to create a story that says something about us. We provide information with a personal semantic value.

When we post and tag a photo on Instagram, we are allowing an AI system to learn what we like and pay attention to, to profile our preferences, to track our interests, and even to calculate the amount of time we spend on posting or describing a photo. We are furnishing data that has economic or political value.

When we post and tag a photo on Instagram, we are allowing a machine-learning system to analyze the correlations we have established between certain words and photos and thus to improve the way it recognizes images. We are providing data that has a computational value (as it feeds human-based computation[35]).

When we post and tag a photo on Instagram, we are subject to the terms of service of the social network or the rules protecting copyright or the protection of personal data of third parties, giving rise to questions of legal responsibility that may require the adoption of automated filters. We are providing data that have legal relevance and computational value (as they test and train the filtering system).

When we post and tag a photo on Instagram, we are posting an image or content today that we may no longer identify with in the future. If the photo is decontextualized and circulates online, we may lose any control we have over this small piece of our life forever, with consequences that are not entirely predictable and calculable. We are providing information that has a semantic, non-personal value, independent of our will.

When we post and tag a photo on Instagram, we are providing more or less extensive access, due to our numerous *followers*, for others to enter our lives and to pass judgment on us, more or less directly, through the expression of comments or criticism. We are providing information with a semantic value, not just personal but shared, that may have significant economic or political repercussions.

When we post and tag a photo on Instagram, we are allowing an AI system to collect data about us (interests, habits, feelings, preferences, etc.) that can function as *proxies*, from which other data can be inferred through statistical correlation. On the basis of the inferred data, abstract profiles of various kinds can be developed, according to which prerogatives, opportunities or rights are granted or denied (i.e., being shortlisted for a job, obtaining a loan, receiving discounts, etc.). We provide data that has inferential value.

When we post and tag a photo on Instagram, we are simultaneously doing all of these things and probably many others. We rarely, if ever, realize how much data and information we are giving away or how many intertwining syntactic and semantic rules we are triggering. This is true not just for Instagram, but also for any other social network and for the Internet as a whole. This is the *everyday revolution* which was referred to earlier: the re-working, often unnoticed or imperceptible, of the syntactical and semantic rules that govern our lives, not in a striking and subversive way, but slowly, quietly and surely.

Notes

1 L. FLORIDI, *The Fourth Revolution. How the Infosphere is Reshaping the Human Reality*, Oxford University Press, Oxford, 2014.
2 L. FLORIDI, *The Fourth Rev., op. cit.*, p. VI.
3 Luciano Floridi, Professor of Philosophy and Chair of Information Ethics at the Oxford Internet Institute, has been working for many years investigating the digital revolution. Among his works, we may recall: L. FLORIDI, *Information: A Very Short Introduction*, Oxford University Press, Oxford, 2010; *The Philosophy of Information*, Oxford University Press, Oxford, 2011; *The Onlife Manifesto: Being Human in a Hyperconnected Era*, Springer, Dordrecht, 2015. The philosopher is also Editor of the series, *The Cambridge Handbook of Information and Computer Ethics*, which, since 2010, has been investigating the impact of information and communication technology (ICT) on the evolution of society.
4 L. FLORIDI, *The Fourth Rev., op. cit.*, pp. 3–4.
5 L. FLORIDI, *The Fourth Rev., op. cit.*, p. VI.
6 On this point, see L. FLORIDI, *The Fourth Rev., op. cit.*, p. 90: "After all, Freud himself was the first to read them as part of a single process of gradual reassessment of human nature. His interpretation was, admittedly, rather self-serving. Yet the line of reasoning does strike a plausible note, and it can be rather helpful to understand the information revolution in a similar vein".

7 The idea elaborated by Luciano Floridi of a *fourth revolution*, which finds in Alan Turing its eponymous hero, and in computational power its conceptual core, has been picked up and echoed even in the field of literature, as evidenced by some recent pages of English writer Ian McEwan's latest novel, *Machines Like Me*, Penguin Random House, New York, 2019, p. 80 *et seq.*, in which Floridi's thesis is taken up.

8 L. FLORIDI, *The Fourth Rev., op. cit.*, p. 93.

9 *Ibid.*

10 *Ibid*: "The history of the word 'computer' is indicative. Between the seventeenth and the nineteenth century, it was synonymous with 'a person who performs calculations' simply because there was nothing else in the universe that could compute autonomously. In 1890, for example, a competitive examination for the position of 'computer' by the US Civil Service had sections on orthography, penmanship, copying, letter-writing, algebra, geometry, logarithms, and trigonometry. It was still Hobbes's idea of thinking as reckoning. Yet by the time Turing published his classic paper entitled 'Computing machinery and intelligence', he had to specify that, in some cases, he was talking about a '*human* computer', because by 1950 he knew that 'computer' no longer referred only to a person who computes. After him, 'computer' entirely lost its anthropological meaning and of course became synonymous with a general-purpose, programmable machine, what we now call a Turing machine".

11 L. FLORIDI, *The Fourth Rev., op. cit.*, pp. 94–96.

12 Of which data (particularly the vast amounts of aggregated data, i.e., Big Data, which is processed by increasingly sophisticated computational systems) constitute the oil, or fuel.

13 L. FLORIDI, *The Fourth Rev., op. cit.*, pp. 7–8: "[…] an iPad2 had enough computing power to process 1,600 millions of instructions per second (MIPS). By making the price of such a processing power equal to $100, the graph shows what it would have cost to buy the computing power of an iPad2 in the past decades. Note that the vertical scale is logarithmic, so it descends by powers of ten as the price of computing power decreases dramatically. All this means that, in the fifties, the 1,600 MIPS you hold in your hands – or rather held, in 2010, because three year later the iPad4 already run at 17,056 MIPS – would have cost you $100 trillion. This is a number that only bankers and generals understand. So, for a quick comparison, consider Qatar's GDP. In 2010, it was ranked 57th out of 190 countries in the world and its GDP would have been insufficient to buy the equivalent of an iPad2 in the fifties, for it was a mere $98 trillion".

14 L. FLORIDI, *The Fourth Rev., op. cit.*, p. 8 (italics not present in the original text).

15 L. FLORIDI, *The Fourth Rev., op. cit.*, pp. 8–9.

16 For simplicity, we will often use this more generic expression in the text to refer to a reality that is obviously much more varied, complex and sophisticated.

17 On this point, see *infra*, chap. 2.

18 L. FLORIDI, *The Fourth Rev., op. cit.*, p. 144.

19 On this point, see *infra*, chap. 8.

20 EU Regulation 2016/679.

21 The reference is to the text by É. DE LA BOÉTIE, *The Politics of Obedience: The Discourse on Voluntary Servitude*, Free Life Editions, NY, 1975.

22 On power, see, among others, M. WEBER, *Economy and Society*, vol. 1–2, University of California Press, Oakland, 2013; H. ARENDT, *The Origins of Totalitarianism*, Penguin, London, 2017; N. LUHMANN, *Trust and Power*, ed. 2, Polity Press, NY, 2017; N. BOBBIO, *Democracy and Dictatorship: The Nature and Limits of State Power*, Polity Press, NY, 2017; M. FOUCAULT, *Power: The Essential Works of Michel Foucault 1954–1986*, Penguin, London, 2012; ID., *Discipline and Punish: The Birth of the Prison*, Penguin, London, 1991; ID., *The History of Sexuality*, vol. 1–3, Penguin, London, 1998; M. MANN, *The Sources of Social Power*, vols. 1–4, Cambridge University Press, Cambridge, 1986–2012; H. POPITZ, *Phenomena of Power: Authority, Domination, and Violence*, Columbia University Press, NY, 2017; S. CLEGG, *Frameworks of Power*, Sage, London, 1989; C. SCHMITT, *Dialogues on Power and Spaces*, Polity Press, NY, 2015; M. CASTELLS, *Communication Power*, Oxford University Press, Oxford, 2009.

23 For the idea of a *microphysics of power*, see M. FOUCAULT, *Discipline and Punish, op. cit.*

24 On this point, see *infra*, chap. 2.

25 I. KANT, *Groundwork for the Metaphysics of Morals*, Cambridge University Press, Cambridge, 1998, p. 42: "In the kingdom of ends everything either has a price or a dignity. What has a price can be replaced by something else as its *equivalent*; what on the other hand is raised above all prices and therefore admits of no equivalent has a dignity. What is related to general human inclinations and needs has a market price; that which, even without presupposing a need, conforms with a certain taste, that is, with a delight in a mere purposeless play of our mental powers, has a fancy price; but that which constitutes the condition under which alone something can be an end in itself has not merely a relative worth, that is, a price, but an inner worth, that is, dignity".

26 M. SERRES, *Times of Crisis. What the Financial Crisis Revealed and How to Reinvest Our Lives and Future*, Bloomsbury, NY, 2015.

27 M. SERRES, *Times of Crisis, op. cit.*, p. 39 *et seq.*

28 M. SERRES, *Times of Crisis, op. cit.*, p. 71.

29 L. FLORIDI, *The Philosophy of Information, op. cit.*, pp. 35–36.

30 In the light of Floridi's information theory, one could further and more correctly distinguish the category of informational objects (which has a more general scope, since it refers to any entity that can be described as a well-constructed set of data that allows one to experience a determined entity at a given level of abstraction) from that of informational agents and patients, who are able to receive, store, retrieve, transform, generate and transmit information. On this point, see L. FLORIDI, *The Philosophy of Information, op. cit.*, p. 35 *et seq.*

31 M. SERRES, *Times of Crisis, op. cit.*, p. 43.

32 L. FLORIDI, *The Fourth Rev., op. cit.*, p. 219.

33 L. FLORIDI, *The Fourth Rev., op. cit.*, p. 47.

34 L. FLORIDI, *The Fourth Rev., op. cit.*, p. 77.

35 L. FLORIDI, *The Fourth Rev., op. cit.*, p. 167.

2

TECHNOLOGY

From instrument to environment

The conception of technology

One of the greatest and perhaps most significant topics of philosophical reflection of the twentieth century that persists to the present day, and which indeed constitutes its essential fulcrum, is the reflection on technology. If it is true that "*philosophy is our time comprehended in thoughts*", as Hegel put it, and if ours is the age of technology, in the sense discussed in Chapter 1, then philosophy today can be none other than a meditation on technology. In fact, there have been so many profound notions of technology proposed since the twentieth century until now that it is impossible to take them all into account[1].

In Chapter 1, I explained that the springboard for this book is a series of arguments introduced by Luciano Floridi in the *Fourth Revolution*. This book, which I take as a meditation on the impact of digital technologies, contains an implicit thesis: namely, that computational power is the driving force of current history and that this power consists primarily in the capacity to create and reinforce the conditions of its own exercise. This means, as already remarked, that we are *enveloping* the world itself around digital technologies; in other words, we are progressively adapting our world and representation of reality to the functioning of artificial agents, devices and processes that employ and make use of computational power.

This thesis is tightly linked to a specific and renewed notion of technology which maintains that technology can no longer be interpreted merely in instrumental terms, or as a means to various ends, but must also be considered in environmental terms, as a process capable of reorganizing the environment in which and with which different agents interact. One could object that this is far from an original thesis, for technology has always contributed to shaping the human environment, representing one of the primary tools at our disposal for reducing complexity and enabling us to adapt to our surroundings. One could further object that whereas technology used to serve humans as a means of defense against the adversities of the environment, today instead, technology poses a very real threat to the environment, which must therefore be defended against it. In reality, neither objection refutes the main premise of the thesis; on the contrary, they actually reinforce it, insofar as they reaffirm that technology has always had an essential impact on the design of our environment.

The peculiarity of my thesis, which will shortly be clarified, consists in the fact that today's technology shapes the environment in such a way that: (1) taking action is no longer the exclusive prerogative of human beings; (2) artificial agents concur in building the environment in which they operate and act; and (3) artificial agents act on the basis of a representation of reality that no longer necessarily coincides with or is comparable to a human one. In other words, the changes brought about by technology are contributing to the creation of a world in which human beings are no longer the only actors, or agents of change. Therefore, humans will no longer only adapt the environment according to their own needs, but also according to those necessary for the functioning of non-human agents. The representation of reality underlying the decision and actions of non-human agents will no longer inevitably be modelled on a human one, but will instead represent the peculiar and autonomous representation of reality generated by those non-human agents.

It is often said that we are currently witnessing a revival or a new wave of interest in the topic of artificial intelligence (AI). Just looking around us, it seems that no topic or concern is more pressing or urgent than that of AI. This perception is undoubtedly reinforced by the vast proliferation of books, seminars, conferences and expert groups on the subject. Yet this is perhaps not the most accurate way of describing what is actually happening: as shall be discussed further later in Chapter 3 the very idea of what AI means is dramatically changing. The three-fold direction this change is taking, as discussed in Chapter 1, suggests a progressive shift from the idea of artificial intelligence to one of *artificial agency*. AI is no longer automatically defined in terms of its ability to reproduce or emulate the functioning of the human mind, but rather in terms of its capacity to act on the basis of a certain representation of reality, meaning its ability to process the quantity and type of data used for this representation.

Having clarified this point, it is now necessary to briefly examine the three classes of technology Floridi proposes in order to understand how the *Fourth Revolution* links the notion of technology to computational power. This provides the germ of the idea to overcome a merely instrumental conception of technology in favor of a more generalized and far-reaching environmental one. It is no coincidence, in fact, that the chapter devoted to Floridi's reflections on technology is entitled *Space*.

The three orders of technology

Luciano Floridi starts his reflection by making a simple but fundamental consideration: one of the traits that most clearly and directly characterizes any technology, in any historical age, is its "in-betweenness"[2]:

Suppose Alice lives in Rio de Janeiro, not in Oxford. A hat is a technology between her and the sunshine. A pair of sandals is a technology between her and the hot sand of the beach on which she is walking. And a pair of sunglasses is between her and the bright light that surrounds her. The idea of such an in-betweenness seems clear and uncontroversial. However, it soon gets complicated.[3]

Floridi thus observes that technology has always played an essential role of mediator between a subject using the technology (referred to by Floridi in the anthropological tradition as the *user*) and the thing that necessitates the use of that technology, or in other words, the thing that prompts the use or creation of the technological tool and which Floridi refers to as the *prompter*[4]. Returning to the example above, if Alice is the *user* who is wearing the sunglasses, the dazzling light of the sun is the *prompter* that prompted the creation and use of those sunglasses. The sunglasses are a form a technology that lies between Alice and the sun; in this case, they are a form of technology that mediates the relationship Alice has with the physical environment. "An inventor is someone who devises an artefact that may satisfy a user's need or want caused by some prompter"[5].

As Floridi notes, however, things are not always so simple. The particular nature of the user and the prompter have led to the existence of what Floridi has identified as first-, second- or third-order technologies. Although this classification largely coincides with the progressive evolution of technology, it is not actually a chronological representation of this evolution: first-, second- and third-order technologies can, in fact, coexist. Moreover, a single technology can occur as first-, second- or third-order, according to the circumstances. Let us briefly examine the three orders of technology in turn.

When the users are *humans* and the prompters are *natural*, technologies may be classified as first order. In this case, technology is in between humanity and nature: the plow, the wheel, the umbrella and the axe are examples of first-order technologies. First-order technologies mediate the relationship that humans have with their environment, allowing them to adapt to it and to satisfy a series of vital needs, such as land cultivation, transportation, protection from atmospheric agents, and gathering wood. Things then get a bit complicated because humans are not limited to using first-order technologies to adapt progressively to the environment; they can also respond to what might be prompted by technology itself. This results in second-order technologies.

In fact, when the users are *humans* and the prompters are *technological*, we may qualify such technologies as second order. In this case, technology is in between humanity and another technology. The screwdriver, the key, the automobile and the engine are examples of second-order technologies. They stand between humans and other technological artifacts and mediate the relationship that humans have with technology: they allow human beings to use certain technologies to meet other vital needs. The screw, for example, is a technology of the first order, which stands between humans and wood, but without the screwdriver it would be difficult, if not impossible, to interact with a screw properly. A key is in between humans and a mechanical lock, a car in between humans and a paved road and so on: "Some first-order technologies [...] are useless without the corresponding second-order technologies to which they are coupled. [...] Second-order technologies imply a level of mutual dependency with first-order technologies (a drill is useless without the drill bits) that is the hallmark of some degree of specialization, and hence of organization"[6]. These technologies are, in principle, linked to the emergence of more complex forms of civilization and socialization, since they presuppose the ability to build technologies based on other technologies. This also means that they constitute a distinctive feature of the human species, since animals, for example, are not able to create relevant second-order technologies, even though they can construct first-order artifacts. Furthermore, from modernity to the contemporary age, technology has played the main role as a prompter: our world is increasingly being built in response to the needs, wants and demands that technology itself suggests:

> The engine, understood as any technology that provides energy to other technologies, is probably the most important second-order technology. Watermills and windmills converted energy into useful motion for millennia, but it is only when the steam, the internal combustion engine, and the electric motor become "portable" energy-providers, which can be placed between users and other technologies wherever they are needed, that the Industrial Revolution turns into a widespread reality.[7]

Engines, watermills or windmills are not arbitrary examples of second-order technologies; they well illustrate a salient aspect of the modern idea of technology, remarked upon repeatedly by Heidegger and Wiener, according to which technology consists in the ability to extract energy from nature and to allocate it to a purpose different from the original. This points to a different articulation of the relationship between technology and the environment, to which we will return shortly. For now, however, let us return to the question of third-order technologies.

The pervasiveness and connectivity of digital technologies means that technologies are capable of communicating and interacting with each other and can thus play the role of users. When both the users and the prompters are *technological*, technologies are considered to be third-order. In this case, technology stands between other forms of technologies and relates them to one another. The Internet of things, or even just a computer connected with a network of other computers, are examples of third-order technologies. Here, technologies are in between other technologies and mediate how they function. This is a distinctive feature of our time:

> Technologies as users interacting with other technologies as prompters, through other in-between technologies: this is another way of describing hyperhistory as the stage of human development when third-order technological relations become the necessary condition for development, innovation,

and welfare. It is also a way of providing further evidence that we have entered into such a hyperhistorical stage of our development. The very expression "machine-readable data" betrays the presence of such a generation of third-order technologies.[8]

This passage highlights some important aspects of third-order technologies. First of all, we are not talking about just a few isolated or irrelevant cases. Most digital ICTs are third-order technologies. In other words, many third-order technologies are those on which the development of individual and collective well-being and hence the existence of our complex information societies depend. Secondly, the success and pervasive spread of these technologies has been determined in part by a specific determining factor: in third-order technologies, not only are the three constituent elements of the functioning of a technology (*user, in-between* and *prompter*) technological, but so is the interface that allows these technologies to communicate and interact. To put it simply, third-order technologies speak a common language, which allows them to communicate and thus weave a complex web of interactions. Floridi rightly emphasizes the importance of the Turing legacy:

> Such a digital uniformity between data and programs was one of Turing's most consequential intuitions. In the infosphere, populated by entities and agents all equally informational, where there is no physical difference between *processors* and *processed*, interactions become equally informational. [...] Digits deal effortlessly and seamlessly with digits.[9]

Thirdly, third-order technologies operate on the basis of a representation of reality (determined by the specific ways in which they process data) which is peculiar to them. In this sense, as we shall later see, the parallel between human and artificial intelligence must be put into proper perspective[10].

When we are confronted with third-order technologies, in which the user, in-betweenness, prompter, interface and protocols are all equally technological, it is fair to ask what role and position are reserved for human beings, who seem to be missing in the scenario just presented. However, humans do not actually disappear from the scene. Instead, they become an integral part of an environment that is now increasingly being defined in technological terms. Third-order technologies (and in particular digital ICTs) are taking an increasingly prominent role in redesigning the environment in which human beings live and interact. This is the third way in which the relationship between technology and environment can be cast: technology is no longer that which allows us to adapt to our environment or to extract energy from the environment to be used for a further and different purpose. Technology shapes the environment itself. This has three key consequences.

Firstly, from a theoretical point of view, it determines a progressive shift from an instrumental to an environmental conception of technology, according to which technology characterizes and tends to shape the environment (context or horizon, etc.) in which we live. We do not always sense this, because our computers sit in front of us and our smartphones are hidden away in our pockets. However, it is now we who are more of an integral part of the world built by connected computers or smartphones than those devices are an integral part of our world. As Ugo Pagallo has rightly observed, if by domicile we mean the location of our main business and interests, the center of our private life and most of our personal data, then our principal domicile today is our smartphone[11]. This conceptual shift, from instrument to environment, should also make it clear that technologies can no longer be merely conceived of as tools (or means) more or less available at our disposal and under our control. Technologies should not also be conceived of as bounded contexts that one can enter or exit like a room. They are processes that deeply involve us and with which we must contend. This leads us to the second consequence.

The fact of being plunged into an environment characterized in technological terms does not necessarily imply that we are always in control of the technological processes that constitute such an environment[12]. To borrow a well-known classification, we can say that humans can be: (1) *in the loop*, meaning that they are an integral part of the process, with the power to deliberate and act within the process itself, for example, by altering its course; (2) *on the loop*, meaning that, although they cannot intervene in the process itself, they maintain a certain power of control over the overall process; (3) *post-loop*, meaning that they have no direct control either over the single phases of the process or its overall progression; they can only intervene *ex post*, to repair or mitigate any harmful consequences of the action delegated to the AI system; (4) *out of the loop*, meaning that they are marginal to some processes and can only deal with the effects produced by the process itself. From telemedicine to drones, from driverless cars to autonomous lethal weapons, there are many areas today in which the degree of involvement of human beings in a given technological process (where a decision or action can be fully or partly entrusted to machines) is a key issue for reflection and discussion. In this sense, the design of the environment by technology does not just designate the construction of a technological environment (such as in the case of home automation or a smart environment) but in broader terms the construction of a technological framework of interactions, processes and decisions to which humans are exposed. This leads us to the third consequence. In some respects, this is the least perceptible yet most relevant consequence.

The evolution of the relationship between technology and the environment does not supplant previous types of relationships between them, but updates those relationships in digital terms. This means that we already use and will increasingly use technology (especially digital technology) in the near future to adapt to the new technologically designed environment. In this sense, technology will also continue to be a form of adaptation to the environment: in fact, many of the current third-order technologies already deal with, for example, the management of digital environments or the progressive adaptation of humans to the functioning of technology. For instance, we have apps that remind us to review the privacy settings on our social network or to change our e-mail passwords. Likewise, the idea of technology as the capacity to extract energy from the environment, in order to use it for a different and further purpose, has not been supplanted. This is one of the most salient features of today's digital revolution. We use technologies *to exploit the resources that the technologically designed environment grants to us*. For example, take the computational power through which we are currently able to extract value from the aggregation and analysis of large amounts of data. It is precisely in the light of this consideration that we can begin to understand how the decentralization of the Internet has made it possible, over time, for power to be concentrated in the hands of a few Big Tech companies. In the next section, we therefore need to return briefly to the subject of network decentralization and concentration.

Network decentralization and concentration

My previous book focused on the decentralization of the Internet as a characteristic feature of the ongoing digital revolution[13]. The decentralized nature of the network has characterized the structure of the Internet as a platform from the start. This has facilitated: (1) *widespread access to the network*: any computer connected to the network allows any user free access to the network and the services of the network, without discrimination between entry points; (2) *end-to-end communication*: the possibility for each node of the network to communicate with every other node of the network without needing authorization from a central authority has allowed and favored the rapid diffusion and circulation of data and information; (3) *online generation of content*: the so-called "Web 2.0" or *user-generated content*, based on the network platform, allows users not only to be passive recipients of content (Web 1.0), but also and above all, to be able to interact online, and to modify and generate content on the Net[14].

Many scholars – including me – have observed and even hoped[15] that decentralization of the Internet would increase the ability of individuals to act both on their own behalves (for example, by increasing individual autonomy, access to information and the construction of social ties) and on the behalf of others (for example, by creating forms of cooperation, sharing and horizontal production of common goods). While some of these promises have been fulfilled, others have been frustrated, so it is quite difficult to give an overall assessment of a phenomenon that is still under way[16]. At the time, however, I had formulated a hypothesis about the possible course of development of the Web or, to be more precise, I had presented an outline of what was likely to affect the course of such a development, which at the time was also a question of power. Let me summarize the implications of those observations[17].

I started from the consideration that digital technologies (like many other technologies) are *enabling* technologies. They allow individuals to do things they were previously unable to do, or to do them more cheaply or easily. Enabling technologies have opened up new possibilities which, when implemented, give rise to new powers. The effect of technology is therefore that of modifying the existing distribution of powers within a given society. An innovative technology is likely to alter the social structure impacted by this redistribution of powers, so that, as I have pointed out on several occasions, the debate concerning a particular technology often concerns how the ensuing redistribution of powers has altered a given social order. Furthermore, the overall effect of the technology in question is best appreciated in the medium term, when it is easier to see which actors benefit most from the redistribution of powers resulting from it.

Thus, the real question to ask is the following: Who has benefited most from decentralization of the Internet? When answering this question, one must bear in mind that the main area of development due to online decentralization is that of content creation. Thanks to our incessant production and sharing of data and information online, we have created and stored more data since the advent of computer connectivity than in the entire history of humanity[18]. In this sense, decentralization of the Internet has stimulated many other recent phenomena, such as the rise of social networks and the entrepreneurial activities of the *sharing economy*, as well as the phenomenon of online concentration[19].

In fact, the very same decentralization of the network that has allowed millions of users to produce and share data online has also allowed the concentration of network power in the hands of just a few major players. Users have no real perception of the value of their shared data. This is because the (economic) value of data derives from the ability to process large volumes of aggregated data from information silos and to extract data of (economic) value. As previously mentioned, the new oil is not only data[20], but also the computational power which makes it possible to extract value from such Big Data. The concentration of power on the Net is not an inevitable outcome of the developing Web or a demonstration of the betrayed promises of the Internet. No, it is the consequence of some big players' ability to develop technologies that show them how to best exploit the resources provided by the new technologically based environment.

This, then, is the takeaway lesson: the latest technologies (in particular third-order digital ICTs) are shaping and redesigning the environment we live in. This does not mean we should abandon them; on the contrary, it makes it even more urgent to create and use technologies that can help us adapt to the new technological environment. The stakes are high. Hanging in the balance, for example, may be a company's success or failure, a political party's victory or defeat, and certain cases of social inclusion or exclusion. It is also imperative to create and exploit technologies that will help us extract energy and resources from the technological environment, in order to store and use them for other purposes, whether they be economic, political, social and so on. Some of the major players, including digital platform owners and service providers, often referred to as "Big Tech", have managed to leverage online decentralization over time and to benefit from their crucial role as intermediators. Their commercial success depends largely on their ability to combine business models based on the extraction of economic value from aggregated data with new forms of life based on the (third-order) technological design of the environment[21]. This strategic position of new intermediation currently affects all aspects relating to digital governance. This crucial topic would merit extensive discussion in its own right[22]. The following section is limited to drawing the reader's attention to the complexity of the question.

Digital governance

There is much discussion today about governance, particularly about digital governance, which for good reason seems to be one of the most pressing issues of our times[23]. It is on the grounds of governance that the impact of the digital revolution can be measured in the plainest terms. As noted above, one of the unforeseen consequences of decentralization of the Net has been the emergence of a new intermediation phase and the progressive affirmation of private actors, owners of infrastructures, platforms and network services.

So much of what we do takes place online today. The private actors providing infrastructures, platforms and services that make all of this possible are thus playing an increasing role in shaping and regulating how these activities are carried out. In response, the public actors at both the national and supra-national levels are seeking to control and regulate these private actors, in order to indirectly control or regulate activities taking place online. In turn, the private actors are subject to pressure from below, as their users express their preferences, demand adjustments and regulations, and call for new forms of governance. One aspect that has gone largely unexamined by scholars is the simple fact of how difficult it is for the owners of infrastructures, platforms and services to govern large communities of users that are so terribly fragmented in terms of culture, habits, standards and values.

Against this backdrop, one main theme emerges, which has been remarked by Jack Balkin with reference to the issue of constitutional freedom of speech and expression of thought[24], arguing that we have moved from a *dyadic* model of governance, based on the dialectic between the rulers and the ruled, to a *triadic*, if not even *pluralistic*, model of digital governance. The pluralistic model is based on the multiplicity of possible relationships between: (1) public actors (states or other supra-national entities); (2) private actors (owners of online infrastructures, platforms or services); and (3) individuals (not only online active users but also passive recipients of what happens online[25]). In this triadic (or pluralistic) structure[26], multitudes of possible relationships propagate, making the multi-agent arrangement of digital governance particularly difficult and complex to manage.

Suffice it to say that new and more complex forms of regulation are added to more traditional ones, such as top-down regulation by public actors or bottom-up regulation by individuals and private actors. Two new forms, in particular, warrant attention: (1) *private digital governance*, which mainly concerns the relationship between public and private actors; and (2) *technological normativity*, which mainly concerns the relationship between private actors and individuals.

The first, private digital governance, is entrusted by public actors to the owners of infrastructures, platforms or services of the network, through the regulation itself of those actors' functions. States (or supranational bodies) create "incentives for private governance"[27]. This can happen: (1) by imposing obligations on private actors, or (2) by granting rights to individuals that they can enforce against private actors, so that these private actors are called upon to interpret and apply the law concerning a complex set of individuals' claims, rights and duties. As we shall later see in some examples[28], this equates to the true privatization of digital governance. There are several reasons for which states (or supra-national bodies) may entrust the role of governance to private actors: firstly, because it is a direct consequence (although not always entirely desired) of regulating their activities, by imposing obligations and responsibilities on them; secondly, because the intermediation role of private actors puts them in a strategic position from a regulatory point of view; thirdly, because, in many cases, they have the organizational and economic resources to bear the costs of governance of complex phenomena; and fourthly, because it shifts part of the political and social responsibility of digital governance from public to private actors, in accordance with the growing expectations of end-users[29].

The second form of governance, technological normativity, refers to the ability of private actors to regulate network user activity through the provision of terms of service, which are accepted through the *notice and consent* model[30], or by incorporating rules or values in the functioning of technological infrastructures, platforms or services. In the latter case, the implicit incorporation of norms or values in the technology works particularly well at producing regulatory effectiveness (i.e., the ability to elicit behaviors that conform to the embodied norms or values); however, it raises issues of formal legitimacy (i.e., conformity to public procedures in the adoption of rules or values), moral desirability or social acceptability[31]. In this case, digital governance is achieved through choices that are not always fair or transparent: the embodiment of rules, standards and values within technology means that their adoption or implementation is not always subject to public scrutiny: this may curtail or eliminate the sphere of interpretation and exception that normally accompanies the application of legal rules[32]. Furthermore, digital governance implemented through the automation of decision-making procedures is likely to restrain the rights or prerogatives of network users (for example, through implicit forms of censorship of speech[33]), without furnishing adequate ways of challenging such violations as typically foreseen within a democratic process.

These new forms of regulation, along with the traditional ones (which in turn become more problematic as a result of digitalization), increase the complexity of digital governance and raise a three-pronged issue.

Firstly, we must acknowledge that we are confronted with a multiplicity of competing actors and regulatory systems; with regard to any relevant aspect of the digital, we must ask ourselves who is exactly regulating whom on the basis of what regulatory system (legal, technological, economic, social, etc.)[34]. The overall regulatory effect in digital governance depends on the relationship between the actors involved at different levels of governance and on the interplay (which can take on competitive or cooperative forms) between the regulatory systems at stake.

Secondly, the complexity of digital governance is such that regulatory choices are likely to create considerable side effects. An emblematic case is the right to be forgotten, which will be examined at greater length in Chapter 4. Imposing a burdensome obligation on a private actor, such as an Internet service provider, may actually backfire, by granting the actor power in the administration and application of its rights as well as the power to exclude those of the competition who cannot afford to comply with the obligation.

Thirdly, digital governance currently raises the need to design an overall institutional architecture, which shall take into account the plurality of actors involved, the interaction between different regulatory systems, the side-effects of collective choices, the trend towards progressive privatization and automation of regulatory solutions, and the need for a social covenant based on trust as the very foundation of digital governance. It is precisely this last consideration that raises the need to rethink the issue of trust in the digital. This is a particularly difficult task, which we will try to sketch out in the rest of this chapter.

Trust in the digital

The problems we have outlined so far have infused a certain degree of mistrust in the users of the Net regarding the institutional capacity to protect their rights and to create a concrete and viable digital governance that is up to the ongoing challenges. The need to renew and strengthen a possible social covenant based on trust between network users, institutional actors and private companies is best exemplified in two recitals of the recent GDPR, which should be quoted in their entirety:

> (6) Rapid technological developments and globalisation have brought new challenges for the protection of personal data. The scale of the collection and sharing of personal data has increased significantly. Technology allows both private companies and public authorities to make use of personal data on an unprecedented scale in order to pursue their activities. Natural persons increasingly make personal information available publicly and globally. Technology has transformed both the economy and social life, and should further facilitate the free flow of personal data within the Union and the transfer to third countries and international organisations, while ensuring a high level of the protection of personal data.
> (7) Those developments require a strong and more coherent data protection framework in the Union, backed by strong enforcement, given the importance of creating the *trust* that will allow the digital economy to develop across the internal market. Natural persons should have control of their own personal data. Legal and practical certainty for natural persons, economic operators and public authorities should be enhanced.[35]

The issue of trust, like that of digital governance, would deserve a specific analysis for its centrality in the contemporary world. It is appropriate here to provide just a few remarks that will be useful for what follows in the book. However, the points made here have not been widely examined in the literature on trust.

Trust is a very complex notion and is defined differently in different fields of research[36]. Diego Gambetta is correct in observing, in general terms, that trust helps human agents to manage their social environments and is present in all human interactions[37]. Without trust in other agents, organizations or infrastructures, human interactions would be weakened and, ultimately, it would be impossible to act. In this perspective, trust has an instrumental value (we need it to achieve a certain goal). Trust is essential when we need to decide or act in contexts of uncertainty characterized by uncertain or incomplete information, or in other words, in most cases, given that uncertainty or incompleteness of information can regard what we know about a certain environment, the behavior of others, or the functioning of a device or process. Trust is structurally characterized by the presence of risk, and in fact trust exists insofar as there is a risk, as Niklas Luhmann pointed out[38], for there is always the risk that trust can be misplaced or betrayed.

These three features (instrumentality, uncertainty, and risk) define the concept of trust in a structural manner. Without delving into the core idea of trust, according to which we believe we can talk of trust with regard both to human and artificial agents[39], it is important here to highlight one feature that allows us to distinguish between two irreducible aspects of trust. In fact, (the granting of) trust takes place in two diametrically opposed situations. Let me examine them.

In many circumstances, the act of trusting allows us to delegate a task and not to perform it ourselves. For example, if A trusts B, A can entrust B to act on his/her behalf[40]: a football player entrusts a teammate with the task of kicking a penalty because she trusts her to score the goal. In other cases, A may abstain from action, trusting in the fact that B will act, even in the absence of an explicit delegation of the task. For example, A trusts B to buy a bottle of wine to take to C's party, even without an explicit arrangement. In other cases, A may trust B in order to reinforce B's sense of self-confidence; in this case, A chooses not to act so that B can act. This would be the case of parents wanting to strengthen their children's sense of self-confidence. There is any number of examples of trust, including more complex scenarios, but the ones just cited all have something in common: trust allows a subject (the trustor) not to act, in favor of another subject (the trustee), who acts in response to explicit or implicit delegation of a task.

This sort of trust is referred to as *intersubjective trust*. This is the form of trust established by means of a relationship between two subjects (whether human or artificial), such that the outcome of a subject's choice not to act is dependent on someone else's action. In these cases, trust is characterized by three elements that qualify the intersubjective relationship and which reflect the three main trust factors: (1) the trustee's trustworthiness; (2) the sharing of a common goal; (3) the trustee's loyalty to the trustor.

Moving on to the second situation. There are many circumstances in which the act of trusting incites us to action. For example, a trustor may have a strong sense of self-confidence and decide to act. A is an expert diver, so she decides to attempt a dive from a particularly high cliff. A is a skilled trader and decides to start up her own business because she trusts her own abilities. In such cases, A chooses to act on her own, without delegating the task to anyone else. This is also the case when a trustor has such confidence in the surrounding environment that she decides to enter it and act within that environment. For example, A decides to perform a transaction through a trustworthy trading system or decides to disclose her personal data in a trustworthy context. In both cases, which represent countless other case, trust causes the trustor to act, and no longer refrain from action, as a result of how the subject perceives the relationship between herself and her surrounding environment.

We can qualify trust in such cases as *systemic trust*. This form of trust is established through the relationship between a subject and an environment, such that a subject decides to act within that environment and thus the outcome depends on her own action. In these cases, trust is characterized, notably, by three elements that qualify the environmental relationship and which reflect the three main trust factors: (1) the trustor's trustworthiness; (2) the security of the environment; (3) the ability to predict the consequences of one's own actions.

It is worth noting that the same phenomenon presides over two different situations: in certain circumstances, trust leads us to act; in others, it leads us to entrust others with the task of acting. In digital contexts, we must be able to distinguish between intersubjective and systemic trust, and to recognize that sometimes both of them may be at play.

On the one hand, there is a growing number of situations in which we entrust others (notably, computational systems [including those who program such computational systems]) with the task of deciding or acting on our behalf. In these cases, we need to ask questions from three points of view: (1) Informationally: To what extent are we able to know and measure the computational system's trustworthiness? (2) Axiologically: To what extent do we share common concerns or purposes with these computational systems? (3) Normatively: How can we prompt or appraise the computational system's loyalty?

On the other hand, there is, as remarked, an increasingly technological design of the environment, according to which we constantly behave in an environment characterized in technological terms. Again, we need to ask questions from three points of view: (1) Informationally: To what extent are we able to grasp and measure our own trustworthiness in such an environment? (2) Environmentally: To what extent can we determine and measure the security of the environment itself? (3) Epistemologically: To what extent can we foresee the consequences of our actions in an environment that is technologically designed?

There is a specific *caveat* that has to be raised as a result of the meditation on trust in the digital world and as a conclusion of this chapter. In today's information societies, which are characterized by the presence of digital ICTs, there is an implicit and progressive shift from the intersubjective trust for artificial agents to the systemic trust for the digital context. This is happening for the obvious reason that the growing delegation of tasks to artificial agents tends to increasingly organize the environment in digital technological terms. This means that the regulatory problem of reliability, responsibility and loyalty, as well as the axiological problem of the values brought into play by the delegation of decisions and tasks to artificial agents, must be grasped, examined and discussed also – and perhaps above all – in the context of the environmental problem (how to build a secure context for a multi-agent system) and of the epistemological problem (how to predict the effects of actions carried out in a technologically designed environment by a multi-agent system).

The tendency to *specifically* trust this or that algorithm, this or that artificial agent, this or that technological device, gives way to the tendency to *generally* trust the digital world, where the environment and the representation of reality will gradually be adapted to the functioning of technologies. As always, this sort of trust involves a risk. However, the kind of risk changes. In intersubjective trust, risk consists in the betrayal of shared goals: the risk being that we no longer understand exactly why we delegated decisions and tasks to machines. In systemic trust, the risk is more radical and consists in the exclusion from the forms of life built in the technologically designed context: individuals, groups or states put their destinies on the line, in relation to the ability to adapt to the technological environment and to the ability to mine energy and resources from that environment, in order to allocate them for further and different purposes.

Notes

1 On technology (and humanism) in the twentieth century, see among others, R. GUARDINI, *Letters from Lake Como: Explorations on Technology and the Human Race*, Eerdamans Publishing, 1994; M. HEIDEGGER, "Letter on Humanism", in M. HEIDEGGER, *Basic Writings*, Routledge, London, 1993; ID., *The Question Concerning Technology*, Harper, NY, 1977; E. JÜNGER, *The Worker. Dominion and Form*, Northwestern University Press, Chicago, 2017; L. MUMFORD, *Technics and Civilization*, University of Chicago Press, Chicago, 2010; N. WIENER, *Cybernetics: Or Control and Communication in the Animal and the Machine*, The MIT Press, Cambridge Mass., 1953; ID., *The Human Use of Human Beings. Cybernetics and Society*, Houghton Mifflin, Boston, 1954; G. ANDERS, *Die Antiquiertheit des Menschen*, Beck, Munich, 1956; M. MCLUHAN, *The Gutemberg Galaxy: The Making of the Typographic Man*, University of Toronto Press, Toronto, 1962; ID., *Understanding Media: The Extensions of Man*, McGraw Hill, NY, 1964; H. JONAS, *Philosophical Essays: From Ancient Creed to Technological Man*, University of Chicago Press, Chicago, 1974; ID., *The Imperative of Responsibility: In Search of Ethics for the Technological Age*, University of Chicago Press, Chicago, 1979; J. ELLUL, *The Technological Society*, A. Knopf, NY, 1964; ID., *The Technological System*, Seabury Press, NY, 1980; A. GEHLEN, *Man: His Nature and Place in the World*, Columbia University Press, NY, 1987.
2 L. FLORIDI, *The Fourth Rev., op. cit.*, p. 25.
3 *Ibid.*
4 *Ibid.*
5 L. FLORIDI, *The Fourth Rev., op. cit.*, pp. 25–26.
6 L. FLORIDI, *The Fourth Rev., op. cit.*, pp. 27–28.
7 *Ibid.*
8 L. FLORIDI, *The Fourth Rev., op. cit.*, p. 31.
9 L. FLORIDI, *The Fourth Rev., op. cit.*, p. 41.
10 On this point, see *infra*, chap. 3.
11 U. PAGALLO, "Profili tecnico-informatici e filosofici", in A. CADOPPI, S. CANESTRARI, A. MANNA, M. PAPA (eds.), *Cybercrime*, Utet, Torino, 2019, pp. 1–32, notably p. 17 *et seq.*

12 In this sense, see L. FLORIDI, *The Fourth Rev., op. cit.*, p. 31: "Essentially, third-order technologies (including the Internet of things) are about removing us, the cumbersome human in-betweeners, off the loop".

13 M. DURANTE, *Il futuro del web. Etica, diritto, decentramento. Dalla sussidiarietà digitale all'economia dell'informazione in rete*, Giappichelli, Torino, 2007.

14 The post in which, in 2005, Tim O'Reilly defined the then emerging Web 2.0 became famous: "Web 2.0 is the network as platform, spanning all connected devices; Web 2.0 applications are those that make the most of the intrinsic advantages of that platform: delivering software a continually-updated service that gets better the more people use it, consuming and remixing data from multiple sources, including individual users, while providing their own data and services in a form that allows remixing by others, creating network effects through an 'architecture of participation,' and going beyond the page metaphor of Web 1.0 to deliver rich user experiences" ("Web 2.0: Compact Definition?", Oct. 1, 2005, radar.oreilly.com/2005/10/web-20-compact-definition.html).

15 In this sense, see especially Y. BENKLER, *The Wealth of Networks: How Social Production Transforms Markets and Freedom*, Yale University Press, New Haven, 2006. Consider also the "Solid" project (*Social Linked Data*), launched by the inventor of the World Wide Web, Tim Berners-Lee, in 2015, in collaboration with MIT, with the aim of creating a completely decentralized platform entirely controlled by users.

16 Nowadays, there are many initiatives aimed at decentralization: think of "Blockstack", the first implementation of a decentralized system based on blockchain, created by the young Muneeb Ali in 2015, or the "Protocols Lab" project, administered by Matt Zumwalt and aimed at building computer systems and tools for a decentralized Web.

17 M. DURANTE, *Il futuro del web, op. cit.*, p. 279 et seq.

18 The World Economic Forum, in a recent article, published online in April 2019, stated that the entire digital universe should reach 44 zettabytes by 2020, accessible online: https://www.weforum.org/agenda/2019/04/how-much-data-is-generated-each-day-cf4bddf29f/.

19 There is already a wide literature on the topic. See, most recently, S. ZUBOFF, *The Age of Surveillance Capitalism. The Fight for a Human Future at the New Frontier of Power*, PublicAffairs, NY, 2019; L. GREEN, *Silicon States. The Power and the Politics of Big Tech and What It Means for Our Future*, Counterpoint, Berkeley, 2019; A. WEBB, *The Big Nine: How the Tech Titans and Their Thinking Machines Could Warp Humanity*, PublicAffairs, NY, 2019; S. MANNONI, G. STAZI, *Is competition a click away? Sfida al monopolio nell'era digitale*, Editoriale Scientifica, Napoli, 2018; F. FOER, *World Without Mind. The Existential Threat of Big Tech*, Penguin Books, London, 2017; J. RIFKIN, *The Zero Marginal Cost Society. The Internet of Things, the Collaborative Commons, and the Eclipse of Capitalism*, Griffin, NY, 2015.

20 Or, to be more precise, as we have previously observed, they are this valuable as long as they find a form of computational power, i.e., the fundamental engine, which can process them and hence extract value from them.

21 To give just a few examples, to "Google" has become synonymous with doing an online search. Facebook is not only the main social network, but also the main social login to network services. Amazon has the overall goal of taking over, in a large part of the world, the entire chain of buying and selling (potentially including credit, storing, exchanging and delivering).

22 On this point, see M. DURANTE, *The Democratic Governance of Information Societies. A Critique to the Theory of Stakeholders*, in "Philosophy & Technology", vol. 28, issue 1, 2015, pp. 11–32; and, with particular reference to the governance of algorithms, M. D'AGOSTINO, M. DURANTE, *Introduction: The Governance of Algorithms*, in M. D'AGOSTINO, M. DURANTE (eds.), The Governance of Algorithms, special issue of "Philosophy & Technology", vol. 31, issue 4, 2018, pp. 499–505.

23 The idea of governance is central in both the academic and the public debate, challenging the concept of sovereignty of nation states, which become one of the holders of power, losing their position of total supremacy. On this point, see U. PAGALLO, "Good

onlife governance: On law, spontaneous orders, and design", in L. FLORIDI (ed.), *The Onlife Manifesto, op. cit.*, pp. 161–177.

24 J. BALKIN, *Free Speech in the Algorithmic Society: Big Data, Private Governance, and the New School of Regulation*, in "UCDL Rev.", 2017, pp. 1149–1210.

25 For which we could borrow Carole Gould's expression of "those affected" – in this case, affected by the effects of the network. For this expression, see C. GOULD, *Globalizing Democracy and Human Rights*, Cambridge University Press, Cambridge, 2004.

26 We could further differentiate the internal composition of the three main actors involved in digital governance as well as detect the presence of other actors due to the sector involved (think, for example, of the current complexity of the multilevel governance of the Internet with regards to the role of ICANN and the multi-stakeholders society). On this topic recently, see R. RADU, *Negotiating Internet Governance*, Oxford University Press, Oxford, 2019; M. MUELLER, *Will the Internet Fragment? Sovereignty, Globalization and Cyberspace*, Polity Press, NY, 2017; L.A. BYGRAVE, *Internet Governance by Contract*, Oxford University Press, Oxford, 2015.

27 J. BALKIN, *Free Speech, op. cit.*, p. 1210.

28 See *infra*, chap. 4.

29 J. BALKIN, *Free Speech, op. cit.*, p. 1198: "Put another way, as online speech platforms govern, and increasingly resemble governments, it is hardly surprising that end-users expect them to abide by the basic obligations of those who govern populations in democratic societies".

30 The "notice and consent" paradigm has been extensively investigated in the current literature. See R.H. SLOAN, R. WARNER, *Beyond Notice and Choice: Privacy, Norms, and Consent*, in "J. High Tech. L.", vol. 14, 2014, pp. 370–414; A. MANTELERO, *The Future of Consumer Data Protection in the EU: Re-thinking the "Notice and Consent" Paradigm in the New Era of Predictive Analytics*, in "Computer Law & Security Review", vol. 30, issue 6, 2014, pp. 643–660; A. KISS, G.L. SZÖKE, "Evolution or revolution? Steps forward to a new generation of data protection regulation", in S. GUTWIRTH, R. LEENES, P. DE HERT (eds.), *Reforming European Data Protection Law*, Law, Governance and Technology Series, Springer, Dordrecht, 2015, pp. 311–331.

31 U. PAGALLO, "On the principle of privacy by design and its limits: Technology, ethics and the rule of law", in S. GUTWIRTH, *et al.* (eds.), *European Data Protection: In Good Health?*, Springer, Dordrecht, 2012, pp. 331–346.

32 U. PAGALLO, *Il diritto nell'età dell'informazione: il riposizionamento tecnologico degli ordinamenti giuridici tra complessità sociale, lotta per il potere e tutela dei diritti*, Giappichelli, Torino, 2014, p. 285.

33 A. RACHOVITSA, *Engineering and Privacy Law by Design: Understanding Online Privacy Both as a Technical and an International Human Rights Issue*, in "International Journal of Law and Information Technology", vol. 24, issue 4, 2016, pp. 374–399.

34 Lawrence Lessig is the precursor of this approach: see L. LESSIG, *Code and Other Laws of Cyberspace. Version 2.0*, Basic Books, NY, 2006. On this issue, see also I. BROWN, C.T. MARSDEN, *Regulating Code: Good Governance and Better Regulation in the Information Age*, The MIT Press, Cambridge Mass., 2013.

35 Italics not present in the original text.

36 On the idea of trust, see, among others, N. LUHMANN, *Trust and Power*, cit. B.C. BAIER, "Trust and its vulnerabilities" and "Sustaining trust", in *Tanner Lectures on Human Values*, vol. 13, University of Utah Press, Salt Lake City, 1991, pp. 109–174; R. HARDIN, *Trust and Trustworthiness*, Russell Sage Foundation, NY, 2002; H. NISSENBAUM, "Will security enhance trust online, or supplant it?", in R.-M. KRAMER, K.-S. COOK (eds.), *Trust and Distrust in Organizations: Dilemmas and Approaches*, Sage, NY, 2004, pp. 155–188; G. SARTOR, "Privacy, reputation, and trust: Some implications for data protection", in *Trust Management* (conference proceedings: The Fourth International Conference on Trust Management, Pisa, 16–19 May 2006) Springer, Berlin, 2006, pp. 354–366; M. TADDEO, *Defining Trust and e-Trust: From the Old Theories to New Problems*, in "International Journal of Technology and

Human Interaction", vol. 5, issue 2, 2009, pp. 23–35; ID., *Trusting Digital Technologies Correctly*, in "Mind and Machines", vol. 27, issue 4, 2017, pp. 565–568.

37 D. GAMBETTA, "Can we trust trust?", in D. GAMBETTA (ed.), *Trust: Making and Breaking Cooperative Relation*, Basil Blackwell, Oxford, 1990, pp. 213–237.

38 N. LUHMANN, "Familiarity, confidence, trust: Problems and alternatives", in D. GAMBETTA (ed.), *Trust: Making and Breaking Cooperative Relation, op. cit.*, pp. 94–107.

39 On the issue of trust in relation to artificial agencies, see M. TADDEO, *Modeling Trust in Artificial Agents. A First Step Toward the Analysis of E-Trust*, in "Minds and Machines", vol. 20, issue 2, 2010, pp. 243–257; M. DURANTE, *What is the Model of Trust for Multi-Agent Systems? Whether or not E-trust Applies to Autonomous Agents*, in "Knowledge, Technology & Policy", vol. 23, issue 3–4, 2010, pp. 347–366; H. TAVANI, *Levels of Trust in the Context of Machine Ethics*, in "Philosophy & Technology", vol. 28, issue 1, 2015, pp. 75–90; M. COECKELBERGH, *Can We Trust Robots?* in "Ethics and Information Technology", vol. 14, issue 1, 2012, pp. 53–60; J. BUECHNER, H. TAVANI, *Trust and Multi-agent Systems: Applying the "Diffuse, Default Model" of Trust to Experiments Involving Artificial Agents*, in "Ethics and Information Technology", vol. 13, issue 1, 2011, pp. 39–51.

40 For an analysis of the effect of trust on delegation decisions, with regards to the economic sphere, see N. GUR, C. BJØRNSKOV, *Trust and Delegation: Theory and Evidence*, in "Journal of Comparative Economics", vol. 45, issue 3, 2017, pp. 644–657.

3

ARTIFICIAL AND HUMAN INTELLIGENCE

The beginning of Faust

The trajectories of artificial intelligence (AI) and human intelligence are likely to continue to diverge for years to come. This is not because AI, as many fear, will be largely removed from human control and judgment[1], but for a subtler and perhaps even more consequential reason. AI will be defined less and less in terms of its ability to approximate human capacity for representing and understanding reality, and more and more in terms of its ability to act upon and reconfigure the nature of that reality. As has been previously observed:

> Artificial intelligence is any technology that we develop and use to perform tasks that would be defined as intelligent if they were created by a human being. This definition belongs to a proposal written in 1955 for a summer research project on artificial intelligence. [...] It is a counterfactual definition, since the capacity of artificial intelligence is defined as intelligent not in itself but when a human being would be defined as intelligent if he were able to achieve the same result. Today, artificial intelligence could be more efficient and more capable of performing a certain task – like winning a GO game – than any human being. This means that human players should be really smart to be just as good. Artificial intelligence is not and above all it does not need to be. We have outlined so far what artificial intelligence does; it is important to specify now what it is: it is a growing resource of ability to act which is interactive, autonomous and learns from itself. It is not necessary to consider artificial intelligence as "intelligent", "conscious" or "similar to life", to pose serious problems to society.[2]

This passage touches on an extremely important point: given its increasing capacity to act, AI may well have disruptive effects upon society. This calls to mind

Goethe's Faust as he ruminates on the translation of the beginning of the Gospel of John: "It says: In the beginning was the *Word*". Not satisfied, Faust tries again:

> It says: In the beginning was the Mind [Sinn]. Ponder that line, wait and see, lest you should write too hastily. Is mind the all-creating source? It ought to say: In the beginning there was Force [Kraft]. Yet something warns me as I grasp the pen, that my translation must be changed again. The spirit helps me! Now it is exact. I write: In the beginning was the Act [Tat].[3]

Action is ranked even higher than power and replaces thought and speech (which can be considered akin to human intelligence). For Goethe, conflation of word and action leaves no space for word to criticize action, thus reducing the space for morality and opening up unlimited possibilities. However, this is not the place for exegesis of Goethe's Faust or to go into the details of the debate on the risks and opportunities of AI.

The AI4People group has recently proposed an *Ethical Framework for a Good AI Society*[4], which critically examines the opportunities and risks posed by AI and sets forth a series of principles and recommendations as part of a broader policy project on the governance of AI. It is worthwhile to briefly refer to this report to gain a specific overview of the opportunities and risks involved in delegating tasks to AI systems.

The report defines four key areas in which AI is likely to have a significant impact on society[5] and thus to affect the development and dignity of human beings: (1) *Who we can become* (concerning the autonomous capacity for self-realization); (2) *What we can do* (concerning human agency); (3) *What we can achieve* (concerning the individual and social capacity to reach specific goals); (4) *How we can interact with each other and with the world* (concerning the degrees of social cohesion that we are able to establish).

If the resources offered by AI are not used efficiently or correctly, these opportunities will inevitably present us with a corresponding series of risks. Examining these risks sheds light on how AI works today as an autonomous form of agency, rather than as an approximation of human reasoning[6].

Who we can become

AI can foster "self-realization, by which we mean the ability for people to flourish in terms of their own characteristics, interests, potential abilities or skills, aspirations, and life projects. [...] More AI may easily mean more human life spent more intelligently"[7]. AI can contribute to human realization, since it provides humans with considerable time to devote to their own development, whether intellectual, cultural, spiritual, and so on. In this sense, AI systems are linked to *increased intelligence* not only because they make more computational power available to humans, but also because they allow humans more time to devote to the development of their own intelligence. We shall return to this important point below, while discussing the impact of ICT and the Internet on human intelligence. What bears noting here is the flip side of the opportunity just examined: "The risk in this case is not the obsolescence of some old skills and the emergence of new ones *per se*, but the pace at which this is happening and the unequal distributions of the resulting costs and benefits"[8]. This, in a nutshell, is the key consideration underlying the present chapter: the overall impact of ICT (understood both as the impact of AI systems on society and as an impact of the Net on human intelligence) is likely to widen the gap between resources enjoyed by individuals, generating a distribution of costs and benefits that may grow increasingly unequal and unfair. This requires: "some intergenerational solidarity between those disadvantaged today and those advantaged tomorrow, to ensure that the disruptive transition between the present and the future will be as fair as possible, for everyone"[9].

What we can do

Thanks to the resources offered by AI systems, we can "do more, better and faster"[10], as the commonly used phrase has it. With greater power comes greater responsibility, and this in two senses: generative and reflexive. In fact, it must be decided *upstream* and in a responsible manner what type of AI systems should be developed, what risks should be taken, what types of use should be favored, and how the resulting costs and benefits should be shared. And it must be decided *downstream* what types of criteria should be used to ascertain and attribute responsibility for the consequences of actions implemented by AI systems. It is not always easy to reconstruct the causal chain of events that triggered a decision or the outcome of a specific action. Not only can this reduce the capacity for human control over the course of events, but it can also make it more difficult and challenging to attribute responsibility to its source. The erosion of human responsibility is thus the risk that accompanies an increased capacity for doing. On closer inspection[11], this risk concerns not only responsibility, but also – and above all – human freedom. There are two closely related reasons for this. First of all, we believe that we are responsible for something to the extent that we are free to act, or at least to the extent that we believe we could have acted differently in a particular circumstance based on a practical counterfactual. In reality, it can be difficult to establish *ex ante* the extent to which we might be free or not to act in a certain way or another. Often, the concrete measure of our freedom is identified, *ex post*, when we are called upon to take responsibility for something within the public judgment. It is within the sphere of reflective judgment that the limits of our freedom are defined, as if the responsibility attributed to us establishes, after the fact, the measure of our (recognized) freedom. The attribution of responsibility generally presupposes an explanation of the course of events, or at least some sort of ordering of a chain of events. This leads to the second reason for which the erosion of human responsibility may impinge upon human freedom: we are free to the extent that we can explain how things happen. As will be examined in greater detail in Chapter 8, the erosion of responsibility risks constraining human freedom if it keeps us from explaining a course of events and thus of predicting and fully appraising the consequences of our actions.

What we can achieve

Delegating decisions and tasks to AI systems can both increase (*augment*) and improve (*enhance*) human abilities by modifying our performance, allowing us to achieve more or better results. This has prompted a number of multidisciplinary debates (ethical, legal, social, economic, etc.) and also raises a general concern regarding expanded and increased human performance[12]. In some cases, AI systems (and more generally all forms of human–machine interaction) can restore tasks and behaviors an individual is no longer capable of performing (AI-based speech synthesis for stroke victims, for example) or increase and improve performance in socially acceptable and ethical ways for the common good (such as the use of AI for medical diagnostics). However, the altered or improved performance stemming from the delegation of decisions or tasks to intelligent systems may sometimes generate advantages that are not necessarily equally distributed throughout society and are available only to those who can afford them. This introduces issues of social equity and questions of ethical, legal and political imperatives. In addition, there are cases where the potential for using intelligent systems generates social expectations that individuals will take advantage of technology to improve their performance (for example, in providing professional services) simply because that technology exists. This raises the thorny issue of the relationship between individual autonomy and social heteronomy. The possibilities opened up by technology are likely to turn individuals' autonomous choices (the willingness to adopt a given intelligent system) into social heteronomous expectations (the more or less explicit demand that individuals should adopt such a system if they want to comply with some social expectation). In my view, the true liberal attitude consists not merely in increasing individuals' choices as an expression of their autonomy, but also and above all in ensuring that these choices are *truly* an expression of their autonomy and not the ill-concealed result of succumbing to heteronomous forces.

As already remarked, there is also a more general problem. The delegation of decisions and tasks to intelligent systems can erode the sphere of human control. This risk can be described in terms of the scenarios mentioned in Chapter 2[13]: (1) *human in the loop*: where the human is still integral to the process and has the power to at least partially intervene in the course of events determined by the AI system; (2) *human on the loop*: where the human being is no longer integral to the process and cannot intervene at single phases of the process, but still has the ability to interact with and monitor its overall progression, providing input in this regard; (3) *human post-loop*: where the human being has no direct control either over the single phases of the process or its overall progression; he or she can only intervene *ex post*, to repair or mitigate any harmful consequences of the action delegated to the AI system. There is also an additional scenario: (4) *human out of the loop*: where the human being is external to the process and lacks any power of intervention. Being "out of the loop" implies the least degree of human control, where one is most exposed to the effects of the autonomous functioning of the AI system. It tends to exclude human control altogether, whereas the first three scenarios attempt to strike a more or less balanced trade-off between delegation and control.

A final point about the erosion of the sphere of human control is worth making. Each delegation of a task or decision is likely to imply a certain degree of confidence that accompanies the progressive loss of control over that task or decision. To a certain extent, we might consider the intelligent system to be an autonomous artificial agent with which we join in a form of intersubjective trust[14], shaped by the characteristics of the artificial agent and the relationship we have with it. However, since the delegation of decisions and tasks to AI systems is becoming so systematic and pervasive, and as these systems begin to communicate and interact with each other, the connotation of trust is becoming less intersubjective and contingent and increasingly widespread and systemic[15]. The transition from an intersubjective to a systemic dimension of trust marks the transition from a loyalty-based perspective to one based on the safety and security of the environment in which we interact with AI systems[16].

How we can interact with each other and with the world

This is the most important aspect highlighted in AI4People's *Ethical Framework*. The development of technology – notably digital ICTs – has not only an instrumental impact on society but also an environmental impact on the world, as it redesigns the environment where individuals operate and interact, making it more complex. This environmental complexity is coupled with the emergence of global problems that raise issues of coordination and collaboration between public and private actors at a supranational level. For this reason, technology based on AI systems is increasingly called upon to contribute to the solution of coordination and collaboration problems through mechanisms that exploit the intensive use of data and algorithms[17]. These systems can thus be designed in such a way as to favor the adoption of certain behaviors, without imposing them but suggesting their adoption through "self-nudging" systems[18]. One again, this comes with both risks and opportunities:

> "Self-nudging" to behave in socially preferable ways is the best form of nudging, and the only one that preserves autonomy. It is the outcome of human decisions and choices, but it can rely on AI solutions to be implemented and facilitated. Yet the risk is that AI systems may erode human self-determination, as they may lead to unplanned and unwelcome changes in human behaviors to accommodate the routines that make automation work and people's lives easier. AI's predictive power and relentless nudging, even if unintentional, should be at the service of human self-determination and foster societal cohesion, not undermining of human dignity or human flourishing.[19]

This passage underlines once again how computational power and its various expressions, including AI systems, algorithms and other computational models, tend to adapt the world and its representation to the exercise of their power. The risk is that by accepting the advantages they bring, we are gradually and almost imperceptibly accommodating our behavior – without premeditation, oversight or consideration of the possible consequences – to the functioning of devices, mechanisms and processes that make decisions and perform tasks in an automated way. This is not a governmental conspiracy with some hidden agenda, but rather the joint outcome of only partially desired and planned choices. This can be illustrated with a simple example.

I do not like driving. I look forward to being able to have cars that drive themselves and getting around in one. This is the part that concerns what I consciously desire. I would not be able to plan or assess how these self-driving cars should represent their route to guarantee safety on the road, nor how we should adapt the environment to the virtual representation of the world run by driverless cars. That part I would leave to others, allowing them to design and evaluate the cars, and to establish safe driving procedures and rules. A third part – perhaps the most decisive for the success of the overall operation – is others explaining what will happen if things go wrong and who will be called on to find a solution. The jigsaw that brings together each of these small parts of the puzzle is the teleological discussion on goals: in other words, the possibility for a public forum on evaluating, weighing and balancing the opportunities and risks:

> Public acceptance and adoption of AI technologies will occur only if the benefits are seen as meaningful and risks as potential, yet preventable, minimisable, or at least something against which one can be protected, through risk management (e.g. insurance) or redressing. These attitudes will depend in turn on public engagement with the development of AI technologies, openness about how they operate, and understandable, widely accessible mechanisms of regulation and redress.[20]

This is a very important theme which we will come back to again and again through the course of this book: there is no possible regulation or governance of the digital without public discussion (from political, legal and ethical standpoints) about the social goals (and the standards for evaluating such goals) of AI systems, whose operations are likely to affect socially relevant values and assets. There is one issue in particular that any ambition of regulation or governance of the digital has to face when entrusting decisions or tasks to AI systems: the need to explain the delegation process, with particular reference to the effects of the decision or task delegated.

This need has deemed necessary, as shall be seen later in the book[21] and which epitomizes two different needs – the understanding of processes and the accountability of actors – as the AI4People correctly remarked, in examining current approaches to the ethical problems of AI systems:

In all [the approaches], reference is made to the need to *understand* and *account* for the decision-making processes of artificial intelligence. [...] The addition of this principle, which we synthesise as "explicability" both in the epistemological sense of "intelligibility" (as an answer to the question "how does it work?") and in the ethical sense of "accountability" (as an answer to the question: "who is responsible for the way it works?"), is therefore the crucial missing piece of the jigsaw [...] for AI to be beneficent and non-maleficent, we must be able to understand the good or harm it is actually doing to society, and in which ways; for AI to promote and not constrain human autonomy, our "decision about who should decide" must be informed by knowledge of how AI would act instead of us; and for AI to be just, we must ensure that the technology – or, more accurately, the people and organisations developing and deploying it – are held accountable in the event of a negative outcome, which would require in turn some understanding of why this outcome arose.[22]

Naturally, this inescapable need for explanation clashes with considerable epistemological problems, both intrinsic and extrinsic[23]. From an intrinsic standpoint, we are dealing with the issue of the *black box society*, that is, the problem of understanding how a system works, given the limits of *reverse engineering* such AI systems; to put it differently, it is one thing to know how a system is built, but another thing altogether to understand retrospectively how it works, or rather, how it came to a certain decision. From an extrinsic standpoint, the explanation of the effects produced in terms of responsibility clashes with an extrinsic problem that stems from the degree of complexity of the agent system, which is increasingly constituted by multi-agent systems where responsibilities are spread out and more difficult to retrace and assign[24].

The delegation of decisions and tasks to intelligent computational systems seems to be an irreversible process; one which is not intended to transform the understanding of human intelligence but instead to reshape, at least in part, the ethical, legal, etc., boundaries of human agency. However, this poses not only a practical but also an epistemological question, which will challenge human intelligence in a completely different way. Machines, using computational models, need to be provided with a specific knowledge base and representation of the world. We can ask ourselves which agent – the human or the artificial – will be adapting to the other's representation of the world. The answer is far from certain, nor can it be taken for granted. On the contrary, those who harness a form of computational power will probably find ways to implement it and to adapt the world to its deployment. This carries the obvious risk for asymmetries in the exploitation of these resources, and may alter the starting conditions of those who invest in the sector, generating scale economies and concentrations of power and potentially promoting social exclusion and discrimination. These possible outcomes must also be taken into account, along with the risk of erosion of the sphere of human control, autonomy and self-determination.

In addition to comparing artificial and human intelligence, it is also important to consider the impact that ICTs, most notably the Internet, have on human intelligence and cognitive abilities. The topic has attracted widespread debate on a single question: Does the Internet make us smart or stupid? The attentive reader will recognize this as the debate between Nicholas Carr and David Weinberger[25], which is summarized briefly here as a prelude to some final remarks regarding the risks of AI.

Does the Internet make us smart or stupid?

In 2010, Nicholas Carr published the book, *The Shallows: What the Internet is Doing to Our Brains*. David Weinberger countered by publishing his text, *Too Big to Know. Rethinking Knowledge Now That Facts Aren't the Facts, Experts Are Everywhere, and the Smartest Person in the Room Is the Room*, in 2011. The debate on the impact of the Internet on the cognitive abilities of users and notably on the formation of online knowledge actually dates back a few years, and has featured optimistic or moderate positions[26] as well as highly critical positions[27], over time and up to the present day[28].

There are a number of reasons for which these two authors stand out from the fray. Firstly, because they have both correctly highlighted the idea that the network platform constitutes a real *medium* of communication and knowledge. Secondly, because they have recognized that this medium affects not only the contents communicated (according to the famous teaching of Marshall McLuhan: "the medium is the message"[29]) but that it affects also and above all the cognitive abilities of users (summarized in terms of stupidity and intelligence). Thirdly, because both have suggested the idea that the network constitutes, for better or for worse, a new representation of knowledge, either in its dense network of connections or in its fragmentation. Finally, because their reflections reveal an issue that emerges from careful reconsideration of their main theses, which will be the focus of the conclusion of this chapter, to formulate a hypothesis that differs at least in part from those of Carr and Weinberger.

Nicholas Carr's main critical observations and David Weinberger's counter-arguments are presented below. It should be kept in mind these arguments have been the subject of much discussion not only between the authors, but also by many other authors interested in the ongoing debate.

Nicholas Carr's perspective: Internet makes us stupid

Carr's perspective can be divided into four main critical observations and corresponding concepts: (1) meaning; (2) memory; (3) attention; (4) in-depth analysis.

The impact of the Internet on the construction of meaning

In general, Carr argues that the pursuit of knowledge has always been mediated by technology (such as simple writing instruments or the more complex printing press), and that this has affected not only the form content takes, but also the way humans have produced and consumed that content, developing particular cognitive abilities and creating specific representations of knowledge (a specific *mindset*) along the way[30]. We all have direct experience with the particular technological tool that is the book, around which the elaboration and use of knowledge have been organized for centuries. The tools mediating knowledge affect how meaning is constructed. The Internet significantly modifies our relationship with reading and writing. Writing is traditionally understood as being characterized by the principles of non-immediacy of the world (it allows us to relate to things that are absent, far away, or merely imagined), of linearity (writing tends to represent knowledge as something that develops in an orderly manner according to a logical process that moves from a beginning to an end), and of self-reflection (both writing and reading imply a private relationship with oneself, a space for analysis and reflection)[31]. According to Carr, Internet-mediated meaning construction is primarily based on a more immediate and direct relationship with the world; it tends towards the non-linear and contains hypertext links that vie for our attention and fragment content; it does not allow us to reconstruct a unitary framework of meanings (and in a riff on the old adage, Carr remarks: "We do not see the forest when we look on the web. We do not even see trees. We only see twigs and leaves"[32]). The Internet tends to produce an image of knowledge and a mindset as something necessarily fragmentary, discontinuous and disjointed.

The impact of the Internet on memory

As also noted by Viktor Mayer-Schönberger in another context[33], Carr reminds us that the Internet has changed our relationship with memory and, consequently, with oblivion. Whereas forgetting was once the rule and remembering the exception, this relationship has been reversed: the Internet has become a gigantic repository of memory, where the (more or less indelible) traces of our passage, of our communications, of anything that concerns us remain. This delegated and outsourced form of memory has largely supplanted our need to remember, for our memories are just a click away. The other side of the coin, however, is information overload, to which we are routinely subjected. This constant barrage of information makes it increasingly difficult for us to select, assimilate and sediment it, memory-based processes that nourish our capacity for thought and reflection[34]. While we are not compelled to remember, because we have delegated and outsourced our memories, we are induced to forget, because the incessant flow of data overwhelms our ability to bring order to the mass of data available and to remember the relevant pieces of information. Memory storage and reproduction, as we shall later see[35], are therefore subject to the functioning of the Internet and its governance, with consequences for both individual and collective memory; they are therefore also helping to reshape not only the construction of personal identity but also that of society. In fact, there can be no civilization without memory. Those who govern the Internet also govern the institution of memory. This is all the more significant when we come to realize that the Net not only captures and records the traces of memories that we continually leave online. It contributes to our forgetting. Through the very accumulation of memory, the Internet also creates oblivion.

The impact of the Internet on attention

One of the most highly debated issues related to the impact of the Internet and more broadly of ICTs, social media and mass media on people's cognitive abilities is that of attention. It has often been remarked that in the communication society, where it is crucial to build communication networks, processes and devices, information plays a central role, since it represents the most precious resource and the true currency of exchange. In the current information society, where communication has become ubiquitous and information sharing is incessant, the most valuable resource has become attention. And it is as precious as it is rare. What scholars decry (and Carr is just one of many) is that the speed and fragmentation of online communication (which would have further extended the speed and fragmentation of traditional mass media communication) are impeding or diminishing people's capacity for attention and concentration. Others suggest that it is not so much a question of diminishing attention spans as a shift in attention from traditional (for example, paper-based) media to other forms of audiovisual or digital media. And still others argue that there are different types of attention (distinguishing, for example, between the extensive and continued attention required to understand a complex text from the intense and focused attention needed to perform a complex task) and that the impact of the Internet and ICTs should be assessed more comprehensively, that is, by taking into account these different forms of attention. What seems clear is that the cognitive and epistemological question of attention (how the ability to pay attention contributes to the elaboration and the diffusion of knowledge) is today largely inseparable from the economic and political question, mediated by network platforms, that concerns the capturing of attention understood as a scarce and ephemeral resource[36]. We must remember Clay Shirky's claim[37] that the success of Web 2.0 derives not so much from having allowed users to generate content on the Net as from having provided them the opportunity for reaching a relatively wide audience. This audience is currently the real *capital* of attention that many seek.

The impact of the Internet on our critical thinking

Ultimately, according to Carr (and many others), the Internet has contributed to making us, if not more stupid, at least more superficial. It has weakened our capacity for analysis. Underlying this critical observation is an implicit and crucial notion worth examining. When referring to the ability to improve our knowledge or understanding of something, we often speak in terms of spatial metaphors, for example, we talk about expanding the "depth" or "breadth" of knowledge and moving beyond "superficial" or "shallow knowledge". However, the ability to advance our knowledge also rests on a temporal foundation: the power to go back over things and think them through again is, in a certain sense, a way of bending time back; the origin of the term "reflection" itself comes from the Latin meaning first to "bend or turn back", and later to "turn one's thoughts back on".

The Internet has opened up so many opportunities that just did not exist in the analog world. I remember when I went to Louvain to prepare the bibliography for my PhD thesis and spent an entire week making seven thousand photocopies. Today, it might have taken me about a day to download the same material. But what would I have done with the time left over? That is the *real* question we need to be asking: What are we doing with all the time we are saving? The Internet gives us quicker and easier access to information; AI systems and artificial robotic agents free us from unnecessary chores; algorithms allow us to spend less time making decisions. But where does all of that time − some of which used to be spent reflecting on and "turning back" our thoughts − actually go? In the library in Louvain it took me time to choose what needed to be photocopied and time to sort all the copies I finally made. It was only natural that I used that time thinking about what I was doing; the time went to good use, and was not completely wasted. Of course, if I had had more time, I could have spent it doing further research on my topic. Thanks to digitization, we have gained time; but again, what are we doing with it? We cannot raise serious issues about the overall (cognitive, epistemic, social and political) effects of digitization, the superficiality or depth of network effects, or the dialectic between ease and difficulty (which is more relevant today than the true/false dialectic[38]), without considering the issue of time gain. It is not enough to ask whether the consumption of online content allows us greater understanding. We need to ask the broader question as to whether the time digitization is saving us is somehow systematically swallowed up, or whether it remains at our disposal.

David Weinberger's perspective: the Internet makes us smarter

The merit of Weinberger's perspective, like Carr's, mainly consists in the fact of recognizing that: (1) knowledge is increasingly and pervasively mediated by technology and digital ICTs that mark a clear discontinuity with traditional ICTs; (2) technological mediation affects not only how knowledge is formed but also the cognitive abilities of network users; (3) the medium of the network produces a new representation and conception of knowledge. We can summarize Weinberger's position according to the following main aspects[39]: (1) abundance; (2) connectedness; (3) permissionlessness; (4) publicness.

The abundance of resources on the Internet

Information overload is one of the most persistent aspects of the effects of digitalization: as network users, we produce more data than we could ever consume and end up being overwhelmed by the abundance of data available. Weinberger suggests that this is a general representation that tends to hide the fact that we usually deal with more limited and specific digital contexts, in which this abundance is likely to result in much faster and more efficient access to the useful resources we seek. What changes is our relationship with the selection filters of reliable and relevant information. These filters now operate mostly *ex post*: users gather first and then they select. This also changes the representation of knowledge: "But the new infrastructure does not only open up a world of abundance: it makes abundance evident, and this changes our way of conceiving knowledge. Although we can only see one form at a time, we know that this is full of links that will lead to other links. […] In this world of abundance knowledge is not a library but a musical lineup that suits our current interests. Not truthful content, now and forever, but fairly good arguments for our current task. Not a kingdom, but a road that takes us where we are going"[40]. This is not a completely new problem. We have always had to reduce the complexity of reality and the overabundance of information[41], in order to produce the knowledge necessary to interact with the world: renewing and refining the ability to synthesize information is hence an integral part of the development of human intelligence and of its ability to adapt to the new informational environment. However, this capacity cannot be measured in merely general terms but rather with reference to "our current task".

The increasing connectedness of the Internet

Knowledge is made up of a dense network of references and interconnections[42]. Today this is hastened by the hyper-textual structure and visible links of digital platforms. In the pre-digital age, the connections were established by other means: think of knowledge spreading through courts of law or academic institutions; think of individuals' ability to make connections through the power of intellect or to establish a web of relationships between sources of knowledge or to answer questions formulated elsewhere or at other times; think of their ability to refer to someone else's works in the dense web of references in a book or article. Weinberger's observation that the Internet has increased the empirical capacity of traditional communication systems to create connections is undoubtedly correct. What he perhaps neglects to address is that the Net's web of hyperlinked information paradoxically reduces the amount of imaginative effort required to associate distant and detached elements. For Weinberger, the main point to note is that the Internet has produced or made more perceptible a conception of knowledge as a network of references and connections that can run in every direction and is thus essentially boundless. "Links also change the basic topology of knowledge. People will continue to write long works because the complex knowledge needs time to unravel, like any narration. But the Internet and its connections accustom readers to see every text that develops an idea as something that lives inside an interconnected and viable web. […] The links are subverting not only the knowledge as a system of fixed points, but also the accreditation mechanism that supported that system. […] Thus, the connections that we all encounter on each Web visit radically transform the form of knowledge, the role of authorities and titles, and the reasons and points where we allow our research to stop"[43].

As mentioned before, the focus here is not to discuss the merit – or lack thereof – of statements that have already been the subject of ample debate (such as the online progressive loss of authoritativeness engendered by the Net). Such statements are difficult to appraise in the absence of clear empirical data on the subject (if there may be such a thing); in fact, one limit of the many debates about the Internet is that they are formulated in ways that do not allow verification in terms of validation or refutation. Instead, we would like to highlight another essential point that concerns a common truism: the technical infrastructure of the Internet opens up a world of new opportunities. There is certainly truth to this statement, since the Internet is an enabling technology. However, there is a particular aspect of the infrastructural element of the Internet that often goes unremarked, even by scholars such as Weinberger who have written extensively on the topic. This aspect may be clarified through a parallel with Floridi's concept of infraethics[44]. Floridi explains quite clearly that infraethics consists of different facets (actions, processes or devices) that can facilitate or hinder morally good or bad actions, without being morally assessable themselves. The fact that these facets can give rise to a dual use or result does not necessarily imply that such a use or result is perfectly symmetrical in its positive and negative consequences. In other words, an infraethic element is like a pipeline carrying water. The fact that the pipeline is intact, in good working order and being used for the proper purpose (transporting a stream of water), does not necessarily imply that the quality of the water is particularly good. In fact, the procedural aspect does not necessarily guarantee that the substance of the matter is high quality; it merely satisfies one of the conditions that make high quality possible. Conversely, a rusty pipeline might affect the quality of the water without preventing its flow. In this case, the procedural aspect does not fail but is flawed; it is therefore likely to negatively affect the substance of the matter. So while a well-designed and properly functioning infrastructure does not necessarily guarantee a positive outcome (even though it is intended to)[45], an ill-designed or malfunctioning infrastructure can lead to negative consequences. For this reason, recurring references to the infrastructural element in Weinberger's and others' work must be read with caution. The importance of designing quality infrastructures is indisputable. However, it must be realized that their normal functioning does not lead inevitably to positive outcomes, and that their improper use normally implies *in and of itself* a negative outcome[46].

The permissionless structure of the Internet

Open access, with its "permissionless" dimension is one of the most salient and defining features of the Internet. Growing numbers of people access ever-expanding online resources each day. This is something we tend to overlook, take for granted, or even condemn, although at the same time, very few of us would willingly stop going online. Freedom of access has made knowledge less exclusive by integrating not only the production of new data and information, but also much of the knowledge base created offline. The expression "traditional" used to refer to things that existed offline. Early on, for example, when Web 2.0 was just giving rise to online user-generated content, traditional offline (professional) journalism was distinguished from online (non-professional) journalism. This distinction has fallen into disuse. Now we tend to distinguish between traditional online journalism and non-professional online journalism. Traditional institutions have migrated online, while retaining an offline dimension. From this perspective, the Internet is no longer subject to comparison but rather a battleground. However, Weinberger identified a major benefit of free access, which recapitulates the thesis of his book. It is not the individuals but the network itself that has become more intelligent: "The network becomes systematically more intelligent when all this is made more available. Not only individuals can find it and use it; when the information is made programmatically accessible to other computers, the developers invent the way to increase their value by aggregating them, linking them and mixing them. Traditional institutions must be great contributors to the network if the new infrastructure is to move towards knowledge and not into obtuse ignorance"[47]. This consideration is all the more interesting as Weinberger could not entirely have foreseen how it would have become possible to increase the value of information by "aggregating, linking and mixing it". I repeat here what I have already said[48]: it is the decentralization of the network (which has favored the production, circulation and sharing of data in a distributed way) which has allowed the collection, aggregation and concentration of such data in the hands of few actors capable of extracting from this mass of data other data of great economic (political, social, etc.) value.

Public knowledge on the Internet

Weinberger correctly remarks that the Internet has provided us not only with wider and freer access to information resources, but also and above all with a public space where we can make use of such resources: "In reality we have not limited ourselves to providing everyone with access to these works: we have created a new type of public space for them. The pages within this space aggregate links, each of which reflects in some way on the meaning and value of the work. Even the web of links has a meaning and value, which can be taken and put back on the network"[49]. This ability to exploit network effects, to create further knowledge and to extract value from created and shared knowledge, is a crucial aspect of the network, which cannot be taken for granted. Weinberger himself is aware of this. He recognizes that digital literacy is required in order to transform the opportunities of the network into reality, to share the cognitive surplus that the network itself produces, and to fully exploit the advantages deriving from network effects. At the same time, he recognizes the risk of new forms of division and social exclusion: "Say something ridiculously technodeterministic in the presence of Eszter Hargittai and she will show you the data that shows that if you put someone in front of the network you will not necessarily become an enthusiast, an expert or even just an internet user. Hargittai is a sociologist who loves the web, but at least as much as she loves data; and her meticulous studies have allowed her to discover that success with the internet varies according to the same old factors: class, income and education. We must therefore *teach* everyone how to use the net"[50]. However optimistic and naive this last sentence may be, Weinberger highlights a key aspect that leads us to the conclusions of the present chapter, in which I try to formulate a third hypothesis, since I am not entirely convinced of either thesis that the Internet makes us more stupid or smarter.

A third hypothesis as a conclusion

Careful reconsideration of Carr's and Weinberger's theses, combined with Barabási's analysis of the unequal distribution of information online, raises the possibility of a third hypothesis: the Internet makes us neither more stupid nor more intelligent. For either to occur would require the Internet to be the only *medium* presiding over the distribution of information as the formation and communication of knowledge. However, this is not the case (at least not yet). Even the youngest generations are exposed one way or another to different sources and channels of information, communication and knowledge. Although the impact of the Internet does not start on a blank slate, it clearly helps to shape the environment in which we live. For this reason, its impact is neither merely deterministic (it affects us totally) nor merely instrumental (it does not affect us at all but is only a tool in our hands). This leads us to the third hypothesis (merely a hypothesis, because there is not enough empirical data to turn it into a thesis[51]): *The Internet makes the smart even smarter and the dumb even dumber.*

In this perspective, one can perhaps speak of an *amplification effect* of the Internet. It seems to us that this is actually what Carr and Weinberger (and many others) have long implied: those with good cognitive tools, intellectual resources, and a sufficient degree of attention and curiosity tend to improve and enrich their starting condition by means of network effects. Those who possess these characteristics only to a limited extent will tend to worsen and further impoverish their starting condition as a result of the same network effects. We can say that the Internet *amplifies* people's starting conditions. It is as if every swimmer, in order to win a competition, increased the frequency of their strokes: those who already possess high endurance qualities are at an advantage, while the others risk being overwhelmed and cut out because of the overly intense rhythm.

If it can be demonstrated and proven, this network amplification effect would pose serious problems for democracy. No matter how democracy is defined, it is generally agreed that individuals should be able to change their starting conditions, particularly within a context (the Internet) in which a large part of their lives is carried out both publicly and privately. We are faced with a new iteration of the familiar problem of social mobility, both upwards and downwards, translated into informational and cognitive terms. Those in unfavorable situations must be provided opportunities to improve their plight (upwards), just as those who already enjoy favorable situations should be encouraged to strive to improve their standing, even at the risk of falling (downwards). In both cases, social immobility is a problem but, of course, upward (informational and cognitive) social immobility is a more discernable and worrying fact, which profoundly reverses the seminal ideal of the Internet, which was precisely that of providing greater opportunities to those from disadvantaged backgrounds. There would be no more biting and dangerous betrayal than this.

This is an important point to emphasize since it perfectly encapsulates what we have already observed in relation to the risks and opportunities of AI. At present, we can assess it both with reference to artificial and human intelligence: the risk (and the opportunity) is that artificial or human intelligence becomes the battlefield where the challenges of innovation may be won, but where division and social exclusion may also develop and spread, once again calling into question the crucial issue of power. Whenever we hear about stupidity on the Net or about network intelligence, we must understand that the issue at stake concerns users' cognitive abilities as well as their social mobility, accompanied by the risk of division and exclusion. Whenever confronted with a question of artificial or human intelligence, we must realize that what is at stake is not just the individual sphere of control, autonomy and self-determination. It is also a question of social equity that must be reconciled with the development and growth of current information societies.

Notes

1 On this point, see A. TETI, "Intelligenza artificiale: la meta finale", in A. TETI, *PsychoTech – Il punto di non ritorno*, Springer, Milano, 2011, pp. 27–59; M. SHANAHAN, *The Technological Singularity*, The MIT Press, Cambridge Mass., 2015. Conversely, and almost in contrast to what has been said, there is also an important tendency to create forms of collaboration between artificial and human intelligence, between humans and computers (from human-computer interaction to human-based computation, up to the forms of collective intelligence of multi-agent systems). In this perspective, see the recent T.W. MALONE, *Superminds. The Surprising Power of People and Computers Thinking Together*, Little, Brown and Company, NY, 2018.

2 L. FLORIDI, *et al.*, *AI4 People – An Ethical Framework for a Good AI Society: Opportunities, Risks, Principles, and Recommendation*, in "Minds and Machines", vol. 28, issue 4, 2018, pp. 689–707, p. 689.

3 J.-W. GOETHE, *Faust*, Anchor, NY, 1990, p. 153.

4 L. FLORIDI, *et al.*, *AI4 People – An Ethical Framework, op. cit.*

5 L. FLORIDI, *et al.*, *AI4 People – An Ethical Framework, op. cit.*, p. 690.

6 As I have remarked elsewhere, the word intelligence derives from the Latin with a double meaning. It can stem from the etymology of *intus-legere*, indicating the ability to understand in depth and adequately represent reality, or from *inter-legere*, indicating the ability to efficiently choose between alternatives. From the etymology of the word, two lines of research that have characterized the study of artificial intelligence over time seem to emerge: cognitive or artificial intelligence in the strong sense (strong AI), which is aimed at reproducing the mechanisms of the human mind, and engineering or artificial intelligence in the weak sense (weak AI), which is aimed at emulating human behaviors, or at least at obtaining the results derived from such behaviors. The idea of artificial intelligence as an autonomous form of agency (in which the analogy with some form of human intelligence tends to vanish) can be seen as a radicalization and definitive

affirmation of engineering or weak AI. In our opinion, this would not fully make sense of the ongoing revolution, characterized as already seen by a triple connotation: (1) the fact that action is no longer the exclusive prerogative of human beings; (2) the increasing delegation of decisions and tasks to automated artificial intelligence systems based on an ever-increasing computational power; (3) the tendency to adapt the world and its representation to the deployment of computational power. For the etymology of the word and the taxonomy of AI studies and law, see M. DURANTE, *Intelligenza artificiale. Applicazioni giuridiche*, vol. 2, Utet, Torino, 2007, pp. 714–724.

7   L. FLORIDI, *et al.*, *AI4 People – An Ethical Framework, op. cit.*, p. 691.

8   *Ibid.*

9   L. FLORIDI, *et al.*, *AI4 People – An Ethical Framework, op. cit.*, p. 692.

10   *Ibid.*

11   See, *infra*, chap. 8. On this point, see also P. AURUCCI, *Applications and Security Risks of Artificial Intelligence for Cyber Security in the Digital Environment*, in "Journal of Ambient Intelligence and Smart Environments", vol. 23: Intelligent Environments, 2018, pp. 308–317.

12   There is a wide literature on the subject. See, *inter alia*, N. BOSTROM, *Superintelligence. Paths, Dangers, Strategies*, Oxford University Press, Oxford, 2016; E. PARENS, *Shaping Our Selves. On Technology, Flourishing, and a Habit of Thinking*, Oxford University Press, NY, 2014; N. AGAR, *Truly Human Enhancement. A Philosophical Defense of Limits*, The MIT Press, Cambridge Mass., 2013; J. SAVULESCU, R. TER MEULEN, G. KAHANE (eds.), *Enhancing Human Capacities*, Wiley-Blackwell, Hoboken, 2011; M.J. SANDEL, *The Case Against Perfection. Ethics in the Age of Genetic Engineering*, Harvard University Press, Cambridge Mass., 2007; J. HARRIS, *Enhancing Evolution. The Ethical Case for Making Better People*, Princeton University Press, Princeton, 2007; R. KURZWEIL, *The Singularity Is Near. When Humans Transcend Biology*, Viking, NY, 2005; L. KASS, *Life, Liberty and the Defense of Dignity. The Challenge for Bioethics*, Encounter Books, NY, 2004; J. HABERMAS, *The Future of Human Nature*, Polity Press, NY, 2003; F. FUKUYAMA, *Our Posthuman Future. Consequences of the Biotechnology Revolution*, Farrar, Straus & Giroux, NY, 2000.

13   See, *supra*, chap. 2.

14   L. FLORIDI, *et al.*, *AI4 People – An Ethical Framework, op. cit.*, p. 693.

15   *Ibid.*

16   In this sense, see also L. FLORIDI, *et al.*, *AI4 People – An Ethical Framework, op. cit.*, p. 692.

17   L. FLORIDI, *et al.*, *AI4 People – An Ethical Framework, op. cit.*, p. 693.

18   The expression "nudge" was made famous by the studies of Richard Thaler and Cass Sunstein (R.H. THALER, C.R. SUNSTEIN, *Nudge: Improving Decisions About Health, Wealth, and Happiness*, Penguin, London, 2009). It suggests the idea that current governance is not to be exerted through the imposition of obligations, but by nudging people: this consists in designing processes and mechanisms in such a way as to embody norms or value choices within them. We can speak of *self-nudging* when processes or mechanisms are designed in such a way as to enable us to make choices. This does not exclude that the possibility to make some choices or adopt some behaviors may be, more or less patently, prompted by the specific design of the processes and mechanisms.

19   L. FLORIDI, *et al.*, *AI4 People – An Ethical Framework, op. cit.*, p. 694.

20   L. FLORIDI, *et al.*, *AI4 People – An Ethical Framework, op. cit.*, pp. 694–695.

21   See, *infra*, chap. 7.

22   L. FLORIDI, *et al.*, *AI4 People – An Ethical Framework, op. cit.*, p. 700.

23   Among many others, see S.T. MCKINLAY, *Evidence, Explanation and Predictive Data Modelling*, in "Philosophy & Technology", vol. 30, issue 4, 2017, pp. 461–473. For an introduction to the topic of scientific explanation, see J. WOODWARD, *Scientific Explanation*, in "Stanford Encyclopedia of Philosophy", accessible online: https://plato.stanford.edu/entries/scientific-explanation/.

24   See M. DURANTE, *What is the Model of Trust for Multi-Agent Systems?, op. cit.*

25   See respectively, N. CARR, *The Shallows: What the Internet Is Doing to Our Brains*, Norton & Co., NY, 2011, and D. WEINBERGER, *Too Big to Know. Rethinking Knowledge Now That*

Facts Aren't the Facts, Experts Are Everywhere, and the Smartest Person in the Room is the Room, Basic Books, NY, 2011.

26 For a positive or moderate approach, the main references remain those of: Y. BENKLER, *The Wealth of Networks, op. cit.*; D. TAPSCOTT, A. WILLIAMS, *Wikinomics. How Mass Collaboration Changes Everything*, Portfolio, NY, 2006; C. SHIRKY, *Here Comes Everybody: The Power of Organizing Without Organizations*, Penguin, London, 2008, and ID., *Cognitive Surplus: Creativity and Generosity in a Connected Age*, Penguin, London, 2008.

27 For a critical approach, the main references are those of: A. KEEN, *The Internet Is Not the Answer*, Atlantic Books, London, 2015; J. LANIER, *Who Owns the Future?*, Simon & Schuster, San José, 2014; L. SIEGEL, *Against The Machine: Being Human in the Era of the Electronic Mob*, Serpent's Tale Publishing, London, 2008.

28 For more recent versions of this debate, see L. PACCAGNELLA, A. VELLAR, *Vivere online. Identità, relazioni, conoscenza*, Il Mulino, Bologna, 2016; M. TEGMARK, *Life 3.0: Being Human in the Age of Artificial Intelligence*, Alfred Knopf, NY, 2017.

29 M. MCLUHAN, Q. FIORE, *The Medium is the Message: An Inventory of Effects*, Penguin Books, London, 1967.

30 N. CARR, *The Shallows, op. cit.*, p. 20: "[…] media aren't just channels of information. They supply the stuff of thought, but they also shape the process of thought".

31 N. CARR, *The Shallows, op. cit.*, p. 20 et seq.

32 N. CARR, *The Shallows, op. cit.*, p. 115.

33 V. MAYER-SCHÖNBERGER, *Delete. The Virtue of Forgetting in the Digital Age*, Princeton University Press, Princeton, 2009.

34 It is significant what was observed in L. FLORIDI, *The Fourth Rev., op. cit.*, p. 72: "ICTs increase the endurance effect, for in digital environments it is easier to identify and reidentify exactly the same thing through time. The problem is that the virtual may or may not work properly, it may be old or updated, but it does not grow old; it 'outdates', it does not age. If you think of it, nothing that outdates can outdate more or less well. […] The effect, which we have only started to experience and with which we are still learning to cope, is a chronological misalignment between the self and its online habitat, between parts of the self that age (e.g. my face) and parts that simply outdate (e.g. the picture of my face on my driving license)". And more broadly, on the subject of the construction of personal identity, see again p. 72: "Recorded memories tend to freeze and reinforce the nature of their subject. The more memories we accumulate and externalize, the more narrative constraints we provide for the construction and development of our personal identities. Increasing our memories also means decreasing the degree of freedom we might enjoy in redefining ourselves. Forgetting is part of the process of self-construction".

35 See, *infra*, chap. 4.

36 There are at present a considerable number of studies concerning the economics of attention. What is important to remember in this regard is that attention is not only relevant as a resource to be gained (for example, when we seek the attention of others) but also as information, that is, as an indication of what we pay attention to: our attention reveals our preferences, searches, habits, how we use social media, and so forth. All this information (i.e., *metadata*), which concerns how we allocate our attention, is a resource from which further economically or politically relevant information can be extracted (for example, it can be used to profile consumers). The responsiveness and timeliness with which this economically and politically relevant information is collected (and through which consumers' profiles are continually being updated) ensure that attention is constantly requested: it therefore follows that attention must necessarily be a waning resource, that is, not long-lasting, in order to be continuously renewed. The cognitive transience of attention is the correlative of the industrial mortality of goods. On this issue, see recently S. ZUBOFF, *The Age of Surveillance Capitalism, op. cit.*

37 C. SHIRKY, *Cognitive Surplus, op. cit.*

38 As we shall see, for example, in the chapter on the issue of fake news (*infra*, chap. 6), the problem is not so much the representation of truth or falsehood, but the challenge of

accessing relevant contents, that is to say, contents that allow us to better understand theoretical questions or to behave more adequately in relation to practical matters.

39 See D. WEINBERGER, *Too Big to Know, op. cit.*, in particular chap. 8.

40 D. WEINBERGER, *Too Big to Know, op. cit.*, pp. 228–229.

41 In this perspective, see P. FEYERABEND, *Conquest of Abundance: A Tale of Abstraction versus the Richness of Being*, University of Chicago Press, Chicago, 2001.

42 A.-L. BARABÁSI, *Linked. The New Science of Networks*, Perseus Books, NY, 2002, p. 45.

43 D. WEINBERGER, *Too Big to Know, op. cit.*, pp. 230–231.

44 L. FLORIDI, *The Fourth Rev., op. cit.*, p. 218.

45 See L. FLORIDI, *The Fourth Rev., op. cit.*, p. 193: "To rely on another analogy: the best pipes (infraethics) may improve the flow but do not improve the quality of the water (ethics); and water of the highest quality is wasted if the pipes are rusty or leaky. So creating the right sort of infraethics and maintaining it is one of the crucial challenges of our time, because an infraethics is not morally good in itself, but it is what is most likely to yield moral goodness if properly designed and combined with the right moral values. The right sort of infraethics should be there to support the right sort of values. It is certainly a constitutive part of the problem concerning the design of the right multi-agent systems".

46 A different example can be given to clarify the point: imagine we need to establish a rule to allow proper communication, that is, the rule about "taking turns when speaking". Compliance with this rule (which is a procedural or infraethic condition) does not necessa-rily produce relevant or meaningful discourse, but it certainly produces an ordered discourse (moreover, respecting this rule is likely to determine over time an ethical consequence: a greater sensitivity for the respect of others deriving from the practice of listening to them and allowing them space to speak). The violation of this rule not only produces disordered discourse, but also and above all, discourse devoid of meaning (which not only negatively affects the procedural dimension, i.e., the form of communication, but also the substantive one, i.e., the content of the communication).

47 D. WEINBERGER, *Too Big to Know, op. cit.*, pp. 247–248.

48 M. DURANTE, *Il futuro del web, op. cit.*, p. 110.

49 D. WEINBERGER, *Too Big to Know, op. cit.*, p. 233.

50 D. WEINBERGER, *Too Big to Know, op. cit.*, p. 248. Weinberger refers to the following texts: E. HARGITTAI, *The Digital Reproduction of Inequality*, Routledge, London, New York, 2018, pp. 660–670; D. GRUSKY, *Social Stratification*, Westview Press, Boulder, Colorado, 2008, pp. 936–944; ID., *Digital Na(t)ives? Variations in Internet Skills and Uses Among Members of the "Net Generations"*, in "Sociological Inquiry", vol. 80, issue 1, 2010, pp. 92–113.

51 Our hypothesis echoes, from the point of view of the impact on cognitive abilities and knowledge formation, Barabási's famous thesis regarding the distribution of information through network connections, according to which the topology of the Web would be governed by a *power law distribution* of links in and out of network nodes. To put it briefly, a huge number of websites have few visits or links; few websites are moderately connected; very few websites have a very high number of visits or links. The *power law distribution* identifies an asymmetric distribution of the connections of non-random net-works; as far as the Internet is concerned, this distribution is characterized by a rather low number of highly visited websites and by a so-called long tail consisting of a large number of websites with few visits and links. On this point, see A.-L. BARABÁSI, *Linked, op. cit.* It is significant that the author has already brought up, in reference to this topological distribution, the substantial anti-democratic character of the network (p. 51): "The most intriguing result of our Web-mapping project was the *complete* absence of democracy, fairness and egalitarian values on the Web. We learned that the Web topology prevents us from seeing anything but a mere handful of the billion documents out there".

4

MEMORY AND OBLIVION

The burden of memory

"Everything in life is memory, except the thin border of the present"[1]. Individual and collective memory is a key human cognitive mechanism and thus plays an essential role in our lives: "without it we would not be able to speak, read, recognize objects, orient ourselves in the environment in which we live or entertain personal relationships"[2]. To put it concisely, in the words of Jonathan Foster, "we are what we remember"[3]. Oblivion plays an equally fundamental role, for it allows us to cancel or suppress parts of our personal histories, thus making the past bearable and allowing us to redesign our futures. In this sense, one may say that we are also that which we forget.

Memory and oblivion contribute to the definition of who we are, to the construction of our individual and collective identities, and to the formation and preservation of knowledge. The dialectic between memory and oblivion is subject to change and differs for every society and historical epoch. However, its ability to shape our personal histories follows a long-established canon or norm that we largely take as given: forgetting is easy and remembering is hard. Even though forgetting is not a matter of volition (one cannot simply decide to forget[4]), the constant accumulation of data, information and memories taxes our memories, so that recollection requires considerable cognitive effort. In fact, people with prodigious memories are often treated like geniuses. The emergence of digitalization and the progressive rise of the Internet and ICTs has changed things. As Victor Mayer-Schönberger acutely observed:

> Since the origins of humanity, forgetting has been the norm and remembering the exception. Today, with the advent of digital technology and global networks, this balance has been reversed, so much so that forgetting has become the exception and remembering the norm.[5]

The relationship has been turned upside down: it is now difficult to forget and easy to remember. Whenever we send text messages, go online, use a network-connected device, pay by credit card, interact on a digital platform, or post or comment on a social network, we leave a nearly indelible trail of data and metadata in our wake. With the former (data), we leave a trace[6] of our actions. With the latter (metadata: that is data on data), we leave traces of the traces we have left. Both data and metadata are extremely revealing of our activities, habits, dispositions, preferences, and so on. Both are a mine of data from which to extract new and additional information. "We are our information"[7].

For example, when we send a message via Whatsapp, the content of the message – the data – is protected with an *end-to-end* encryption system, so that the message can only be read by the sender and the receiver: its content is made inaccessible to everyone else, including the messaging system itself. Whatsapp wants to establish a climate of trust with its users by guaranteeing them protection and security through the anonymity of their conversations. No one can spy on our Whatsapp exchanges. This is the noble cause of protecting the confidentiality of our conversations. However, there is also a flip side to the coin: the content of our conversations is often less interesting than how they take place.

In fact, we leave a long trail of metadata when we send a message, including information about who we are writing to, the length of the message and what time it is sent, how often we use the recipient's name, and so on. This metadata is often more revealing of our communication habits than the message's actual content. But most importantly, metadata is not protected. The business model underlying the messaging system is based on the power to access and manipulate our data or metadata in exchange for an otherwise free service. Data protection does not necessarily imply metadata protection.

This example illustrates three points.

Firstly, in the digital world, not only is our data stored indefinitely, but so is our metadata: we have outsourced not only the memory of what we do, but also of how we act and leave traces of our traces. This capturing of metadata – the memory of memory – is occurring to an unprecedented extent.

Secondly, as difficult as it is for users to keep track of the entire life cycle of their data, it is even more difficult to keep track of their metadata. Metadata is certainly less visible, and users may not be aware that it is being tracked or even exists. Yet what and how much information can be inferred from such metadata?

Thirdly, in today's information society, what is remembered and what is forgotten in the mass of data, metadata and information about us constitutes our identities. It is thus in each individual's best interest to have the greatest possible control over it.

How much control do we or should we have? This chapter addresses this question by examining the individual's right to control what happens to personal data and to have a say in what is remembered and what is forgotten. Over time, assertion of this right has evolved into recognition of the right to be forgotten, that is, the power to remove one's own digital traces[8]. It becomes a question of guaranteeing an individual's right to remove or to have their data removed from the Net. This power is presented as the expression of autonomy through which individuals can represent, describe and project their own narrative in the infosphere[9].

However, whenever a right is recognized, much more happens than simply recognizing the legitimacy of a subjective claim on the part of an individual. Along with recognition comes a complex and multifaceted institutional arrangement that regulates intersubjective relations by delegating to a third authority the interpretation, administration and application of this legal relationship. In fact, we may reductively say that x enjoys a right y, without perceiving the web of relationships that the existence of this right implies. By recognizing the right to be forgotten, we delegate to an authority the power to rule on memory and oblivion, defining the terms and ways in which this right is actually applied. It is far from a trivial matter.

Technology alters power relations within society by affecting how they are distributed and exercised[10]. In this case, technology does so via an institutional process that implies recognition of a right, which affects some constitutive factors of a democratic society. These factors – memory, oblivion, truth, knowledge and so forth – should not be a monopoly, or even a prerogative, of any authority. Without going into extensive technical and legal detail, this chapter aims to outline the real consequences of this institutional process. While aiming at rebuilding a climate of trust[11] between users and Big Tech, this process has led to a specific institutional arrangement where the balance between memory and oblivion affects not only concrete power relations, but also knowledge and the representation of reality.

The *Google Spain* judgment

Like every narrative, this saga too has a main character: the Spanish lawyer Mario Costeja Gonzáles. Mr. Costeja had a burning desire: *to be forgotten*. Ironically, he will now be remembered forever. But it is best to start from the beginning. In 1998, the Spanish newspaper *La Vanguardia* published a series of notices of default and foreclosure sales in both its online and print editions. As an owner of one of the properties sold, Costeja was mentioned in the notices. Years later, in 2009, he contacted the newspaper, complaining that a Google search on his name still led to the 1998 news story as the top result. Despite how much time had passed, or the fact that the property had been sold and his debts repaid, his name was permanently linked to the episode, compromising both his personal and professional image.

Let us stop to reflect for a moment on the exact nature of Costeja's complaint. What he was arguing was that the information posted about him on the Net gave a fixed and outdated impression of him, a photograph of the past that tainted the present and threatened to damage his standing in society. A similar case in an offline context had already been litigated in Italy in the nineties, culminating in an important ruling by the Italian Court of Cassation that recognized: "the legitimate interest of every individual not to remain indefinitely subject to further damage to their honor and reputation by the repeated publication of news legitimately pub-lished in the past"[12]. From then on, the right to be forgotten has been conceived in the Italian courts as a fine balance between two conflicting interests: the right of the individual to remove news stories and that of the public's right to know. The application of this right therefore required (and still requires) striking a delicate balance[13] between fundamental rights, such as the right to construct one's own informational identity, and the right of the community to the free circulation of data, freedom of expression and the right to information[14].

So what happened next in the case of our Spanish lawyer? Although Costeja Gonzáles asked *La Vanguardia* newspaper to remove the news story about him from its online site, his request was ignored. He approached Google to ask it, as an Internet service provider, to make the news inaccessible by removing links to sites containing his name. This request met with no better luck. In 2010, Costeja Gonzales turned to the Spanish Data Protection Authority to present his case. The matter wound its way through the courts, eventually reaching the EU Court of Justice, which issued the now-famous 2014 *Google Spain* ruling siding with Costeja and recognizing the right to be forgotten. With this ruling, the Court gave rise to a complex institutional archi-tecture that constitutes the real point of interest in this chapter, since it still plays a crucial role in digital governance. The constant tension between memory and oblivion seriously affects the redistribution of power accompanying the shift from an offline to an online world. At an even more fundamental level, it also has a profound effect on the advancement and dissemination of knowledge.

The point of discussing this complex institutional architecture is to underline the wide variety of actors and interests at stake, which therefore go well beyond the relationship individuals have with their own personal histories. The case of Costeja Gonzáles involved the interest of the individual to maintain his own informational identity; that of the community in the free circulation of information and free speech; that of the online site in the making and dissemination of news; that of the search engine, whose business model consists precisely in indexing the news and allowing retrieval and access. These interests are different and in some cases con-flicting, and one could assign them different degrees of meaning and importance. That is what the Court of Justice essentially did with its decision, the consequences of which probably went beyond its original intentions. The model and balance of relationships that the explicit recognition of a *right to erasure (right to be forgotten)* provided for in Article 17 of the GDPR is unlikely to change[15]. But what exactly did the Court of Justice rule in 2014?

We can refer to "Article 29 Working Party" (thus named because it consists of the European supervisory authorities pursuant to Article 29 of Directive 95/46/EC) whose "Guidelines on the implementation of the Court of Justice of the European Union Judgement on *Google Spain*"[16], recaps the main points of the decision:

1. *Search engines as data controllers*
   Because the activity of search engine operators consists in the processing of personal data, these actors qualify as data controllers pursuant to the European

legislation on personal data protection. In other words, the indexing of search results is considered to be a case of personal data processing and Google is thus subject to application of European Union legislation as is the owner of the site publishing the information. It is an essential part of the ruling that, for the purpose of the case in question, it held Google responsible, for the first time, for the process of indexing the news.

2.   *Fair balance between interests and fundamental rights*
    The Court wanted to rank the priority of the interests at stake, stating that "in the light of the potential seriousness of the impact of such processing on the fundamental rights to privacy and data protection, the rights of the data subject prevail, as a general rule, on the economic interest of the search engine and that of network users to have access to the personal information through search engines". However, the judges in Luxembourg acknowledged that in the specific case a fair balance between the relevant rights and interests, with regards to the nature of processed data and to the public interest in the accessibility of information, had to be struck. This point of the ruling is particularly relevant in terms of digital governance: on the one hand, it affirms the prevalence of the interest of the *individual* over the more *general* right to the free circulation of data[17]; on the other hand, the actual implementation of such interests relies on maintenance of a delicate and difficult equilibrium.

3.   *Limited impact of delisting on access to information*
    According to its report[18], the Article 29 Group believed that the impact of the delisting process on the rights of freedom of expression and access to information would be very limited, since they expected the European supervisory authorities for the protection of personal data to maintain a judicious balance among the different conflicting interests. This turned out not to be the case. As we shall see shortly, the balancing act was performed neither by the supervisory authorities nor by the domestic courts, but substantially and almost exclusively by Google.

4.   *No information is removed from its original source*
    The Court's decision found for the individual's right to delisting, meaning that the individual's name no longer appears in the list of results obtained when running the name through a search engine. However, this right does not extend to deleting the link from result lists based on other searches. The original information remains accessible by using other search terms or by directly accessing the site that originally published it. The Court did not require the erasure of the news for various reasons: because accessing the news occurs to a large extent through search engines (so that limiting access actually would mean blacking out the news); because removing data from the network is a technically complex and burdensome operation; because direct access to the news, although extremely limited, guarantees a partial balancing of the interests at stake.

5.   *No obligation for the data subject to contact the original website*
    Subjects intending to avail themselves of the right to be forgotten are not required to contact the site of origin. Data subjects can address their request

directly to the search engine, asking it to dissociate their name from the search results. Moreover, the search engine is not even required, as a general rule, to inform the webmaster of the pages related to the delisting process that some pages will no longer be found starting from searches based on a given name. In other words, and unlike the US *notice and take down system* often invoked in this regard[19], in relation to a request for delisting, there is no fair hearing of all the parties involved: the controversy essentially seems to concern the individual exercising the right to be forgotten and Google as the main, if not exclusive, search engine in Europe.

The effects of the decision

There are other technical points in the judgment to which there is no need to call attention[20] here. It is important, instead, to draw some clear conclusions from what has been said so far. The Court wanted to restore power to network users and to give them greater control over their data. Individuals should be the ultimate arbiters of what the network can remember or forget about them. Under the protection of the law, this would lead them to strengthen their fiduciary pact with Big Tech in the network and continue to circulate their data, well aware of their increased power of control over the life cycle of their data. For this reason, the Court recognized the power of individuals to claim, under given conditions, the dissociation of their name from the results of a search, thus forcing the search engine to proceed with the delisting.

In this way, the Court identified the search engine owner as the recipient of the delisting request, making it the main player in the affair. Because the vast majority of searches in Europe are conducted via Google, the Court has effectively entrusted Google with a key role. If we analyze the decision not from a strictly legal point of view (the search engine is a data processor = Google is the main search engine = Google is the main data processor), but from the point of view of digital governance, we can ask why the Court actually gave Google such a central role. The reasons are essentially three.

In the first place, it was precisely with regard to Google that the Court wanted to reinforce the users' atmosphere of trust, reaffirming, however, that the right of individuals prevails, *as a general rule*, over the opposing economic interests of the search engine. With the decision, the Court intended to restore a condition of greater equilibrium and to redress the growing imbalance between individuals and Big Tech.

Secondly, Google profits (and earns) most from the mechanism of circulation and indexing of data. It is therefore reasonable that it should also be the one that is called on first to respond to distortions in the functioning of the system (based on the systematic preservation of memory), from which it derives huge profits. It is also in the best position technically and economically to remedy these distortions.

Thirdly, the application of a right imposes heavy costs in terms of time and resources. It is, indeed, a matter of creating a system that is capable of receiving and evaluating claims according to transparent criteria, of providing a swift response, and of developing methods of interpretation that ensure consistent decisions in the still culturally fragmented European area. The Court decided that these costs should not be borne by domestic courts or supervisory authorities, but by Google, which has the necessary resources to afford them.

Empirical data from 2014 to 2018 tend to validate this strategic design[21]. Let us analyze them briefly, before turning to the critical issues raised by the ruling.

In 2014, when the Court of Justice ruled on the *Google Spain* case, about five years had passed since Costeja González first contacted the newspaper *La Vanguardia* with his request. In the first four years following the ruling, Google processed over seven hundred thousand requests for delisting from all over Europe pertaining to more than two million Web pages. At first, Google's legal staff, a many-tiered organization spread across all of the member states, had to revise their evaluation procedure, which took eighty-five days on average. At the time of writing, the average time to process a delisting request is four days. No national supervisory authority or court could have kept that pace. Most requests for delisting (around 56%) are rejected by Google. Another considerable portion is accepted. However, the most interesting aspect lies in the fact that very few of the requests rejected by Google[22] are subsequently subjected to a review process by a supervisory authority or a national court. This means that Google regularly performs the role of judge both in the first instance and as a last resort in the interpretation and enforcement of the right to be forgotten. In other words, it is Google which has the task and power to shape the online contours of memory and oblivion.

Although the Court intended to strengthen the power of individuals and to limit that of Big Tech, it in fact gave Google a sort of monopoly on the enforcement of the right to be forgotten. Time will tell us whether it was a Pyrrhic victory, but it has certainly been the subject of numerous critical observations from the standpoint of both legal and digital governance. We should briefly say something about this. To these critical remarks, rather well known in the international debate, it is also necessary to add a, less apparent but equally significant, final remark.

There are three main reasons for criticizing the ruling of the Court of Justice or, to put it in a better way, for criticizing how the right to be forgotten has been applied and will probably continue to be applied in Europe[23].

The private enforcement of a right

"In the case of the right to be forgotten, the European Union has not only ordered Google to comply with European law; it has essentially handed off enforcement of the right in the first instance to Google"[24]. In doing so, it has in fact outsourced a task and given rise to a singular private enforcement of the right to be forgotten, due to the fact that "the large private enterprises that constitute the digital infrastructure have the technical and bureaucratic capacity to regulate and govern speech, through blocking, filtering, and removing content, through otherwise controlling access to their facilities, and through digital surveillance". As a result, companies such as Google "have also created private bureaucracies to govern their end-user communities in the interests of the community (and the company's profits)"[25]. This inevitably raises a significant democratic question in the information society, since "companies that began as technology companies soon discover not only that they are actually media companies, but that they are also governance structures"[26]. It is one thing to move away from a traditional model of government, involving actors who previously had no direct voice and representation, towards a broader model of governance. It is yet another to delegate a crucial role in the governance of delicate institutional and social balances to private entities.

Segmentation of the information market

As already noted, delisting does not keep people from accessing the originally published information through a search with other terms or through other search engines or even by directly accessing the original website containing the information. Furthermore, the search engine operator, to whom requests for delisting are addressed, can accept or reject these requests without necessarily having to involve those who originally published the news in the decision-making process. For some scholars, this is an "odd consequence", since:

> Members of the public can still learn what happened to Costeja, but they must pay a much greater price to do so. Although members of the public can no longer search on Costeja's name, they can still learn about his attachment proceedings if they search public records, or creatively design new forms of Google searches that do not use his name or inspect printed copies of La Vanguardia's archive. All this costs extra time and money. The architecture created by Google Spain thus skews the distribution of information toward those with resources to spend on information acquisition. This is surely an odd consequence for a society that celebrates open and equal access to information.[27]

This means that the Court's decision indirectly produces an unjustified differentiation, on the one hand, between network users who more or less have the means to acquire information and, on the other, between search engine operators who have or do not have the resources to stay on the market and afford the costs of enforcing such a complex right.

The contrast with the rule of law from a procedural point of view

It has been correctly remarked that Google's balancing of conflicting interests is not necessarily or substantially different from that put into place by national courts in balancing the rights of privacy and freedom of information. However, this balancing act poses serious issues from the procedural point of view, that is, in relation to the mechanism with which all of the actors concerned are involved (or not) in the case:

The procedures Google has followed when implementing the CJEU's *Google Spain* decision are inconsistent with the due process provisions of the U.S. Constitution—and with fundamental, shared notions of due process generally. A fundamental component of due process is that individuals be accorded *notice* and an *opportunity to be heard* by an impartial decision-maker *before* a decision affecting their rights is rendered. Even assuming that Google is such an impartial decision-maker, the procedure by which it is administering delisting decisions is deficient because—pursuant to the guidance provided by European data protection authorities—Google provides neither notice nor an opportunity to be heard to the affected content providers before their free speech rights are determined.[28]

The fact that Google may be diligent in informing the parties involved does not mean that it is required to do so or that the involvement of the concerned actors is effective. This delicate procedural aspect is and remains a serious democratic problem even when compared with the rule of law in Europe[29].

The paradox of oblivion

These reasons for criticism have signaled certain serious and perilous distortions in the structure of the architecture to which the Court's decision gave rise. However, these distortions are not limited to the enforcement of the right to be forgotten which affects the access to information and hence to knowledge; they directly concern the creation of knowledge. As a matter of fact, another crucial aspect in this complex affair only came to light some years later and can be read about in an interesting report entitled: "Three Years of the Right to be Forgotten"[30].

This report, written by a series of authors affiliated to Google, aims to explain, with full transparency, how European citizens have resorted to the right to be forgotten. Accordingly, it provides a lot of useful data and descriptions about who files the most requests in Europe, what kind of requests are made most often and about what topics, in which contexts, how requests are examined, and so on. It provides a very good panorama of the entire situation, although one which is necessarily seen from a distance. Nonetheless, the report contains an extremely important passage, even if its implications may not immediately be evident:

> Our analysis broadly expands on the information currently available in Google's Transparency Report. Following the transparency report's same standard, in the course of our analysis we never discuss details that might de-anonymize requesters or draw attention to specific URL content that was delisted. This emphasis on privacy creates a fundamental tension with standards for reproducible science. We cannot directly reveal a sample mapping between URLs and our annotations, nor can we reveal the exact URLs requested and the justification for delisting verdicts.[31]

What are really getting at? Apparently, this long passage is merely informing us that, for privacy reasons, Google cannot tell us everything it knows. It cannot directly reveal to us "a sample mapping between URLs and our annotations", that is, the annotations with which Google evaluates, examines and processes the requests. This is because "privacy creates a fundamental tension with standards for reproducible science". But what scientific knowledge (science) is the report talking about? The report is actually telling us that the overall volume of requests over time has generated a huge and unexpectedly up-to-date record of data and metadata concerning how European citizens enforce their right to be forgotten; this is a large database from which Google is able to extract knowledge. Knowledge that, paradoxically enough, Google cannot share with us for privacy reasons!

Analysis of our delisting requests makes it possible to draw a rather precise picture of how our sensitivity to privacy and data protection is created, in the tension between memory and oblivion, and how this sensitivity affects access to information in time and space. *Google records what we want to forget and remembers how and when we want to forget it.* Our attitudes and sensitivities constitute an endless wealth of information. Requests for delisting are currently providing the basis for producing new memory. From this systematically stored and annotated memory, it is possible to mine new knowledge. One can try to predict what we would like to forget and therefore what we want to remember. And if one can predict it, maybe one can also influence it. We do not know exactly what kind of knowledge Google is able to extract from the huge database that the Court's decision made possible.

The Court wanted to limit Google's power as a reaction to widespread sentiment in Europe. We presume it did not succeed. On the contrary, the architecture generated by the decision handed Google more power. Not only power deriving from the administration and enforcement of a right, but above all, power that derives from the creation of knowledge. The latter aspect seems to us even more relevant than the first, since it is less visible and therefore less subjected to discussion and scrutiny. Moreover, it is certainly more capable of affecting, over time, our sensitivity towards the past, our ability to remember and forget, and the construction of our informational identity. In a word, our knowledge.

Notes

1 Michael Gazzaniga cited by J.-K. FOSTER, *Memory: A Very Short Introduction*, Oxford University Press, Oxford, 2008.
2 J.-K. FOSTER, *Memory, op. cit.*, p. 3.
3 *Ibid.*
4 See P. ROSSI, *Il passato, la memoria, l'oblio. Otto saggi di storia delle idee*, Il Mulino, Bologna, 2013.
5 V. MAYER-SCHÖNBERGER, *Delete, op. cit.*, p. 1. On this subject, see also F. THOUVENIN, *et al., Remembering and Forgetting in the Digital Age*, Springer, Dordrecht, 2019.
6 On the relationship between identity and trace, see M. DURANTE, "Rethinking human identity in the age of autonomic computing: The philosophical idea of trace", in

M. HILDEBRANDT, A. ROUVROY (eds.), *Law, Human Agency and Autonomic Computing. The Philosophy of Law meets the Philosophy of Technology*, Routledge, London, New York, 2011, pp. 85–103.

7 L. FLORIDI, *The Fourth Rev., op. cit.*, p. 78.

8 There is an extensive literature on the subject of the right to be forgotten. See, among others, recently, F. WERRO (ed.), *The Right To Be Forgotten: A Comparative Study of the Emergent Right's Evolution and Application in Europe, the Americas, and Asia*, Springer, Dordrecht, 2020; M. TZANOU, "The unexpected consequences of the EU Right to Be Forgotten: Internet search engines as fundamental rights adjudicators", in M. TZANOU (ed.), *Personal Data Protection and Legal Developments in the European Union*, IGI Global, Hershey, PA, 2020, pp. 279–301.

9 See U. PAGALLO, M. DURANTE, "Legal memories and the right to be forgotten", in L. FLORIDI (ed.), *Protection of Information and the Right to Privacy. A New Equilibrium?* Springer, Dordrecht, 2014, pp. 17–30.

10 For this thesis, see M. DURANTE, *Il futuro del web, op. cit.*, pp. 284–289.

11 In this sense, the reference to trust contained in the GDPR, to which we have already referred in chap. 2, is highly significant.

12 Italian Court of Cassation, sentence n. 3679/1998.

13 On the balance between fundamental rights, see G. PINO, *Conflitto e bilanciamento tra diritti fondamentali. Una mappa dei problemi*, in "Etica & Politica", issue 1, 2006, pp. 1–57; M. DURANTE, *Dealing with Legal Conflicts in the Information Society. An Informational Understanding of Balancing Competing Rights*, in "Philosophy & Technology", vol. 26, issue 4, 2013, pp. 437–457; M. SUSI, "The Internet balancing formula", in M. SUSI (ed.), *Human Rights, Digital Society and the Law. A Research Companion*, Routledge, London, 2019, pp. 178–194.

14 In this sense, see F. PIZZETTI, "Il prisma del diritto all'oblio", in F. PIZZETTI (ed.), *Il caso del diritto all'oblio*, Giappichelli, Torino, 2013, pp. 21–63, p. 34, where it is remarked that the right to be forgotten can be considered as "a point of equilibrium between the respect for the rights of the personality, on the one hand, and the freedom of information and the expression of thought, on the other".

15 Article 17. Right to erasure ("right to be forgotten").

16 14/EN WP225: Guidelines on the implementation of the Court of Justice of the European Union on Google Spain and Inc v. Agencia Espanola de Protección de Datos (AEPD) and Mario Costeja Gonzáles, C-131/12, accessible online: http://www.datap rotection.ro/servlet/ViewDocument?id=1080.

17 14/EN WP225, p. 5.

18 14/EN WP225, p. 10.

19 On critical procedural aspects, see D.C. NUNZIATO, *Forget about it? Harmonizing European and American protections for privacy, free speech, and due process*, in "GWU Law School Public Law Research Paper No. 2017", vol. 52, 2017, pp. 1–20; U. PAGALLO, M. DURANTE, "Human rights and the right to be forgotten", in M. SUSI (ed.), *Human Rights, Digital Society and the Law, op. cit.*, pp. 197–208. On the substantial critical aspects, see K. BYRUM, *The European Right to Be Forgotten. The First Amendment Enemy*, Lexington Books, NY, 2018.

20 This refers, in particular, to the subject of DPIA (*Data Protection Impact Assessment*), 14/EN WP225, p. 11.

21 *Google's Transparency Report*, Google Europe Public Policy, 2018, accessible online: https://transparencyreport.google.com/eu-privacy/overview.

22 *Ibid.*

23 As remarked by J. BALKIN, *Free Speech, op. cit.*, p. 28 *et seq.*

24 J. BALKIN, *Free Speech, op. cit.*, p. 34.

25 J. BALKIN, *Free Speech, op. cit.*, p. 29, 35.

26 J. BALKIN, *Free Speech, op. cit.*, p. 35.

27 R. POST, *Data Privacy and Dignitary Privacy: Google Spain, the Right to be Forgotten, and the Construction of the Public Sphere*, in "Duke Law Review", vol. 67, 2018, pp. 981–1072, p. 1066.

28 D.-C. NUNZIATO, *Forget about it?, op. cit.,* p. 14.
29 On this point, see U. PAGALLO, M. DURANTE, *Human Rights and the Right to Be Forgotten, op. cit.,* pp. 17–30.
30 T. BERTRAM, *et al., Three Years of the Right to be Forgotten,* 2018. In the report, authors are mentioned as being affiliated with Google; accessible online: https://blog.acolyer.org/2018/03/22/three-years-of-the-right-to-be-forgotten/.
31 T. BERTRAM, *et al., Three Years, op. cit.,* p. 4: "Our analysis broadly expands on the information currently available in Google's Transparency Report [14]. Following the transparency report's same standard, in the course of our analysis we never discuss details that might de-anonymize requesters or draw attention to specific URL content that was delisted. This emphasis on privacy creates a fundamental tension with standards for reproducible science. We cannot directly reveal a sample mapping between URLs and our annotations, nor can we reveal the exact URLs requested and the justification for delisting verdicts".

5

DATA, INFORMATION AND KNOWLEDGE

Data, information and knowledge

The epistemic impact of digitalization and, more specifically, of ICTs on our world touches on three basic notions addressed in this chapter: data, information and knowledge. Much could be said about the philosophical debate on these notions, but that is not our concern here. Our task instead is to outline some useful working definitions that shed light on their conceptual core. This will allow us to better understand the epistemological consequences of the impact of technology due to the specific characteristics of each of these essential epistemic notions. In fact, the words "data", "information" and "knowledge" are frequently confused in the rhetoric that surrounds information technology. This confusing and overlapping use of the terms has kept us from truly understanding and addressing several issues that are typical of the digital context, particularly those concerning the relationship between the syntactic and semantic dimensions in the creation of knowledge. To help explain the meaning of these notions, we make reference to Luciano Floridi's information and knowledge theory[1].

The conception of data

Much of the confusion can be traced to the notion of data. There are two reasons for this. In the first place, the terms data and information are often used interchangeably or as synonyms, although technically they represent two different notions that should be kept conceptually distinct. Secondly, the definition of data depends on the epistemological context of reference; in this case, the specificity of the context in question is not a source of confusion but, on the contrary, a potential source of an array of concepts, all of which possess or claim their autonomy[2].

It therefore seems important to articulate a minimal and unitary definition of data. To this end, we can refer to the diaphoric interpretation of data which, while referring to the notion of information, allows us to keep the two concepts distinct:

> The fact is that a genuine, complete erasure of all data can be achieved only by the elimination of all possible differences. This clarifies why a datum is ultimately reducible to a *lack of uniformity*. Donald MacCrimmon MacKay highlighted this important point when he wrote that "information is a distinction that makes a difference". He was followed by Gregory Bateson, whose slogan is better known, although less accurate: "In fact, what we mean by information – the elementary unit of information – is a difference which makes a difference." More formally, according to the *diaphoric interpretation* (*diaphora* is the Greek word for "difference"), the general definition of a datum is:
>
> Dd) datum = $_{\text{def.}}$ x being distinct from y, where x and y are two uninterpreted variables and the relation of 'being distinct', as well as the domain, is left open to further interpretation.

In other words, a datum can be defined as a *lack of uniformity* in the world or, to put it more simply, a point of discontinuity, a difference that signals a difference. A sound that breaks the silence or a black dot on the white page constitutes in itself a datum or, more precisely, the difference between the sound and the silence, between the black dot and the white page constitutes a lack of uniformity, a discontinuity that makes us perceive a difference. The difference that can be grasped as such is the essence of the datum; it is the possibility of perceiving something as given. The lack of uniformity, which characterizes and defines data, may be perceived, according to Floridi, in three main ways[3]:

1. data as *diaphora de re*: a difference that is perceptible in the real world (such as a sound that breaks the silence, or a red light on a black background);
2. data as *diaphora de signo*: a difference that is perceptible between at least two physical states of a system or signals (such as the highest or lowest voltage of an electric charge, or the dots and dashes in Morse code);
3. data as *diaphora de dicto*: a difference that is perceptible between two symbols (such as the difference between two letters of the alphabet).

These are the different levels at which data can be captured. This does not mean that, due to the position or context in which these data are perceived, data in "(1) may be either identical with, or what makes possible *signals* in (2); and signals in (2) are what make possible coding of *symbols* in (3)"[4]. What is important to remark with Floridi is that these differences are a lack of uniformity, mere points of discontinuity, "pure data or proto-epistemic data, that is to say, data before it is interpreted in epistemic terms. As 'fractures in the fabric of being', they can only be posited as an external anchor of our information, for dedomena are never accessed or processed independently of a level of abstraction"[5]. In this sense, the world is full of data, because "total and absolute uniformity is as rare in the universe as complete randomness is"[6]. Therefore, it is possible to gather data in isolation or, as happens more often, in connection with other data; for this to be possible, it is necessary that such data be well formed from the syntactic point of view[7]. We will soon return to this extremely important point. Before doing so, two further categories of data must be specified[8], and will often be referred to in this book: *metadata*, which constitute indications about the nature of other data (for example, the time of day a message is sent constitutes metadata about the data-message); and *derived data*, which can be extracted from other data whenever the latter are used as an indirect source for the search for patterns, indications or inferential evidence in relation to elements other than those directly inferable from the data in question. For example, a credit card purchase is likely to provide a direct datum (a given purchase) and an indirect datum that can be derived from it, such as the fact that the subject was at a particular store when the purchase was made.

Having made this clarification, we examine below how the notion of data, while distinct from that of information, nonetheless affects the concept of information.

The concept of information

The concept of information as intended here is that presented by Floridi in terms of semantic information. This is the current and most common concept of information[9], which analyzes information in terms of its constituent elements. Needless to say, there are different notions and notably different possible taxonomies of information[10]. The general definition of information from the semantic point of view presupposes that of datum.

Floridi observes that, for a long time now and in many epistemological contexts (from information science to the theory, methodology, analysis and design of information systems, from database management and processing to decision theory), a general definition of information in terms of *data + meaning* has been adopted. This is the very definition of information as semantic information, so that information is made up of well-constructed and meaningful data. For a piece of information to reveal anything about some state of the world, it must consist of data that are well connected to each other, which can be associated with a semantic content, that is to say, some meaning. More analytically, it is possible to say that: (1) semantic information includes data; (2) data are well constructed from a syntactic point of view, meaning that such data "are grouped together based on rules that govern the system, code or language that is analyzed. Syntax must be understood in a broad sense (and not only in linguistic terms), like what determines the shape, construction, composition or structure of something"[11]; (3) well-formed data have meaning. The semantic dimension is coupled with the syntactic one. "'Meaningful' means that the data must comply with the meanings of the system, code or language in question. Even in this case, let's not forget that semantic information is not necessarily linguistic"[12].

This determines a crucial consequence, to which we will return in the following analysis: data can, as a rule, be elaborated and processed syntactically, by syntactic engines, whereas information must be elaborated and processed at a semantic level, by semantic engines. Syntactic engines, such as computers or any other computational system, can usually elaborate and process data syntactically *better* (faster and more efficiently) than any human being. Semantic engines, such as human beings, are capable of elaborating and processing data from a semantic point of view, by attributing to them extremely well-articulated semantic contents: treating them as information and organizing them into composite forms of knowledge. The process of signification, whereby x counts as y, is a complex process both in the recognition phase (when we recognize the meaning of something) and in the performance phase (when we attribute a given meaning to something). This is much more difficult for a machine, if not impossible. For a machine to work, a minimum proto-semantic capacity is required, that is, the ability to distinguish and process a difference (according to the principle of identity and not contradiction).

We will return to this crucial point shortly. For the moment, we need to focus on one last aspect that serves to introduce the next section of this chapter. Possessing one or more pieces of information means knowing some aspects or elements of a given reality; it means knowing *that* things are in a certain way, not *because* they are that way. For this reason, adding other information to the information in our possession does not necessarily improve or change the situation. Sometimes it offers us a more complete or in-depth representation of the facts, but it does not necessarily allow us to have access to knowledge. From this point of view, the online dissemination of information increases the number of people who are likely to know that p (that things are in a certain way) but does not necessarily increase the knowledge of why p (why things are in that way). This militates against the idea that knowledge is a progressive and indiscriminate accumulation of information, likely to result eventually in some form of knowledge. For this reason, we will focus on the idea of knowledge as a network of questions and answers.

The conception of knowledge

Every authentic cognitive inquiry or true undertaking of thought rests on the ability to question. There is nothing more difficult in the search for knowledge than to construct the relevant and pertinent questions, from which any investigation and reflection can take its departure. Formulating the question is, if anything, more difficult and pertinent than coming up with the answer, since every answer is obtained within the confines established by the question.

This crucial importance of this aspect of any cognitive activity is frequently overlooked. There is no possible description or representation of reality that has not previously been the subject of a question. When we describe x in terms of y (which gives us the erroneous impression that x possesses some reality independent of the characteristics y_1, y_2, etc., with which we can portray it at different levels of abstraction[13]), we are implicitly answering a question we raised about x. This point was grasped clearly by Floridi, who posited it as the foundation of his theory of knowledge:

Each piece of semantic information is a response to a question, which, as a whole, raises further questions about itself, which require the correct flow of information to receive adequate response, through an appropriate network of relationships with some information source.[14]

Let us take this one step at a time. In reality, we possess many pieces of information, which we have obtained through various means: through observation, through inference, through learning from others, through searching online, and so forth. From these pieces of information, we try to build a more complete and organized representation of reality. We are unable to create such a representation as long as each piece of information remains mutually independent of the others, as long as each piece cannot *account for the* others, that is, it cannot explain how these pieces are connected together:

It is known that Plato discussed the importance of incorporating truths (our information packages) into the correct network of conceptual interrelations that can "offer reasons" (*logon didonai*) for such truths, so as to obtain their knowledge.[15]

We must be able to account for or offer reasons for why things are in a certain way (or, to put it more technically, we must account for the network of conceptual relationships that exist between different pieces of semantic information). This network of relationships does not exist by itself but has to be built. The portrait of knowledge as a network is a suggestive and correct image. What is wrong in certain current representations of knowledge (borrowed from the image of online networks) is to think that this network exists in and of itself and does not require a complex process of conceptual construction[16]:

The relevant semantic information lacks the necessary relationship structure that allows different information packages to account for each other. Consequently, in order for the relevant semantic information to become known, they must be incorporated into a network of equally relevant questions and corresponding correct answers. A network of information flows [...] satisfies this criterion, where it ensures that the erotetic deficit, which the semantic information that serves as a goal *or* possesses by default, is satisfied by the flow of correct answers, offered by the adequate information source f.[17]

To put it more simply: knowing does not mean accumulating a vast amount of information resources, but being able to construct (and maneuver within) a conceptual network of questions and answers[18].

Syntactic engines: inferential and predictive knowledge

Digital technologies are endowed with an extraordinary computational power with which they syntactically process increasing amounts of data. Their ability to process data ever more efficiently and rapidly enables them to transform inputs into outputs, with the result of identifying statistical recurrences, extracting correlations, producing inferences, generating predictions, building profiles, etc., namely, of producing a form of knowledge that is widely exploited in the economic, political and social fields (and in a growing number of other areas as well, including the law). Not surprisingly, this form of knowledge is particularly applicable in these areas, since its inferential and predictive nature has a strong regulatory impact: it allows us to predict behaviors and therefore to influence them. This can result in more or less direct forms of conditioning. Examples include sales strategies based on customer profiles (*price discrimination*), the production of false news (*fake news*) to reinforce feelings or influence the orientations of people, and the systematic selection of information (*filter bubble*) that corresponds to the already consolidated interests of users. Conditioning can also be indirect, such as when a person has a personal stake in being included within a particular category based on statistical correlations. For example, if a credit institution is offering special loan rates to individuals who possess qualities x and y (statistically correlated to the ability to repay the loan but devoid of any causal relationship), it is in the best interest of loan seekers to show that they possess qualities x and y.

We could list countless examples and will in fact return in the course of our discussion to some problematic aspects related to the normative impact of inferential and predictive knowledge[19]. Here we need to focus on a different point, which is relevant from the epistemological point of view. Digital technologies are not able to process data semantically. They cannot ascribe meaning to or make sense of things the same way human beings do. At most, they can perform proto-semantic operations[20]. Machines are therefore exceptional syntactic but not semantic engines. As we will see below, human beings are still the main, if not the only, semantic engines. This generates two very relevant tendencies: the tendency to tackle and solve semantic problems in syntactic terms (*reduction to the syntactic level*) and the tendency to rely on human semantic engines to tackle and solve semantic problems (*human-based computation*). Let us touch briefly on what these two tendencies mean.

Firstly, machines have the resources (in terms of the amount of memory, sharing and availability of data) and are programmed in such a way (based on increasingly sophisticated computational models able to learn from experience) that they reduce the representation of reality to a series of elements, operations, processes and data that can be processed syntactically, so as to adapt it to their mode of operation:

> We do not have semantically proficient technologies. But memory outperforms intelligence, so it does not matter. There are so many data, so many distributed ICT systems communicating with each other, so many humans plugged in, such good statistical and algorithmic tools, that purely syntactic technologies can bypass problems of meaning and understanding, and still deliver what we need: a translation, the right picture of a place, the preferred restaurant, the interesting book, a good song that fits our musical preferences,

a better priced ticket, an attractively discounted bargain, the unexpected item we did not even know we needed, and so forth.[21]

More importantly, this implies the progressive replacement of an immediate and direct experience of reality with an increasingly mediated and indirect experience, through what has been defined as a "proxy culture"[22], that is, a culture in which certain experiences and actions are made vicariously possible by the fact that "something represents and replaces (and acts in place of) something else"[23] (such as when we have no direct experience with a hotel or restaurant but rely on a recommendation system such as Tripadvisor). On the one hand, the experience is no longer immediate and direct; on the other hand, the mediated and indirect experience, which functions as a proxy, is generated on the basis of a computational model that projects its algorithmically elaborated representation of reality onto the world. This flattens both the representation of reality and our way of experiencing it to a syntactic dimension, which in the long run is likely to become an increasingly inadvertent and pervasive interface between us and the world.

Secondly, there are areas and circumstances in which machines need access to a semantic understanding and interpretation of reality – one which is based on meaning. In this case, computation can be based on the ability of integrating human activity as a semantic engine, within the syntactic procedure. This can occur through a form of cooperation between *human* and *machine* (*human-computer interaction*)[24] or by entrusting semantic tasks to human beings (*human-based computation*)[25], which may be implicit (as in the case of reCAPTCHA or Instagram) or explicit (as in the case of Amazon Mechanical Turk)[26]. The reason of interest is not only epistemological (these forms of cooperation produce a mediated and indirect welding of the syntactic and semantic levels) but also and above all technological (according to the environmental interpretation of technology that we have already pointed out), as human beings become an integral part of the process of adapting the world to the way machines work, as Floridi once more acutely observed:

> One of the consequences of enveloping the world to transform it into an ICT-friendly place is that humans may become inadvertently part of the mechanism. The point is simple: sometimes our ICTs need to *understand* and *interpret* what is happening, so they need semantic engines like us to do the job. [...] Other examples of useful employment of human brains by smart systems multiply daily. [...] The winning formula is simple: smart machine + human intelligence = clever system.[27]

As we have said before and will specify later when discussing Lynch, digital technologies tend to reshape the environment in which we live and to prompt the development of practices, habits and behaviors that are real *forms of life*, understood more specifically as a set of syntactic and semantic rules that structure human experience. This also means that the delegation of decisions and tasks to machines operating on the basis of computational models is likely to produce forms of dependence deriving from the fact that the use of these computational models is connected to the forms of life they contributed to creating. For example, at a certain point, choosing a hotel or a restaurant will be entirely dependent on knowledge produced by an online recommendation system. In this regard, there is a further epistemological aspect to which attention must be drawn: that concerning the ability to experience reality as produced by the progressive accumulation and sharing of data.

The growing amount of data that we accumulate and process – often referred to as Big Data[28] – raises an intrinsic epistemological problem, which no longer concerns *information overload*, that is, the idea that such a huge amount of data would overwhelm our ability to experience it. We are now used to operating within this huge amount of data, as we will see later in Lynch's words. Further, its abundance no longer necessarily feels daunting, since the availability of data is the main prerequisite of the exercise of computational power. In fact, an entirely different issue arises in this regard, stemming from the need to extract increasingly specific information from the data available for tailoring to specific needs:

> The real epistemological question with big data is *small patterns*. Precisely because so many data can now be generated and processed so quickly, so cheaply, and on virtually anything, the pressure both on the data *nouveau riche*, such as Facebook or Walmart, Amazon or Google, and on the data *old money*, such as genetics or medicine, experimental physics or neuroscience, is to be able to spot where the new patterns with real added-value lie in their immense databases, and how they can best be exploited for the creation of wealth, the improvement of human lives, and the advancement of knowledge. This is a problem of brainpower rather than computational power.[29]

We need to know how to ask questions ("what you are or may be looking for"[30]), to kickstart knowledge creation. As already mentioned, while it is certainly possible to extract correlations, produce inferences and generate predictions by processing huge amounts of data, this does not necessarily mean being able to elaborate scientific knowledge ("we do not do science by mere accumulation of data"[31]). As will be clarified later in Chapter 7[32], this has provoked widespread concerns, which are well summarized in Judea Pearl's latest book, aptly entitled *The Book of Why*[33], where the American computer scientist and philosopher, winner of the ACM Turing Award in 2011, emphasizes the importance of re-establishing a representation and understanding of reality based on a theory of causality or, more precisely, of *causal inference*, against the excessive emphasis placed on the ability to extract knowledge from correlations based on the analysis of Big Data:

> Some tens of thousands of years ago, humans began to understand that some things cause others and that tinkering with the former can change the latter. No other species grasps this, certainly not to the extent that we do. From this

discovery came organized societies, then towns and cities, and eventually the science- and technology-based civilization we enjoy today. All because we asked a simple question: Why? Causal inference is all about taking this question seriously. It posits that the human brain is the most advanced tool ever devised for managing causes and effects. Our brains store an incredible amount of causal knowledge which, supplemented by data, we could harness to answer some of the most pressing questions of our time. [...] We live in an era that presumes Big Data to be the solution to all our problems. [...] But I hope with this book to convince you that the data are profoundly dumb.[34]

We will return to this issue later, but one point is important to mention here that touches closely on the question of power. As already remarked elsewhere[35], technology has a peculiar relationship with power. In particular, enabling technologies create possibilities: when these possibilities are implemented, they are a means to power for those who have access to their implementation. Access to technologies and implementation of powers is not necessarily distributed in an egalitarian way; they provide greater power to some people, but limit the power of others. For this reason, the spread of technology is likely to alter the distribution of existing powers within society. Often, the debate concerning the regulation of a particular technology does not concern the technology as such – its merits or demerits – but rather the underlying redistribution of power that it entails.

This is also true when a technology consists in producing an inferential or predictive type of knowledge that serves as the basis for machine-based decisions or actions. In such cases, a computational model produces some form of knowledge useful for completing a task, deciding a case, contributing to a practice, and so forth, which then competes with the same knowledge produced by other sources. This sort of competition can alter the distribution of power between competing sources. For example, a subject (or society as a whole) may be asked to choose which source of knowledge, human or computational, should be entrusted with making legal or medical decisions. This competition is also likely to create a technological divide, due to the different degree of implementation of the possibilities generated by a technology, or in other words, to the different capacity to exploit the resources provided by computational models. To cite a recurrent motif in many law schools but easily applicable to further contexts, AI systems applied to the law will not supplant lawyers; lawyers who know how to use AI systems will replace lawyers who do not know how to use them.

Semantic engines: semantic capital

As already remarked, Luciano Floridi stressed how computers, and particularly AI computational systems, are exceptional syntactic engines, capable of processing and transforming data into output at a pace and with an efficacy that human beings cannot match. However, human beings remain the main semantic engines, namely, those who are most capable of performing an extraordinarily complex operation such as attributing meaning to things. This ability characterizes the accumulation of what Floridi qualifies as semantic capital and constitutes one of the salient features, if not the most decisive today, of the *singularity* of the human species. Let us see how semantic capital is defined by Floridi, first in general terms and then more analytically:

> There is a wealth of resources – including ideas, insights, discoveries, inventions, traditions, cultures, languages, arts, religions, sciences, narratives, stories, poems, customs and norms, music and songs, games and personal experiences, and advertisements – that we produce, curate, consume, transmit, and inherit as humans. We use this wealth – which I shall define more precisely as *semantic capital* in the next section – in order to give meaning to, and make sense of, our own existence and the world surrounding us, to define who we are, and to develop an individual and social life.[36]

As human beings, we make sense of our lives and of the surrounding world through the creation and accumulation of resources that constitute a true form of capital, a reserve of wealth, although this capital is not defined in economic terms either by analogy or by logical deduction, but originally in semantic terms. Contrary to long-standing tradition in thinking, as Floridi remarks, the emphasis should be placed on the term semantic and not on capital, in a non-economic perspective[37]. Floridi then defines semantic capital in more analytical terms, as he did with the general definitions of data and information, to highlight some salient aspects:

> (SC) Semantic Capital = $_{def.}$ any content that can enhance someone's power to give meaning to and make sense of (semanticise) something.[38]

Semantic capital is broadly and generally defined as *content*, with implicit reference to the notion of well-constructed and meaningful data (but without necessarily implying the notion of information, which in Floridi's theory presupposes the idea of truth[39]). It is interesting and important to observe that this semantic capital is characterized by the fact that it gives human beings a specific power: that of giving meaning to and making sense of something (that is, the power to semanticize reality). This is directly related to the issue of computational power. It is not actually, in Floridi's view, a generic skill or ability of human beings, but, as in an analytics of existence[40], a power that characterizes the real *singularity* of human beings:

> This is another key element in the definition: persons have semantic capital, animals and robots do not, but most importantly cannot. On the one hand, animals handle only meaning at most, but never sense. They may be told to have cultural capital, but this seems closer to Bourdieu's economic concept. They do not have narratives within which meanings are embedded: they may feel the flames, but have no reflective sense of the *vestigia*, their past and future. On the other hand, robots only handle syntax, not even meaning,

and syntactical flames can leave no scar, in the same sense in which the simulation of a fire cannot burn. One may object that families, friends, teams, groups, organisations, institutions, political parties and whole nations can all have semantic capital. Of course, but the reply is obvious: this is true only insofar as they are made of past, present, or future persons. Any organisation without the persons constituting it is devoid of both meaning and sense. Semantic capital is not the only thing that defines us, but it is certainly what defines *only* us.[41]

The formation of semantic capital is thus obtained through a three-layered progression, which brings into play the ability to provide things with meaning; to put this meaning within a framework or narrative that more generally gives sense to the human experience; to subject experiences to revision through the reflective ability to critically reconsider and rework the past. This last point is important. The correct representation of reality as well as the understanding of life do not occur, usually, in the immediacy of events but require, more often, a certain lapse of time (they are obtained *post festum*). Likewise, Floridi observes that preserving the coherence of our existential narration requires a profound work of "re-semanticisation"[42], that is, the capacity to give a different interpretation of the past (which nonetheless maintains the truth value of the facts narrated). Meaning, sense and reflexivity are a human patrimony and they play an inalienable role both at the individual and social level, since the production, conservation and transmission of semantic capital are not so much the product of an individual as they are the outcome of a collective process. In this context, it is essential to have contexts, notably public and institutional, that are separate from automated processes, where human beings can still exercise their sphere of reflexivity; for example, consider the social value that the interpretation and enforcement of law have in the context of the so-called "hard" court cases[43]. There are, in fact, multiple circumstances that put social capital at risk, which are to be taken into account specifically with regards to the effect of digitalization:

> Semantic capital risk can occur through projects about, or wrong investment in, content that fails to semanticise. Five kinds of risks are then logically possible: the simple (a) loss of semantic capital; the presence of semantic capital that is (b) unproductive; the productive presence of semantic capital that turns out to be (c) underused or (d) misused; and the presence of semantic capital that, although properly used, (e) depreciates through time.[44]

As is easy to infer, all these risks are brought into play by the impact of ICTs. Not only because the formation, conservation and transmission of semantic capital have always been mediated and influenced by, if not even dependent on, these technologies, but also because these technologies tend to produce their own representation of reality, at least partly concurrent with that produced by the human work of semanticization. Floridi has a very balanced approach to the overall impact that digital ICTs are likely to have on the formation of social capital that can be summed up in terms of new opportunities and challenges:

> Each stage in our technological development has generated new opportunities and new challenges. Digital technologies are not an exception. They both exacerbate the risks [...] and offer new forms of availability, accessibility, utilisation, and capitalisation of semantic capital. Just think of the debate on fake news on the one hand, and the consumption of digital photographs on the other. [...] What may be worth highlighting are rather two factors that will deserve an independent discussion. On the one hand, digital technologies provide an increasing reservoir of smart agency (Artificial Intelligence) that could support us in the fruitful management of our semantic capital. I am not referring just to curation [...] but, more importantly, to the possibility of augmenting our abilities to take advantage of the wealth of semantic capital already available, to use it and enrich it more effectively and efficiently, and hence semanticise our lives and realities better. On the other hand, the digital itself is generating new forms of semantic capital that would have been otherwise impossible, in terms of experiences, new cultural forms, scientific progress, games, music, images, fashions, and so forth. Semantic capital is no longer just analog, it is also increasingly digital, and may not be generated solely by human agents.[45]

This last remark is particularly significant, since it emphasizes the epistemological dimension of computational power. AI systems are far from being able to reason as the human mind does, from giving meaning to things as human beings do or from reflecting over their decisions or actions. Perhaps they will never be able to do these things, given the difficulty of integrating the syntactic and the semantic. However, these systems are able to modify reality through their decisions and actions, and this presupposes the ability to generate an autonomous model of reality that is instrumental to their functioning and affects our way of acting, deciding and making sense of the world. In this perspective, as Floridi keenly observes, semantic capital is no longer produced solely by human beings. This is the corollary of the fact that agency is no longer the exclusive prerogative of the human species.

There is thus a general lesson we must learn from these reflections on semantic capital. The semanticization of reality is not only an ability but also a form of power. However, this form of power implies the performance of a task. Floridi is perfectly aware of the fact that the exercise of computational power, while being solely or mostly syntactic, is capable of producing a specific model of reality that can affect and sometimes overturn our representation of reality. This means that our lives and reality are both increasingly decoded in terms of data to be processed (*datification*), elements to be calculated (*quantification*) or results to be predicted (*prediction*). It also means that we are increasingly prompted to adapt the world and our lives to a representation of reality that is instrumental to the functioning of computational models that characterize intelligent systems, algorithmic decisions or artificial agents. For this reason, the process of semanticization of reality is not only a capacity or a power, but mainly a task, and not a task to be renounced lightly: "Our identities, lives, experiences, interactions and representations of the world we inhabit and share would be pointless and empty (i.e. lacking any meaning or sense), if our semantic capital did not fill them with value. Minds cannot bear the meaningless and the senseless, and they fill this vacuum with any semantic capital they may have or create"[46]. It is thus a complex task that brings the problem of knowledge into play.

The problem of knowledge: Michael Lynch

Michael Lynch, an analytical philosopher who has dedicated most of his studies to the issue of truth[47], recently highlighted and emphasized the relevance of our epistemic responsibility towards knowledge in the information age[48].

The premise of his reasoning shares a similar perspective to that emphasized in this book: digital ICTs mediate our approach to knowledge and therefore to our representation of the world not only because they constitute the main tools of acquisition, creation and dissemination of knowledge, but also and above all because they now constitute the environment, that is, the *forms of life*, within which our existence largely takes place:

> Digital data is something that is no longer drowning us. We are adapting to life under water, we are breathing it all in, becoming digitally human. Information is the atmosphere – what the philosopher Luciano Floridi calls the infosphere – of our lives. But the fact that we live in the infosphere, that is becoming ordinary, doesn't mean that we understand it, nor how it is changing us and what Ludwig Wittgenstein might have called our form of life. A form of life, as I mean it here, is the myriad practices of a culture that create their philosophies, but also, in Stanley Cavell's words, their "routes of interest and feeling, sense of humor, and of significance, and of fulfillment of what is outrageous, of what is similar to what else". As I read him, Wittgenstein thought that once a set of practices is ingrained enough to become your form of life, it is difficult to substantively critique them or even to recognize them as what they are. That's because our form of life is "what has to be accepted, the given". We can no longer get outside of it.[49]

We need to examine how these digital forms of life affect our way of knowing. As already observed with Floridi's epistemic theory, knowledge is also a specific and gradual practice for Lynch. From the standpoint of its specificity, Lynch correctly remarks that knowing something is different from having an opinion about it. To have an opinion, it is enough to have a set of more or less accurate information. To know something, one needs to have accurate information, but even that is not enough: when we make a lucky guess, even if we come up with accurate information, it derives from the uncertain basis of chance. The foundation of our opinions and beliefs is crucial, because it is on this basis we make decisions and act. As Lynch recalls, knowledge is actionable information, meaning information we can work with and base our actions on. It is reliable. As Lynch observes, this allows us to arrive at a *minimal definition of knowledge*, by which "knowing is having a correct belief (getting it right, having a true opinion) that is grounded or *justified*, and which can therefore guide our action"[50]. According to Lynch, the way in which a belief can be founded or justified varies considerably and can consequently give rise to a cline of knowledge. Receptive knowledge, where we receive correct information coming from reliable sources, is lowest on the cline. This includes, for example, information we receive from reading a manual or searching online using reliable websites. Next on the cline is a more active type of knowledge, when we learn information through direct experience, are capable of evaluating the sources, or have reasons to give credence to information. This includes, for example, information gained from observing facts, when we are skilled ourselves, or are drawing on what we know to be reliable information. Finally, we reach the type of knowledge that Lynch describes in terms of understanding. This occurs when we have not only learned something, but we have also learned the *reason* for it: "understanding is what the scientist is after when trying to find out *why* Ebola outbreaks happen (not just predict how the disease spreads)"[51].

Lynch's paradigm of understanding also brings into play what we have already seen as a decisive element in Floridi's theory of knowledge, i.e., the network of questions and answers: "understanding not only gets us the 'why,' it brings with it the 'which' – as in which question to ask. Those who know, do. But those who understand also ask the right question – and therefore can find out what to do next. Asking questions was Socrates' special skill. It is perhaps for that reason that the Oracle of Delphi famously told Socrates that he was the wisest man in Athens. According to Plato, Socrates himself said that all he knew was that he didn't know much. And maybe he didn't. [...] Socrates was a champion not of knowledge per se but of understanding"[52].

Lynch's thesis is that digitalization affects these three forms of knowledge differently. Indeed, the overall effect is in some respects controversial, since the Internet is likely to expand the lowest and most basic form of knowledge on the cline: receptive knowledge. However, at the same time, it would produce an information coordination problem concerning our more active cognitive ability to gain experience and provide reasons, as it could lead to less general understanding. Let us proceed gradually, and break this down into three critical aspects for discussion.

Firstly, the Internet has tended to increase our receptive capacity, based on an alleged *democratization* of knowledge. This has seemingly happened in three respects[53], by introducing: (1) the most widely available knowledge, since, according to the familiar catchphrase, the Internet makes "more information to more people" accessible, shared and widespread; (2) the production of more inclusive knowledge, involving a growing number of people in the formation of online content in various ways and with different purposes; (3) more transparent knowledge, by creating freer and less controlled platforms and outlets of communication, at least in principle, and thus by providing the opportunity to disclose information that would otherwise have remained hidden. Without wanting to disregard these effects, Lynch expresses doubts, however, about the effective democratization of knowledge: "not all changes in the economy of knowledge – even those that can legitimately be described as 'democratizing' – are leading *societies* to become more democratic"[54]. In several respects, the democratization of knowledge, meaning the development of more inclusive and available production and distribution of epistemic resources, has not much diminished what Lynch defines as "epistemic inequality"[55], and defined by others as "epistemic injustice"[56]. In fact, equality or epistemic justice is possible only if a network user is recognized as "*a full participant in the economy of knowledge*"[57]. This will only happen when users are no longer considered as mere tools involved in content creation, which is the basis of the knowledge economy, but are substantially and knowingly included in the decisions, strategies and benefits generated by this form of economy.

The next point is that the Internet also affects the second form of knowledge, which relates to our most active capacity to be reasonable, that is, to rely on reasons as the basis of our beliefs. Lynch observes that digitization can raise an "information coordination problem" in this case[58]. Actually, every society has to face this problem, "since no society can survive without its citizens trading information with each other"[59]. It is not just a matter of exchanging information, but primarily a matter of offering reasons, mutually, for believing in something (in this context, as Lynch notes, by reason we simply mean a consideration for which something can be deemed to be true). If we want to be more than merely passive receivers of knowledge, we must exchange reasons, asking for and providing reasons for which something can be believed to be true. To be truly autonomous, we need a relationship based on mutual understanding. In this sense, we must "believe based on *reasons we can own* – stemming from principles you would, on reflection, endorse"[60]. However, it is exactly here that an extremely important problem arises:

> But if the principles we use to evaluate one another's information are forever hidden from view, they aren't of much use. In order to solve the information coordination problem, we can't just live up to our *own* standards. We need to be willing to explain ourselves to one another in terms we can *both* understand.[61]

A series of well-known trends in social networking – from the polarization of opinions to the fragmentation of reason; from the virtualization of reality to the weakening of the ontological marks of truth – makes this reciprocal explanation difficult and exacerbates the problem of online information coordination. This is also likely to create wider consequences at the epistemic and democratic levels already mentioned. From the epistemic viewpoint, this problem affects the notion of truth. Whatever the notion of truth is, it can be understood, at a minimum, as never depending entirely on us. Lynch remarks that truth does not necessarily require a superior or unconditional standpoint ("the view from nowhere"[62]), but rather some degree of objectivity. We are objective when we are sensitive to someone else's reasons, when the sensitivity for others' reasons makes us aware of our own limitations. Obviously, whenever this form of sensitivity is reduced or affected by the problem of information coordination, the very notion of democracy, understood as an unavoidable "space of reasons"[63] in an open society, is put into crisis. Finally, according to Lynch, this sensitivity or need for mutual explanation tends to call into question the image, so dear to Weinberger, of knowledge as a network[64] and of its emergence as a network effect, since the exchange of reasons requires a dimension of relationships that goes far beyond the formation of inferential knowledge based on the aggregation of individual preferences.

And finally, the Internet affects the third and most relevant form of knowledge: that which Lynch defines in terms of understanding. The critical observations just outlined can help us better appreciate the idea of understanding as suggested by Lynch:

> So, understanding is a kind of knowing that involves grasping relationships – the network, or parts and whole. But crucially, the relationships you grasp when you understand something aren't just correlations. To truly understand, you also need to know what *depends* on what – *why* the spread of a certain disease is related to hand-washing habits or why having good apples depends on having a certain amount of rainfall.[65]

Understanding, in the sense just outlined, involves not only the ability to understand the cause of something, but also some overall representation of the whole, that is, of the network of questions and answers, to use Floridi's expression, which allows us to follow a flow of information and to provide others with an explanation that is not based on mere correlation. As will be discussed in more detail later in this book[66], the need for mutual explanation cannot be satisfied by inferential knowledge based on statistical correlations, recurrent pattern extractions from Big Data analysis or clusters of individual preferences. Lynch correctly observes that explanations based on the understanding of a causal nature have something specific in themselves, since:

> [They] make us aware of why things hang together, which in turn allows us to see that understanding is a matter of degree – the larger and more coherent the set of information one has about apples, trees, etc., and the greater one's reflective and intuitive awareness of coherent connections between one's beliefs about those matters, the greater one's understanding. The greater you grasp the whole, the better able you are to fully explain the phenomenon in question.[67]

Understanding, therefore, presupposes an active, reflective and intuitive dimension, which, according to Lynch, is difficult to reconcile with the substantial passivity of downloading, systematic online searches, connections or selections of news suggested by algorithmic procedures, or in other words, of the growing delegation of knowledge creation to automated and external sources, which make us "more vulnerable to the manipulations and desires of others"[68]. In Lynch's lucid analysis, there are a number of critical observations and concerns that can be agreed upon, together with some commonsensical remarks, which focus on the relevance of our epistemic responsibilities. Unlike those who insist on the need to revise the business model underlying the networked data economy (economy-based solutions) or those who suggest procedural strategies for substantial issues (architecture-based solutions), Lynch highlights our role as autonomous epistemic agents called on to claim and assert a more conscious and active participation in the creation of knowledge, in order to reduce the different forms of epistemic inequality or injustice, even before those of political, economic or social inequity (solutions based on responsibility).

In Lynch's approach, there is obviously no such thing as a clear way out or an overall solution to the problems of online information coordination, understanding and creation of knowledge. However, there is a general consideration, as simple as it is important, which allows us to focus in on one of the most critical considerations made in this book:

> Humans are toolmakers, and information technologies are the grandest tools we have at the moment. Our tool-making nature shapes how we understand the world and our role within it. It encourages us to see the natural environment as something upon which we operate, which we use as means for our own ends, as an extension of the tools we develop to interact with it. So what happens when we extend our tools to the point that they become integrated with our life, when we become the very tools themselves? This is the most salient question about the coming Internet of Us. And it raises a danger that we cease to see our own personhood as an end in itself. Instead, we begin to see ourselves as devices to be used, as tools to be exploited.[69]

Lynch pointedly observes, in accordance with the interpretation of Floridi's analysis we have proposed, that the instrumental conception of technology is progressively giving way to an environmental conception of it[70], according to which technology redesigns the environment and becomes an integral part of our forms of life. However, technology does not limit itself to reshaping the natural environment: the computational power that technology has unleashed tends to adapt the world and its own representation to the functioning of computational systems. In this framework, we need to *reboot*, in the sense that Floridi gives to this term[71], a meditation on the ends that distinguish us as human beings, on our decisions as well as on the standards with which we evaluate these decisions.

Luciano Floridi and Michael Lynch make the same key point. We can delegate tasks but there is something we cannot responsibly give up: "*Understanding is not something I can outsource*"[72]. The creation and conservation of semantic capital is a burden that rests mostly upon us. Thus, we must be vigilant about what seeks to make sense of our lives. Networked knowledge and collective intelligence may serve to suggest answers to the questions we have formulated for the purposes we have chosen for our own sake. However, they should not suggest the questions to ask, make our life choices, or determine the goals guiding our journey.

Notes

1 On this point, see L. FLORIDI, *The Philosophy of Information, op. cit.*; ID., *What is the Philosophy of Information?*, in "Metaphilosophy", vol. 33, issue 1–2, 2002, pp. 123–145; ID., *Outline of a Theory of Strongly Semantic Information*, in "Minds and Machines", vol. 14, issue 2, 2004, pp. 197–221; and ID., *Is Semantic Information Meaningful Data?*, in "Philosophy and Phenomenological Research", vol. 70, issue 2, 2005, pp. 351–370.
2 The concept of data varies according to the area examined: IT, sociological, economic, legal, etc. To remain within the legal framework, and limiting ourselves to the example of personal data protection (which explicitly refers to the notion of data), one finds a double trend. On the one hand, we have a legal definition of personal data (formulated in Article 4.1 of the GDPR, and at the basis of a legal taxonomy of data: we speak in this sense of "special categories of personal data", pursuant to Article 9, GDPR); on the other hand, the very notion of personal data, from the legal point of view, implies the notion of information, since "personal data" is defined, in fact, as "any information relating to an identified or identifiable natural person", pursuant to Article 4.1, GDPR.
3 L. FLORIDI, *The Philosophy of Information, op. cit.*, pp. 85–86.
4 L. FLORIDI, *The Philosophy of Information, op. cit.*, p. 86.
5 L. FLORIDI, *The Philosophy of Information, op. cit.*, p. 85.
6 L. FLORIDI, *Semantic Capital: Its Nature, Value, and Curation*, in "Philosophy & Technology", vol. 31, issue 4, 2018, pp. 481–497, p. 484.
7 *Ibid.*: "All these data sets must be structured, not merely (perceived as) collected together, hence their being well formed from a syntactic point of view".
8 For a complete taxonomy of data, see L. FLORIDI, *The Philosophy of Information, op. cit.*, pp. 87–88.
9 In this sense, see L. FLORIDI, *The Philosophy of Information, op. cit.*, p. 82: "Intuitively, 'information' is often used to refer to user-independent content, declarative (that is, qualifiable in aletic terms), factual and semantic, incorporated into physical devices, such as books, databases, encyclopedias, web sites, television programs, etc., which can be produced, collected, known and processed in various ways".
10 On this point, among others, see J. MCKINNEY, H. EARL, C.J. YOOS, *Information about Information: A Taxonomy of Views*, in "MIS quarterly", vol. 34, issue 2, 2010, pp. 329–344; J. FURNER, *Information Studies Without Information*, in "Library trends", vol. 52, issue 3, 2004, pp. 427–446.
11 L. FLORIDI, *The Philosophy of Information, op. cit.*, p. 84.
12 *Ibid.*
13 L. FLORIDI, *The Philosophy of Information, op. cit.*, p. 46.
14 L. FLORIDI, *The Philosophy of Information, op. cit.*, p. 274.
15 L. FLORIDI, *The Philosophy of Information, op. cit.*, p. 273.
16 L. FLORIDI, *The Philosophy of Information, op. cit.*, p. 274: "[...] we must build a network through which the correct type of information flows from a source *f* to an objective *o*".
17 L. FLORIDI, *The Philosophy of Information, op. cit.*, pp. 278–279.
18 Unlike those who, like Chris Anderson, not many years ago, believed that it was enough to get a huge amount of data to make the numbers speak for themselves. See C. ANDERSON, *The End of Theory: The Data Makes the Scientific Method Obsolete*, in "Wired Magazine", 2008, pp. 1–3.
19 On this point, see, *infra*, chap. 7.

20 L. FLORIDI, *The Fourth Rev., op. cit.*, p. 157.
21 L. FLORIDI, *The Fourth Rev., op. cit.*, pp. 145–146.
22 L. FLORIDI, *A Proxy Culture*, in "Philosophy & Technology", vol. 28, issue 4, 2015, pp. 487–490. See also FLORIDI, *The Fourth Rev., op. cit.*, pp. 63–65.
23 L. FLORIDI, *A Proxy Culture, op. cit.*, p. 487.
24 L. FLORIDI, *The Fourth Rev., op. cit.*, p. 9. On this subject, see also A. SEARS, J.A. JACKO (eds.), *Human–Computer Interaction. Fundamentals*, CRC Press, Boca Raton, 2009; A. MARCUS, *HCI and User-Experience Design: Fast-Forward to the Past, Present and Future*, Springer, Dordrecht, 2015; G.A. BOY, *The Handbook of Human–Machine Interaction. A Human Centered Approach*, CRC Press, Boca Raton, 2017.
25 L. FLORIDI, *The Fourth Rev., op. cit.*, p. 167 *et seq.*
26 L. FLORIDI, *The Fourth Rev., op. cit.*, p. 169.
27 L. FLORIDI, *The Fourth Rev., op. cit.*, pp. 146–148.
28 There is a wide literature on the subject. We limit ourselves to some more recent publications: A. SAID, V. TORRA (eds.), *Data Science in Practice*, Springer, Dordrecht, 2019; S. LEONELLI, *La ricerca scientific nell'era dei Big Data*, Meltemi, Milano, 2018; S.H. CHEN (ed.), *Big Data in Computational Social Science and Humanities*, Springer, Dordrecht, 2018; M. CORRALES, M. FENWICK, N. FORGÓ (eds.), *New Technology, Big Data and the Law*, Springer, Dordrecht, 2018; A.G. FERGUSON, *The Rise of Big Data Policing. Surveillance, Race, and the Future of Law Enforcement*, New York University Press, NY, 2017; C. O'NEILL, *Weapons of Math Destruction. How Big Data Increases Equality and Threatens Democracy*, Broadway Books, NY, 2017; D.E. HOLMES, *Big Data. A Very Short Introduction*, Oxford University Press, Oxford, 2017; M. ZOOK, S. BAROCAS, D. BOYD et al., *Ten Simple Rules for Responsible Big Data Research*, in "PLoS Computational Biology", vol. 13, issue 3, 2017, pp. 1–10; E. VAYENA, J. TASIOULAS, *The Dynamics of Big Data and Human Rights. The Case of Scientific Research*, in "Philosophical Transactions of the Royal Society A: Mathematical, Physical and Engineering Sciences", vol. 374, issue 2083, 2016, pp. 2–14; B. MARR, *Big Data. Using SMART Big Data, Analytics and Metrics to take Better Decisions and Improve Performance*, John Wiley & Sons, Hoboken, 2015; C.L. BORGMAN, *Big Data, Little Data, No Data*, The MIT Press, Cambridge Mass., 2015; V. MAYER-SCHÖNBERGER, K. CUKIER, *Big Data. A Revolution That Will Transform How We Live, Work, and Think*, Houghton Mifflin Harcourt, Boston, 2013.
29 L. FLORIDI, *The Fourth Rev., op. cit.*, p. 16.
30 L. FLORIDI, *The Fourth Rev., op. cit.*, p. 17.
31 *Ibid.*
32 See, *infra*, chap. 7.
33 J. PEARL, D. MACKENZIE, *The Book of Why: The New Science of Causes and Effects*, Basic Books, NY, 2018. We do not wish to enter here into the debate on the subject and limit ourselves to observing that even Pearl's theoretical proposal is certainly not devoid of a certain emphasis placed on the possibility of incorporating causal inference mechanisms in new generation robots that will thus lead the way to forms of strong AI. This appears to be a rather futuristic scenario.
34 J. PEARL, D. MACKENZIE, *The Book of Why, op. cit.*, p. 9.
35 M. DURANTE, *Il futuro del web, op. cit.*, p. 73 *et seq.*
36 L. FLORIDI, *Semantic Capital, op. cit.*, p. 481.
37 L. FLORIDI, *Semantic Capital, op. cit.*, p. 483: "This means that, in each case, the philosophically heavy-lifting work is done by the noun, 'capital', not by the adjective qualifying it, exactly the opposite of what happens with '*semantic capital*', where I shall argue that the whole emphasis is on 'semantic'. [...] In the end, the whole debate on not-yet-economic forms of capital is dominated by a philosophy of economics as *first philosophy*, a tunnel vision that has so far missed what I would argue is really the most important form of capital, the one that far surpasses in value (understood in terms of what we care about, not merely of what we are ready to pay for) any economic capital, and hence any other kind of capital translatable into it."
38 *Ibid.*

39 L. FLORIDI, *The Philosophy of Information, op. cit.*, p. 182 *et seq.*

40 L. FLORIDI, *Semantic Capital, op. cit.*, p. 487: "Semantic capital is the top soil of our lives: it is the ultimate transcendental condition, because it makes possible the other forms of mental life, including the social, political and economic ones, not just because a meaningless and senseless life is not worth living, but because it is simply not liveable".

41 L. FLORIDI, *Semantic Capital, op. cit.*, p. 485.

42 L. FLORIDI, *Semantic Capital, op. cit.*, p. 490.

43 On this point, see U. PAGALLO, *Il diritto nell'età dell'informazione, op. cit.*, p. 289 *et seq.*, in which an analysis of hard legal cases is carried out, starting from the positions of Herbert H. Hart (1907–1992) and Ronald Dworkin (1931–2013). As Jonathan Zittrain correctly observed, what is endangered is precisely "the public understanding of its application eliminating a useful interface", J. ZITTRAIN, "Perfect enforcement on tomorrow's Internet", in R. BROWNSWORD, K. YEUNG (eds.) *Regulating Technologies: Legal Futures, Regulatory Frames and Technological Fixes*, Hart, London, 2007, pp. 125–156. The point has also been made by Bert-Jaap Koops and Ronald Leenes, who state that "the idea of encoding legal norms at the beginning of information processing systems is at odds with the dynamic and fluid nature of many legal norms, which need to breathing space that is typically not something that can be embedded in software", B.-J. KOOPS, R. LEENES, *Privacy Regulation Cannot Be Hardcoded: A Critical Comment on the "Privacy by Design" Provision in Data Protection Law*, in "International Review of Law, Computers & Technology", vol. 28, 2014, pp. 159–171, p. 167. On this point, see also, *infra*, chap. 9.

44 L. FLORIDI, *Semantic Capital, op. cit.*, p. 495.

45 L. FLORIDI, *Semantic Capital, op. cit.*, p. 496.

46 L. FLORIDI, *Semantic Capital, op. cit.*, p. 487.

47 M. LYNCH, *In Praise of Reason: Why Rationality Matters for Democracy*, The MIT Press, Cambridge Mass., 2012; ID., *Truth as One and Many*, Oxford University Press, Oxford, 2009; ID., *True to Life: Why Truth Matters*, The MIT Press, Cambridge Mass., 2004; ID., *Truth in Context: An Essay on Pluralism and Objectivity*, The MIT Press, Cambridge Mass., 1998.

48 M. LYNCH, *The Internet of Us. Knowing More and Understanding Less in the Age of Big Data*, Liveright, London, New York, 2016.

49 M. LYNCH, *The Internet of Us, op. cit.*, p. 10. And again p. 10: "One way to describe the direction in which our culture is proceeding is to say that many of us are starting to *adapt* to what we might call a digital form of life, which takes life in the infosphere for granted, precisely because digital is now integrated into our lives without interruption" (*our italics*).

50 M. LYNCH, *The Internet of Us, op. cit.*, p. 14.

51 M. LYNCH, *The Internet of Us, op. cit.*, p. 16.

52 *Ibid.*

53 M. LYNCH, *The Internet of Us, op. cit.*, pp. 134–137.

54 M. LYNCH, *The Internet of Us, op. cit.*, p. 138.

55 M. LYNCH, *The Internet of Us, op. cit.*, p. 142.

56 M. FRICKER, *Epistemic Injustice: Power and the Ethics of Knowledge*, Oxford University Press, Oxford, 2007. We will return to this problem, from another point of view, in chap. 8, dedicated to the asymmetric distribution of data and rights.

57 M. LYNCH, *The Internet of Us, op. cit.*, p. 146.

58 M. LYNCH, *The Internet of Us, op. cit.*, p. 38.

59 *Ibid.*

60 M. LYNCH, *The Internet of Us, op. cit.*, p. 39.

61 *Ibid.*

62 M. LYNCH, *The Internet of Us, op. cit.*, p. 84.

63 M. LYNCH, *The Internet of Us, op. cit.*, p. 55.

64 See, on this point, M. LYNCH, *The Internet of Us, op. cit.*, chap. 6, notably pp. 111–132, and, *supra*, chap. 3 of this book.

65 M. LYNCH, *The Internet of Us, op. cit.*, p. 165.

66 We will deal more analytically with this problem in chap. 8, dedicated to the asymmetric distribution of data and rights, with regards to the so-called *right to explanation* and, notably, to the debate on Article 22, GDPR. In this sense, see M. HILDEBRANDT, *Learning as a Machine: Crossovers Between Humans and Machines*, in "Journal of Learning Analytics", vol. 4, issue 1, 2017, pp. 6–23, p. 19: "Core to human learning are creativity, humor, and reflection, corresponding with art and ethics, judgment, politics, and law. Creativity and humor combine, detecting the unexpected with both life and death. Instead of succumbing entirely to unconscious learning processes. That is why teaching will remain crucial to democracy. Teaching refers to *explicit presentation and explanation* of knowledge, which can be the object of debate and discussion. LA [learning analytics] may be a great way to *induce* learning processes, as it was, behind a person's back, even if not necessarily wrong or bad, LA must be (re-)configured in a way that allows for critical reflection *on what and on how* we learn".
67 M. LYNCH, *The Internet of Us, op. cit.*, p. 167.
68 M. LYNCH, *The Internet of Us, op. cit.*, p. 187.
69 M. LYNCH, *The Internet of Us, op. cit.*, p. 187 *et seq.*
70 M. LYNCH, *The Internet of Us, op. cit.*, pp. 187–188.
71 L. FLORIDI, *The Fourth Rev., op. cit.*, p. 191.
72 M. LYNCH, *The Internet of Us, op. cit.*, p. 182.

6

TRUTH AND FAKE NEWS

The lawfulness of lying

If I walked into a room and declared, "Rome is the capital of France", I would obviously be stating a falsehood or telling a lie[1]. But would I be held legally liable? Is lying permitted in a state of law? Can people who deliberately spread falsehoods be punished?

It is a matter of common experience to know that nothing would happen to me if I lied about Rome being the capital of France. In other words, in a democratic society and in a state of law, as a rule, uttering a falsehood is permissible, or, more precisely, it carries no significant legal consequences. When, then, is lying forbidden? When is it unlawful to speak an untruth? The answer is when, as in certain cases, lying amounts to committing some other illegal and punishable offense. For example, if I lied when testifying in court, I would face serious criminal charges of perjury, since my false statement would amount to giving false testimony. It is not the misleading or false statement as such that is legally relevant, but the fact that it represents a form of conduct under the given circumstances that the law sees fit to pursue and punish.

The law does not regulate the telling of untruths. However, it does regulate the specific circumstances under which a legally relevant and punishable act (such as rendering false testimony in court) is committed by the assertion of a falsehood. In the philosophy of language, such an assertion is considered to be a performative utterance, which means it is a speech act that actually does or accomplishes something when spoken in the appropriate circumstances. For example, if I provide an inaccurate description of an object while negotiating a sale, not only am I misrepresenting the truth, but I am also conducting bad faith negotiations and betraying the buyer's good faith at the time of stipulating the contract. As with the example of perjury, lying here is strategic and serves an ulterior motive; the act of telling a lie is not legally relevant *per se*, but becomes so in relation to the circumstances in which the ulterior motive is pursued.

To further clarify this point, let us focus for a moment on the structure of the performative as a linguistic act by considering John Searle's theory of the construction of social reality[2]. For the American philosopher, social reality is constructed through social acts, which have the following structure:

X counts as Y in context C

X is an act (or object) that takes on the specific meaning Y (meaning that the act or material object X is the act or social object Y) in a given context C. In that specific context C, collective intentionality attributes to the act (or the object) X a function, which constitutes it as the act (or the object) Y. Marking an electoral ballot with a cross amounts to voting in the context of elections. Stating "I do" during a wedding ceremony implies getting married. The law regulates elections and weddings as well as the conditions required for casting a vote and for getting married. Returning to the example of false testimony, we can see that stating a falsehood (X) counts as providing false testimony (Y) within the context of a trial (C). Once again, the law does not regulate X, but only Y and C. The law first dictates the rules for defining C, the trial, and then when and how Y is configured as false testimony, in C. Note, however, that it does not discipline X as such, i.e., independently of a context C in which X *counts* (is legally relevant) as Y.

It may seem strange that lying is deemed to be lawful unless it equates to doing something else considered by law to be wrong and punishable. Why is it not always illegal to deal in falsehoods? Why are false representations of reality not regularly pursued and sanctioned? There is actually a good reason for this, which is based on an essential principle of legal and democratic civilization: in a state of law and in a democratic society nobody can or should have sole possession of the truth. If we were to charge a public authority (for example, the State) with the responsibility of pursuing and punishing all false statements, we would implicitly be investing this authority with the power to distinguish truth from falsehood and thus, ultimately, the power to declare what is true or false in a given society.

Hannah Arendt has taught us that when the State claims possession of the truth, it paves the way for a totalitarian and anti-democratic regime[3]. Truth constitutes a limit to power, not an instrument for its pursuit, so no one can rightfully claim to possess truth or to have privileged access to it. We must hence always be wary of those who want to discipline and punish the utterance of falsehoods, for this inevitably brings with it the problem of access to truth.

In light of these considerations, the next section addresses the recent phenomenon of fake news, on which much has already been said and written[4]. The discussion touches on several aspects that allow us to reflect on the side issue of the filters of relevance and reliability, whose importance has long been recognized[5]. Before entering *in medias res*, it is worth pointing out an important conceptual distinction: fake news raises a problem for epistemology and democracy, but not for metaphysics. In other words, fake news partially undermines the way in which we represent certain aspects of reality and form opinions, which has a clear impact on democracy, but it does not really affect the question of the existence of truth. This is perhaps easiest to illustrate with an example, for a detailed discussion of post-truth is not the main concern here[6].

Truth is a bit like a precious jar of jam that you hide on the topmost shelf of the larder to keep it from being found. Keeping it out of sight, however, does not mean that the jar ceases to exist. Likewise, the problem of access to truth must not be confused with the problem of the existence of truth. Fake news concerns the former issue, not the latter. Of course in the long run, by hiding the jar, we may forget how good that particular jam is, and end up satisfying ourselves with inferior substitutes[7]. Yet the fact remains that, in order to lie, the truth must exist, and access to truth must be precluded. Understanding the problem of fake news is best tackled from the perspective of access to truth, which in turn involves the filters of relevance and reliability.

The thesis of this chapter is that analysis of the issue of fake news has (understandably) placed great emphasis on reliability, whereas the relevance of news has been wholly or partially neglected. This has created an unjustified delimitation of the problem, which has to be corrected. Let us start by looking at what is meant by fake news. Generally, the term is used in reference to all "false news, with particular reference to those disseminated through the Net"[8]. The phenomenon of disseminating false news has always existed, but it has become increasingly prevalent due to the reach and impact of the Internet. There are many kinds of motivation for creating and spreading fake news. Some of the strongest include the desire to influence public opinion (especially in the political context, for example, to generate consensus, to strengthen beliefs, to create fear or feelings of hatred, to alter the normal course of elections, etc.); the pursuit of economic exploitation through the manipulation of reality (by attracting clicks and generating attention for advertising; the ability to create fake trends or influence popular expectations; fueling needs or helping to profile network users, etc.); the pleasure of lying (shaping images or reality artifacts, reinforcing biases, discrediting other people and their opinions, etc.). The motivations can be grouped into three main categories: political, economic and recreational.

The following factors help to explain why the Internet has been so successful in fueling the increase in fake news:

1. *Network effects*: the characteristics of networks have contributed to the phenomenon insofar as they affect how information is conveyed and accessed. The distribution of information is not always equitable[9], is aggregated into information silos[10] by Big Tech exploiting platforms such as social networks; is filtered through filter bubbles or echo chambers[11], is selected, recommended and offered through *feeds*, whose functioning is not always transparent[12]. More generally, the architectural or design features of networks are capable of influencing how users consume information.

2. *The epistemic characteristics of online communication*: the Internet and the platforms that have been built and developed on it have contributed to spreading a communication system that has negatively influenced the management of attention, the amount spent on discussion and analysis, as well as the ability of people to act as responsible epistemic subjects, or even their ability to be "real interlocutors"[13] of the platform owners.
3. *The gradual removal of the filters of relevance and reliability*: decentralization of the Internet has caused a gradual disintermediation mechanism that allowed the rise of Web 2.0, meaning the online generation of content by network users in a horizontal and distributed way. Over time this has resulted in two further consequences: on the one hand, it has weakened, if not removed, the filters of relevance and reliability, that is to say those mechanisms (procedures and professional figures) tasked with generating or selecting the information deemed relevant and reliable and bringing it to public attention; on the other hand, it has allowed the rise of new intermediaries (the owners of platforms and Internet services) who are not interested in generating content but only in extracting value from its dissemination. These conflicting tendencies are discussed below.

The relevance and reliability filters

Knowledge and communication require access to relevant and reliable information. Reality, whether offline or online, is often so packed with information[14] that we have to use the filters of relevance and reliability in order to select the information that is useful to us. As already observed, scholars have often remarked on the issue of veracity and reliability of information, and it is obviously important to be able to rely on information that we can consider to be true. This allows us not only to decide and act on well-grounded and rational assumptions, but also to communicate with others on an equal footing: information asymmetries are, in fact, often likely to turn into power asymmetries. However, it is certainly not enough for information to be reliable and trustworthy. It is also necessary and, I believe, essential that information be relevant. In other words, information should be able to satisfy the need for which it is sought, the purpose for which something must be known. Indeed, true or reliable information is useful or relevant with respect to the concrete information situation we find ourselves in.

Methodologically, knowledge is therefore a goal-oriented activity, meaning that it cannot be detached from the purpose for which it is sought:

> The attempt to look for something unconditional is equivalent to the understandable but profoundly mistaken commitment to analyze a system (the world itself, for Kant, but it could be a more limited area) independently of any (specification of) the level of abstraction to which the analysis is conducted, questions are asked and answers are offered, *for a specific purpose.*[15]

It is thus not possible to know anything except at a certain level of abstraction, that is, through an interface that mediates the epistemic relationship between the observer and the observed. This means that there is always some level of abstraction at which an investigation is being conducted, at which questions are being asked and answers given. Knowledge is obtained through a network of questions and answers. It is therefore impossible to embark on any investigation without a specific purpose, which frames the question asked and the answer given. This purpose makes the selection and acquisition of information *relevant*.

Relevance is thus not only a key filter for the selection of information, but also an essential attribute of knowledge. This has a direct impact on our analysis: the ability to convey false or unreliable news depends not only on the will to deceive, but also on the concrete relevance that such news has for those who receive it. The literature dealing with online knowledge and communication has often emphasized the fact that the weakening of the traditional filters of relevance and reliability (for example, the selection of the news by professional media) could be offset by the epistemic responsibility of the recipients, who should be expected to verify the reliability of the news themselves[16]. This has only been partly the case, making the issue of fake news all the more urgent and important.

If it is indeed true that an attentive or expert receiver is more difficult to deceive, it is equally true that network users are often neither attentive nor experts. Although in many cases users should potentially be able to verify the credibility of news, they often fail to devote sufficient time or attention to the task. This is where the role of relevance becomes significant. The more relevant a news item is perceived to be, the stronger the recipient's commitment is to verifying its reliability. Also, it is the very relevance of the news, as I noted earlier, that determines the standpoint (or the level of abstraction) from which we approach the content of the news: it explains why the news is being sought and determines the context in which the news carries out its actual informativeness. To put it in terms of the theory of social acts, interest in the news – i.e., the specific purpose for which a question is asked and an answer given – identifies the context C, in which this news is somehow (legally, politically, ethically, socially, etc.) relevant. It is with regards to news that is deemed relevant, in the sense just outlined, that we must investigate its credibility or, in other words, its actual informativeness.

How can we recreate the role played by traditional filters of relevance and reliability in the Internet environment, where an initial phase of disintermediation has been followed by a new phase of intermediation? A suitable approach will have to consider how the new online intermediaries operate and what relationship they have with the other parties involved in the fake news story: public actors and network users.

The new network intermediaries

Jack Balkin has noted that the structure of online expression is triadic[17] and consists of public actors (mainly national governments, but also other supra-national bodies), private actors (mainly digital infrastructure owners such as social media platforms or search engines) and individuals (mainly network users who use digital infrastructures to produce and disseminate online content).

In the analogical world, the structure of mass communication was essentially binary and consisted of public actors (mainly national governments) and public or private subjects (newspapers, radio, television, and all the other traditional outlets of communication) providing information to a wide audience. The public or private subjects producing information also played an essential role as intermediaries, since they served as the filters of relevance and reliability for the information selected and disseminated. Because of this role, these subjects were (and are) subject to regulation by public actors, although the tendency in democratic societies has always been to interfere with the freedom of information as little as possible. While these subjects still exist in the digital world and now have to compete with large numbers of individuals producing content, their role as intermediators in the analogical reality is completely different from that played by the owners of online platforms:

> However, the role of digital infrastructure companies in the twenty-first century is not the same as the role of twentieth century mass media companies. These mass media companies were not conduits for the speech for the vast majority of the people who constituted the audience for their products. Rather, these companies (1) produced their own content, (2) published the content of a small number of creative artists, or (3) delivered content made by other organizations to a mass public. In the twentieth century model, the vast majority of people were members of an audience for mass media products, but very few actively used mass media as speakers or broadcasters. Twenty-first century governors of digital speech, by contrast, make their money by facilitating and encouraging the production of content by ordinary people and governing the communities of speakers that result. New media companies like Facebook, Google, YouTube, and Twitter do not produce most of the content they serve. Rather, their business model requires them to induce as many people as possible around the world to post, speak, and broadcast to each other. Constant production of content by end-users, in turn, captures audience attention. This allows digital media companies to sell advertising, collect data about end-users, and use this information to sell even more advertising.[18]

The new online intermediaries, or owners of digital infrastructures, produce almost no content at all. Instead, they provide a platform for publishing user created content. This means that any regulation or solution to the issue of fake news on the Internet in the current model of communication concerns[19] three potential levels of stakeholders: (1) public actors; (2) private actors; and (3) network users.

The main remedies proposed pose different problems at each of these levels. Let us briefly consider these remedies and the issues they raise, by expanding on Balkin's threefold taxonomy of the new forms of speech regulation[20] to include user-based solutions. We therefore have: (1) forms of regulation determined by public actors; (2) forms of regulation based on collaboration between public and private actors; (3) forms of regulation based on the governance of private actors; (4) user-based solutions.

Forms of regulation determined by public actors

Because the State can decide to regulate online communication more or less strictly, indirect forms of censorship may arise. As Balkin correctly observes, "collateral censorship occurs when the state aims at A in order to control B's speech. If A and B are the same enterprise or the same publication, there is not a significant free speech problem. For example, we hold newspapers liable for defamatory speech published by their reporters, and we hold publishers liable for defamatory content by the authors they publish. On the other hand, if A is an infrastructure provider or conduit like an ISP or a social media site, and B is an independent speaker, then A will tend to overblock and over-censor to avoid liability or government sanction"[21]. This type of problem occurs when the State creates forms of responsibility for new intermediaries, which can result in *ex ante* forms of limiting communication (since the threat of sanctions puts pressure on digital infrastructure owners to impose advance censorship and content blocking or to set up automatic filtering systems) or *ex post* (requiring infrastructure owners to remove certain contents after their publication, with or without having to warn the content creators). This solution is particularly problematic because it can lead to unjustified and hidden forms of indirect censorship deriving from excessive restraints or from automatic over-filtering. Furthermore, the establishment of *a priori* limits on communication can shift the burden of action from the individual to the public or private actor, and along with it, the power to regulate digital communication: "In a world without prior restraints, speakers decide for themselves whether to speak and risk prosecution; they do not have to obtain prior permission from the government"[22].

Forms of regulation based on collaboration between public and private actors

The State can decide to establish forms of collaboration with private platform owners without imposing regulations on them (such as forms of accountability or the threat of sanctions), but by exploiting the resources offered by their digital infrastructures instead. In this way, the State can exercise indirect control over online communications, embedded in the design of digital infrastructures, rather than attempting to achieve control through traditional legal means (not always an easy enterprise). For example, private platforms can be tasked with providing information about online content deemed to be unlawful or with setting up *ex ante* automatic content filters or *ex post* content monitoring and removal systems. From the design point of view, platform owners can be required to create Web pages in such a way as to facilitate users' ability to access reliable information as well as to draw their attention to the type of content produced and to their compliance with general rules of conduct. Likewise, private actors can also be encouraged to shape the terms of service of their applications in such a way as to favor the creation of content that is lawful or otherwise consistent with shared rules of online communities. As already seen in the case of the right to be forgotten, public actors can be motivated to create forms of collaboration with private actors both because of the efficiency of the regulatory solutions implemented at the technological level and because it allows the costs related to the enforcement and monitoring of regulatory solutions to be shifted to private actors, who have the large financial and organizational resources necessary for this purpose. This naturally brings with it two problems on which we have already dwelt: the incorporation of standards in technological devices limits the sphere of dialogue, interpretation and public scrutiny concerning the enforcement of norms; furthermore, the privatization of regulatory solutions is likely to weaken the guarantees provided by the compliance with legal norms in today's democratic information societies. Needless to say, this form of privatization also strengthens the dominant position of these private actors in digital governance. This point will become even clearer in the next section.

Forms of regulation based on the governance of private actors

On their own initiative, private actors can adapt their digital infrastructures or terms of service of their applications in a way that gives rise to a true form of "private governance"[23] of online communication. Thanks to their technological wherewithal and economic and organizational resources, private actors can regulate and control online communication more or less directly. Using their digital infrastructures, they can govern and direct users' communication in ways that are consistent "with their terms of service, end-user licensing agreements, or other internal company policies"[24]. Private actors are driven to take on the governance of online communication not only because of pressure from the State or the desire to strengthen their dominant position, but also because of pressure from network users' expectations that they adopt appropriate procedures and rules of conduct.

   This is an interesting aspect of the phenomenon of digital governance, in which the demand for regulation comes from below and is promoted by the participants in online communities themselves, who aspire to have secure communication even in the context of digital platforms. This request has been taken into account by private actors, and has been used to support a climate of trust between network users and digital infrastructure owners:

> Over time, however, infrastructure owners have faced pressure from two directions. On the one hand, nation states expected them to control and govern their end-users. On the other, the end-users themselves — and other people affected by end-users' speech — expected companies to enforce norms of appropriate behavior. Social media companies and search engines in particular understood that their end-users required increasing amounts of care and regulation. They realized that a substantial aspect of their product was creating

a hospitable environment for end-users, and that meant governing communities of people who used their services.[25]

This has led to a progressive transformation towards a situation where infrastructure owners "soon discover not only that they are actually media companies, but that they are also governance structures"[26]. This is all the more true in terms of fake news, where the pressure from network users on private actors has been felt even more intensely. However, if this pressure has created and is destined to create increasingly extensive and elaborate forms of private governance[27], none of this has necessarily been translated into the true involvement of users in these forms of governance. On the contrary, users' expectations of participation have largely been frustrated, despite the fact that platform owners are not in a position to ignore them entirely nor do they have an interest in doing so[28]. These expectations include:

1. obligations of transparency, notice, and fair procedures;
2. the offer of reasoned explanations for decisions or changes of policy;
3. the ability of end users to complain about the conduct of the institution and demand reforms; and
4. the ability of end users to participate, even in the most limited ways, in the governance of the institution.[29]

There is an important point to be made regarding these expectations. Private governance, although not necessarily based on a process of democratic legitimacy, has the advantage of being implemented very effectively from a procedural point of view, since its normativity is incorporated into choices of code and design, algorithms, mechanisms and technological devices, and the architecture and functioning of digital platforms. However, it is precisely this efficacy that raises problems from the standpoint of procedural legitimacy, since it can result in a lack of information about the rights of users, insufficient transparency in the application of rules, an implicit disproportion of powers between the actors involved, and a weakening of the usual principles of due process This indicates the need (which is not limited to the issue of fake news or online communication, but has a more general scope) for achieving greater power symmetry or at least procedural balance between the actors involved in digital governance:

> Indeed, end-users may accept, to some degree, that companies will take down materials that violate a company's internal policies and expel end-users who are abusive or violate the company's terms of service. But what end-users may especially resent is that the criteria are kept hidden, that the takedowns are done summarily, that the rules are applied arbitrarily, that powerful people and organizations are given exceptions to the rules, and that end-users are booted off the platform without notice and an opportunity to defend themselves. The shift from a binary model of state versus speaker to a pluralist

model of speakers, private governors, and states has the curious effect of making procedural norms especially salient and therefore especially valuable to end-users.[30]

In short, whether based on the regulatory power of public actors or on the governance of private actors, solutions to the issue of fake news are problematic, albeit for different reasons. The State's regulatory power may appear liberticidal or inadequate, since it targets anonymous users, outside its jurisdiction, or artificial agents, which are often a cover for bots. The delegation of regulatory power to private actors, owners of digital infrastructures, can strengthen their dominant position and generate forms of legal responsibility that further segment the online communication market. Private governance can raise issues of indirect censorship and procedural legitimacy, as well as problems of agency, by incorporating value choices in automatic filtering, content removal, and inappropriate reporting of suspected *fake news*. Given these issues, we often emphasize solutions based on the epistemic responsibilities of users.

User-based solutions

At least five courses of action or solutions based on the central role of network users have been outlined in the literature: (a) cognitive education or *media literacy*; (b) the adoption of guidelines or codes of conduct; (c) *fact-checking* based on peer collaboration; (d) combating behavioral dependence; and (e) the architecture of online communication. These remedies tend to have in common users' epistemic responsibility. In other words, it is on the network users themselves to identify reliable information. Let us see what this is all about.

(a) Cognitive education or media literacy

Many scholars have emphasized that user discernment remains the keystone of the system and that the issue of fake news cannot be positively addressed without leveraging the cognitive abilities of users in discerning the truth and in verifying credibility of information. These cognitive abilities vary greatly depending on the context, degree of experience, knowledge and skills, attention management, etc., of network users, as well as the specific user's understanding of the communication mechanisms inherent in digital platforms and notably in social media. The generic motto "verify yourself", which was invoked as a mantra only some time ago, must be updated today in epistemic and cognitive terms. Users need more specific education to increase their media literacy in order to hone their attention, engage critically with the news, learn to decode Web-based communicative strategies, and to resist becoming passive recipients of information dispensed by others. Needless to say, this common-sense request for education immediately raises the question of who is responsible for providing this education. The users themselves? The public actors? The private ones? If we believe that the responsibility rests with the public or private actors, we come head to head with the implicit value choices that such education presupposes and is likely to embody. If we assume that it rests with the users, the implication is that users will take it upon themselves to fill in the gaps about something they are likely not even aware of. From experience, it is never a great idea to ask those who lie at the heart of the problem to try and solve it. The other two categories of solutions address these hurdles to be surmounted.

(b) The adoption of guidelines or codes of conduct

Soft law tools such as codes of conduct, social norms, guidelines, reports or manifestos[31], are recommended as an option for guiding users towards more prudent and informed forms of communication. If they are adhered to, they should generate virtuous practices over time, without requiring other forms of top-down regulation. Such guidelines and codes of conduct usually consist of common-sense rules and advice, and often have the merit of providing helpful suggestions and an appropriate reminder. However, they are mainly supererogatory in nature, meaning that they expect too much from network users ("Check the evidence: check the author's sources to make sure they are reliable. The lack of evidence or reference to experts whose names are not mentioned could indicate that the news is fake"[32]). In fact, the limit of these soft law instruments is precisely in that they often assume the existence of that which is lacking (or that which has now fallen into neglect: the verification of the sources; the acquisition of empirical data; the authority of experts; the principle of interpretative charity; critical analysis; exposure to a variety of sources, etc.).

(c) Fact-checking based on peer collaboration

In the past, it has been hypothesized (and I was quite convinced of the validity of this hypothesis myself[33]) that the filters of relevance and reliability of the news could be reconstituted on the network as a result of the joint activity of users, that is, thanks to horizontal (peer) cooperation, even in the absence of individual central authorities. Although horizontal peer production of goods has provided appreciable results over time[34], it is hard to imagine that effective and systematic fact checking will result from spontaneously coordinated collaborative efforts. For example, the modularity and granularity of an online encyclopedia based on the incremental accrual of knowledge (as well as the emphasis placed on the possibility of creating a collective online work) succeeded in making large online projects such as Wikipedia possible; however, these features are less well associated with the specificity and timeliness required to filter out unreliable news from time to time. Still, many websites dedicated to fact checking have also emerged, although it should be noted that proper fact checking requires dedication and specialized skills[35]. One hopes that other peer initiatives will increasingly reveal which information websites are worthy of attention and epistemic trust. However, this requires a certain detachment from the life of the online communities to which network users belong. This aspect is addressed by the fourth solution.

(d) Combating behavioral dependence

It has rightly been observed that "social media develop behavioral dependence"[36]. Network users are increasingly dependent on social media for a growing number of activities (from entertainment to commerce, from communication to information, etc.). In broader terms, our societies at large are increasingly ICT dependent[37]. Needless to say, the map of our dependencies also draws the map of our fragilities. It is getting harder and harder to combat or even curtail the behavioral dependencies that go hand in hand with the growing part of our lives spent on digital platforms. This form of addiction is made more acute by the fear of missing out on the life of online communities. An important solution to the issue of fake news (and the polarization of online communication) certainly lies in trying to reduce the forms of behavioral dependence that consist in the massive, if not exclusive, consumption of news and information from social media. Once again, this solution is not easily feasible: not only because of the difficulty for many users of dealing with the "metacognitive deficit, that is, the inability to stop and reflect on the meaning of their behavior"[38], but also because behavioral dependence on digital infrastructures tends to acquire the connotation of a real form of life. It is no coincidence that Luciano Floridi has long supported the idea of an "onlife" existence[39], which not only implies the conceptual overcoming of the offline and online dichotomy, but also postulates the need to rethink the very concept of (form of) life.

(e) The architecture of online communication

The last solution does not directly concern user behavior, but how users receive news and information, that is, how they are exposed to online communication. In this case, the problem[40] is that the functioning of news feeds, and more generally of online communication, has the effect of enclosing users in a bubble that filters the contents of communication (the so-called filter bubble). This bubble is a kind of trap of desires[41], governed by algorithms, which personalize for each individual user a set of news, information and content, which is tailored to the wishes, interests, preferences and even ideological beliefs of the user, thus confirming and reinforcing their beliefs and expectations. From a certain point of view, this appears to be a positive effect of the architecture of online communication, since it allows users to permanently access their desired content. On the other hand, it conceals a threat to democracy and, in the present context, to knowledge, for it reduces users' exposure to different points of view. This diminishes their ability to access different sources of information, to compare news items, and to analyze them; hence, it is likely to exacerbate the risk of falling victim to fake news. Since this problem is found at the level of the architecture of online communication, the suggested remedy is found on the same plane. The solution would be that of building the architecture of online communication in such a way as to favor the serendipity of information[42], that is, the chance for users to be exposed to a variety of content and information they would otherwise not be privy to. This is an interesting solution, because it addresses the ethical, political and epistemic issue of reduced plurality of viewpoints at a procedural or infraethical level, to use Floridi's words[43], namely, at the architectural level of online communication design.

In sum, the solutions we have mentioned emphasize users' epistemic responsibility, despite the issue of how difficult it is for users to select, filter and access relevant and reliable information. From the start, we have emphasized the point that this epistemic responsibility cannot be based solely on reliability but must also, and perhaps above all, be based on relevance. The following section explores this more in depth, according to the epistemic distinction between truth and distance from truth.

The distinction between truth and distance from truth

A very important but perhaps not sufficiently explored aspect of Luciano Floridi's information theory allows us to discuss the topic of relevance in conjunction with that of network users' epistemic responsibility regarding fake news.

As we have seen, there are good reasons that militate against an excessive regulation of fake news, whether carried out by the public authorities or privately owned platforms. For this reason, the idea of insisting on users' epistemic responsibility is not misplaced, if put into the proper perspective. In fact, we cannot claim that the reliability of information is entirely entrusted to users. In many cases, users are simply incapable of verifying the news; in others, they are not interested, since no matter how unreliable it may be, it tends to reinforce their previous beliefs and merge with them into a dangerous crucible. It is precisely in the light of these cognitive limits (which concern the access to or interest in the truth) that relevance, that is to say the ability of information to satisfy the purpose for which it is sought, becomes useful.

From this point of view, one should recall the crucial distinction drawn by Floridi between truth and distance from truth[44]. Once again, it is not our interest here to delve into the intricate philosophical debate on the nature of truth, but to make some considerations on the informativeness of statements. Floridi astutely observes that, seemingly paradoxically, the ability of a false statement to convey information (its informativeness) can be greater than that of a true statement. How is that possible? The key lies in the distinction between truth and distance from the truth, conceived in terms of the information conveyed. While truth expresses a certain correspondence (conformity or congruence) between the content of some piece of information and a state of the world, distance from truth measures the capacity of a sentence to approximate that state of the world, or to the understanding of a situation that has been taken as a *target*, as a relevant goal, of the communication taking place.

For example, imagine a context C, in which it seems important to acquire some information. Let us assume that Bob is organizing a dinner party at home, but has no idea how many people Alice has invited. For Bob, the number of guests is a relevant piece of information (which constitutes his target) in context C, organization of the dinner party. Alice has decided to invite eleven people but for some reason is unable to relay this information to Bob. The latter receives two pieces of information from mutual friends. Paul tells him that more than two people have been invited. Monica tells him that twelve people have been invited. The first is true information, while the second is false information, in the sense that it does not accurately portray the reality (namely, the content of the statement does not correspond to the state of the world). From another standpoint, however, the first piece of information is certainly farther from the truth than the second is.

In fact, even though the second statement conveys false or inexact information, its information capacity is higher than that of the true information Bob received, because the information it conveys is less distant from the purpose concerning context C, which makes communication relevant in the given situation. Simply put, the inaccurate information allows Bob to organize the dinner more effectively than the true information would allow. The interesting fact that emerges from Floridi's theory is that the (measurement of) distance from truth is made possible by having assumed a certain informative goal in a given context. The pursuit of the goal in the current situation makes it relevant to obtain some information: it made it more important and urgent to get relevant information than merely truthful (precise or reliable) information.

Distance from truth thus becomes an inverse measure of the relevance of information: the less distant information is from truth, the more relevant it is. In other words, information is as relevant as it approximates us to or makes us achieve the goal for which communication is pursued within a given context. This perspective is certainly not the solution to the issue of fake news, but at least it shifts attention from the mere content of the news (reliability) to the identification of the purposes (relevance) for which the communication is set in motion in a specific context. What is important is that communication has a real information capacity for network users, in the sense just outlined. However, this requires us to ask the right question, that is to say, to identify the context in which the acquisition of information meets a certain purpose.

Once again, the issue of digital governance does not concern, in the case of fake news, the content communicated, but rather the purpose of communication. The debate about fake news must be, in my opinion, a debate about goals. For example, the proliferation of fake news today in the field of political communication is more revealing of the unease in assessing the relevant goals of online political communication than of users' failure to verify the reliability of the news. We must ask ourselves if and when a piece of news becomes relevant to us; if and when knowledge is still a goal of communication. We must ask ourselves in what contexts it is relevant to acquire news that allows us to reduce our distance from the truth. In fact, there is no representation of facts independent of the purpose for which a question is asked. As in the case of the performative we examined at the beginning of this chapter, it is not communication (the statement of truth or falsehood) that can or must be regulated as such, but only the contexts in which the communication of facts is relevant in relation to the purposes or values that are brought into play in such contexts. Information becomes knowledge only if we are able to situate it within a network of meaningful and purposeful questions and answers.

The relevance of information

The thrust of this chapter suggests that fake news cannot and should not be subject to regulation as such. It can only be regulated indirectly, when disseminating false information amounts to a legally relevant behavior from a given standpoint. We thus need to pay close attention to the specific circumstances in which lying is relevant (from the legal point of view, but not exclusively), or in other words, when it is important to measure how far we really are from the truth, and to ask what legal asset or underlying value the lie jeopardizes. It must be recalled, however, that the distance from truth is not simply measured in relation to the truth of specific statements, but in relation to their actual informational capacity. In the age of fake news, it is not enough to ask whether an answer is reliable; it is even more important to ask why a particular question is being posed. In fact, the reliability of an answer cannot be judged and verified without relating it to the concrete purpose underlying the question. Relevance does not prevent network users from being deceived by unreliable information. However, it does help us to identify problematic contexts, the purposes for which questions are raised and answers are sought, and the distance from truth that makes communication effective and productive. The question is not so much whether an answer is merely reliable, but whether it provides us with adequate information (by increasing our information capital) about a given fact, context or situation, where there is a purpose or value we consider relevant.

Notes

1 For the purposes of this chapter it is not necessary to distinguish between falsehood and lying. It seems intuitive that we are not necessarily lying every time we utter something false. We might be misrepresenting reality by mistake or in jest, without intending to lie. In these cases, we generally refer to the fact of giving rise, through statements, to an inaccurate representation of reality. On lying, see, among others, A. TAGLIAPIETRA, *Filosofia della bugia. Figure della menzogna nella storia del pensiero occidentale*, Bruno Mondadori, Milano, 2008.

2 J. SEARLE, *The Construction of Social Reality*, Free Press, NY, 1996. The philosophical roots of Searle's social ontology may be found in John Austin's theory of linguistic acts: J.-L. AUSTIN, *How to Do Things with Words*, Harvard University Press, Cambridge Mass., 1962.

3 H. ARENDT, *Truth and Politics*, first published in "The New Yorker", February 25, 1967, and reprinted with minor changes in *Between Past and Future*, 1968. From the same author, see also *Lying in Politics. Reflections on the 'Pentagon Papers'*, first published in "The New Yorker", November 18, 1971, and reprinted in *Crises of the Republic: Lying in Politics*, Mariner Books, Boston, 1972.

4 On this subject, see recently J. FARKAS, J. SCHOU, *Post-Truth, Fake News and Democracy. Mapping the Politics of Falsehood*, Studies in Global Information, Politics and Society, Routledge, London, 2019; Y. BENKLER, R. FARIS, H. ROBERTS, *Network Propaganda. Manipulation, Disinformation, and Radicalization in American Politics*, Oxford University Press, Oxford, 2018; G. RIVA, *Fake news. Vivere e sopravviver in un mondo di post-verità*, Il Mulino,

Bologna, 2018; G. PITRUZZELLA, O. POLLICINO, S. QUINTARELLI, *Parole e potere: libertà di espressione, hate speech e fake news*, Egea, Milano, 2017.

5 On this point, see M. DURANTE, *Il future del web, op. cit.*, in particular pp. 259–265; E. PARISER, *The Filter Bubble: What the Internet Is Hiding From You*, Penguin, London, 2012.

6 On this, see recently L. MCINTYRE, *Post-Truth*, The MIT Press, Chicago Mass., 2018.

7 It is no coincidence that, in another context, Luciano Floridi raised the question of a proxy society, progressively built on access to intermediaries or surrogates instead of immediate and direct experience. This is a contribution we have already mentioned: L. FLORIDI, *A Proxy Culture, op. cit.*

8 G. RIVA, *Fake News, op. cit.*, p. 7. By "fake" we intend to refer not only to what is false, but more generally to what is counterfeit, shoddy, second-hand, or in other words, not just to news designed to deceive someone, but also to news that is manufactured to create confusion and divert attention.

9 On this point, see L. BARABÁSI, *Linked. The Science of Networks, op. cit.*, for example, p. 51.

10 On this point, see M. PUASCHUNDER, *Nudging in the Digital Big Data Era*, in "European Journal of Economics, Law and Politics", vol. 4, issue 4, December 2017, pp. 18–23.

11 As described in E. PARISER, *The Filter Bubble, op. cit.*

12 M. TURILLI, L. FLORIDI, *The Ethics of Information Transparency*, in "Ethics and Information Technology", vol. 11, issue 2, 2009, pp. 105–112.

13 We have tried to clarify the meaning of this expression in M. DURANTE, *The Democratic Governance of Information Societies.*

14 On the issue of information overload, see L. FLORIDI, *Big Data and their Epistemological Challenge*, in "Philosophy & Technology", vol. 25, issue 4, 2012, pp. 435–437; ID., *The Logic of Being Informed*, in "Logique et analyze", vol. 49, issue 196, 2006, pp. 433–460. Paul Feyerabend had coined the already mentioned expression of the *conquest of abundance*, to allude to the epistemic practice of reducing abundance and making abstraction from experience. On this point, see P. FEYERABEND, *Conquest of Abundance, op. cit.*

15 See L. FLORIDI, *The Philosophy of Information, op. cit.*, p. 59 (*our italics*). For an analysis of the method of the levels of abstraction, see M. DURANTE, *Ethics, Law and the Politics of Information. A Guide to the Philosophy of Luciano Floridi*, Springer, Dordrecht, 2017, pp. 11–14.

16 J. BALKIN, *Free Speech, op. cit.*, p. 1189. In this sense, see also Y. BENKLER, *The Wealth of Networks, op. cit.*

17 More precisely, it could be defined as pluralist, since each actor could be specified in further figures, but, in this chapter, we can continue to refer to a tripartite structure. See on this point J. BALKIN, *Free Speech, op. cit.*, pp. 1191–1192.

18 J. BALKIN, *Free Speech, op. cit.*, p. 1192.

19 See in this sense what is remarked by J. BALKIN, *Free Speech, op. cit.*, p. 1188: "The substantive problem of free expression in the early twenty-first century is that the practical ability to speak online is affected by power struggles among these various groups. Our practical ability to speak is shaped by (1) our relationship to the state; (2) our relationship to the owners of the digital infrastructure that we use to speak; and (3) the relationships of cooperation, cooptation, and coercion between states and digital infrastructure owners".

20 J. BALKIN, *Free Speech, op. cit.*, p. 1179 *et seq.*

21 J. BALKIN, *Free Speech, op. cit.*, p. 1176.

22 J. BALKIN, *Free Speech, op. cit.*, p. 1177.

23 J. BALKIN, *Free Speech, op. cit.*, p. 1182.

24 *Ibid.*

25 J. BALKIN, *Free Speech, op. cit.*, p. 1183.

26 J. BALKIN, *Free Speech, op. cit.*, p. 1181.

27 J. BALKIN, *Free Speech, op. cit.*, pp. 1208–1209: "To solve a perceived problem of speech regulation, a wide variety of public and private actors urge infrastructure owners — in this case, social media companies — to develop their own programs, algorithms, and bureaucracies, and to help end-users make decisions about what kinds of news stories they should read and trust. In other words, our new pluralist system of speech regulation

encourages platform owners to develop ever more extensive and elaborate systems of private governance."

28 In this sense, see J. BALKIN, *Free Speech, op. cit.*, p. 1198: "Online speech platforms may often frustrate these expectations of procedural and participatory fairness. But online speech platforms will find that they cannot ignore them entirely. These expectations point to the ways that online speech platforms will have to accommodate their end users in the future. Moreover, they point to the kinds of reforms that democratic governments may eventually try to require of online speech platforms as they become indispensable features both of commerce and democracy within democratic nation-states."

29 *Ibid.*

30 J. BALKIN, *Free Speech, op. cit.*, pp. 1197–1198.

31 For an overview of these instruments, see G. RIVA, *Fake News, op. cit.*, p. 151 *et seq.*

32 See http://www.mondodigitale.org/it. This suggestion is very indicative because it requires users to evaluate three elements, the crisis (and sometimes the refusal of it) is at the beginning of the fake news phenomenon: the validation of sources; the evidence provided by data; the principle of authority of the experts.

33 The reference is to M. DURANTE, *Il futuro del web, op. cit.*, p. 187 *et seq.*

34 On this point, see M. DURANTE, *Il futuro del web, op. cit.*, pp. 197–203, in which, specifically, the case of Wikipedia, Google and Slashdot were analyzed.

35 G. RIVA, *Fake News, op. cit.*, p. 145 *et seq.*

36 G. RIVA, *Fake News, op. cit.*, p. 146.

37 In this sense, see U. PAGALLO, *Il diritto nell'età dell'informazione, op. cit.*, p. XIX *et seq.* On this point, see also L. FLORIDI, *The Fourth Rev., op. cit.*, p. 6 *et seq.*

38 G. RIVA, *Fake News, op. cit.*, p. 146.

39 L. FLORIDI (ed.), *The Onlife Manifesto, op. cit.*

40 E. PARISER, *The Filter Bubble, op. cit.*, p. 13.

41 Often also referred to as an *echo chamber*, in which individual users seem always to be listening to themselves, since they are constantly confronted with things that are personalized and tailored to them.

42 In this sense, see recently C.R. SUNSTEIN, *#Republic: Divided Democracy in the Age of Social Media*, Princeton University Press, Princeton, 2017, which first raised the case and opportunity. See also on this topic E. PARISER, *The Filter Bubble, op. cit.*, p. 54.

43 L. FLORIDI, *The Fourth Rev., op. cit.*, p. 218 *et seq.*; ID., *Infraethics*, in "The Philosophers' Magazine", issue 60, 2013, pp. 26–27.

44 L. FLORIDI, *The Philosophy of Information, op. cit.*, p. 327.

7

THE GOVERNANCE OF ALGORITHMS

The use of algorithms

Since 2014, an algorithm has sat on the board of directors of a Hong Kong-based venture capital firm. VITAL, which stands for *Validating Investment Tool for Advancing Life Science*, is the first robot manager to play a major role on the board of Deep Knowledge Ventures (DKV), a company specialized in biotechnology. The company's CEO, Dmitry Kaminskiy, told interviewers that "VITAL is an equal member of the board because its opinion (which is actually the result of its analysis algorithm) will be considered the most important". He explained that all "investment decisions will be made after VITAL has processed all the data". The statement issued by DKV to justify its adoption of the technology is significant: "human beings are emotional and subjective. They can make mistakes. Machines, on the other hand, can choose the right path based on intuition and logic. Combined with the experience of the company's investors, it will be possible to minimize risks"[1]. It hardly comes as a surprise that VITAL version 2.0 is currently under development[2].

This is not an isolated phenomenon, but one of many examples of a movement that is currently sweeping the planet. Our modern information societies are growing increasingly dependent on the use of ICTs[3]. We are delegating more and more tasks and decisions to machines, artificial agents or expert systems that utilize some form of artificial intelligence, basing their decisions and actions on algorithms. We are growing reliant on algorithms to make choices and perform tasks that were traditionally reserved for humans, in almost every sphere of human activity. The wide-scale adoption of algorithms is a by-product of one of the fundamental characteristics of our world on which this book dwells: agency is no longer the exclusive prerogative of human beings. Some further examples can help to illustrate the pervasiveness of this phenomenon.

Algorithms largely govern the functioning of complex systems, such as the stock market in international finance[4] or the indexing and ranking of search engine results, according to "popular rule", which now largely affects the creation of knowledge[5]. Choosing candidates, recruiting employees, screening mortgage applicants; these and countless other operations are increasingly the outcome of choices based on automated data processing directed by algorithmic procedures. As Frank Pasquale has remarked, if the use of algorithms is now ubiquitous, their relevance, i.e., their ability to affect the fabric of human relations, depends on the importance and sensitivity of the context in which they are adopted:

> Algorithms are increasingly important because businesses rarely thought of as high-tech have learned the lessons of the internet giants' successes. Following the advice of Jeff Jarvis' *What Would Google Do?*, they are collecting data from both workers and customers, using algorithmic tools to make decisions, the desirable from the disposable. Companies may be parsing your voice and credit record when you call them, to determine whether you match up to "ideal customer" status, or are simply "waste" who can be treated with disdain. Epagogix advises movie studios on what scripts to buy based on how closely they match past, successful scripts. Even winemakers make algorithmic judgments, based on statistical analyses of the weather and other characteristics of good and bad vintage years. For wines or films, the stakes are not terribly high. But when algorithms start affecting critical opportunities for employment, career advancement, health, credit and education, they deserve more scrutiny. U.S. hospitals are using big data-driven systems to determine which patients are high-risk – and data far outside traditional health records is informing those determinations. IBM now uses algorithmic assessment tools to sort employees worldwide on criteria of cost-effectiveness, but spares top managers the same invasive surveillance and ranking. In government, too, algorithmic assessments of dangerousness can lead to longer sentences for convicts, or no-fly lists for travelers. Credit scoring drives billions of dollars in lending, but the scorers' methods remain opaque. The average borrower could lose tens of thousands of dollars over a lifetime, thanks to wrong or unfairly processed data.[6]

The intensive use of algorithms in our information societies is determined not just by the delegation of tasks and decisions to machines, but also by the technological reshaping of our environment. In fact, the world that surrounds us is increasingly defined in strictly technological terms. In this environment – which is made up of the Internet of Things (already evolving into the Internet of Everything), multiple network platforms, the Cloud, intelligent environments, smart applications (including the widespread network of sensors and actuators that enable *Smart Cities*) – a growing number of entities (devices, systems, agents, machines) are ruled by a set of algorithms in their continuous production, collection, sharing, aggregation and processing of data.

There are therefore two processes at work. We are not only outsourcing decisions and tasks to algorithms; we are also increasingly adapting the environment to their functioning, that is, to the use of devices that function on the basis of algorithms. The environment itself has become a venue for the collection, sharing, aggregation and production of the data that drives the functioning of such devices. I have long insisted on this point: acting in the environment and interacting with it has always required us to represent the reality in which we act and with which we interact. To the extent that a growing number of decisions and actions are entrusted to machines, even the representation of reality with which they are equipped is adapted to their needs and their way of functioning. *We create an epistemology of and for machines.* This is the most salient aspect of contemporary epistemology: knowledge, model and representation of reality and of the world are increasingly elaborated so as to be useable by machines, whose performance improves in proportion to how closely the environment and its representation are accommodated to their way of functioning.

The delegation of decisions and tasks to algorithms affects not only the practical sphere of action, but also implies an overall reconfiguration of the environment and, with it, the epistemic modelling and representation of the world. The passage by Frank Pasquale quoted above is important precisely in that it helps us to understand the benefits and pitfalls intrinsic to the systematic recourse to algorithms in our information societies. Both the opportunities and the potentially serious trade-offs are rooted in the way algorithms are structured and function. It is therefore well worth examining the structure of algorithms in more depth. Without going into too much technical detail, a straightforward definition of algorithm should suffice to identify the main problems associated with their use.

In the general sense, algorithms are "coded procedures for transforming input data into a desired output, based on specific calculations"[7] or, to put it even more broadly, they are sets of rules for solving a problem in a finite number of steps. This definition is sufficient to allow us to understand the potential benefits and pitfalls, the expectations, and the issues raised by the delegation of decisions and tasks to algorithms.

On the one hand, algorithmic delegation carries the promise of a *proceduralization* of the world, that is, the promise to efficiently solve problems and obtain results based on well-codified and hence controllable and governable procedures. Algorithmic delegation can also relieve human beings of disagreeable or difficult tasks, allowing them to spend the time, resources and energy saved on more rewarding pursuits. This is certainly a prospect worth contemplating; however, the benefits must be weighed against the potential challenges.

Algorithmic delegation raises problems at each phase of the algorithmic process: (1) input; (2) procedure; (3) output. The main (ethical, legal, epistemic, etc.) problems affecting algorithms occur at one or a combination of all three phases. Current debate often focuses on just a single phase, but the most troublesome issues actually involve all three, each of which is likely to have a negative impact on the others.

There are questions that concern: (1) the make-up of the knowledge base (the *input*), meaning the set of data, information and knowledge that defines the epistemic base required for solving the problems within the machine's specific context of operation, or more simply stated, within the model and representation of the world the machine relies on in order to decide and act; (2) the mechanism for processing and calculation (the *procedure*), i.e., the set of instructions given to the machine which allows it to draw conclusions from the knowledge base acquired and to adopt solutions to the problem posed, transforming the input into output. In other words, it is the syntactical mechanism through which the machine operates; (3) the expected result (the *output*), i.e., the concrete decision or action implemented by the machine. The latter can also be instructed (through machine learning systems) to learn from experience, that is, to be trained with a dataset (containing training data) in order to learn how to perform a task, by improving the accuracy of its output.

Each of these phases raises challenging epistemic questions related to the formalization of knowledge, the relationship between the syntactic and semantic levels, the use of learning systems, and so on. They also raise normative questions pertaining to the ethical, social and legal consequences of predictions and decisions generated by machines. The latter questions are the most pressing, and have sparked international debate due to widespread concern over their growing magnitude and urgency[8]. Here, we limit discussion to the main ethical, social and legal issues arising at each phase of the algorithmic process[9].

Input, procedure and output

Input

For a machine to perform a task through an algorithmic procedure, it must have access to a set of data that constitutes its knowledge base[10]. A knowledge base, one may recall, is a specific representation of the world used by every agent to make decisions and to behave. At the input stage, a classic issue of agency arises[11]: the way the representation of the world is modeled plays a decisive role on the decisions, predictions and operations carried out by the machine. The selection of data that constitutes the knowledge base can be affected by cognitive bias and, more generally, can be guided by implicit value choices, since the programmer's cognitive biases and values may differ from those of the people to whom the output of the algorithmic procedure applies. Clearly, this can raise serious ethical, social and legal problems. Let us consider a case in which we want to develop a software intended to assess a person's risk of future criminal conduct[12], in terms of the likelihood that the defendant will re-offend ("recidivism risk"), before the trial. The algorithm's knowledge base can be constructed using statistical data taking into account elements such as socioeconomic status, family background, neighborhood crime, employment status, all of which may include references to gender and race, to calculate the statistical likelihood of an individual's criminal risk. This knowledge base is used by the programmer to create an abstract profile of people at risk for recidivism. The program can subsume the concrete profile of the defendant within the abstract profile; hence, elements such as gender or race, included within the socioeconomic status, family background, neighborhood crime, or employment status, may end up affecting the final screening more than overall consideration of the defendant's personal history[13].

The problem of agency in this example (the incorporation of cognitive biases or values in the creation of the knowledge base) arises at two different levels: the meta-problem of delegation and the meta-problem of standards. We will consider both more closely at the end of this chapter. For now, it is important to note that if a decision is delegated to a machine whose knowledge base incorporates cognitively or axiologically biased inputs that affect the final decision, then any error made during the initial phase is propagated throughout the entire procedure, and may produce discriminatory results as the output. If these biases are difficult to detect (how the training data were selected, for example) or if the procedure is opaque (how the chosen inputs affect the output), it can be difficult to recognize the discriminatory effect and therefore to challenge the final decision. This is one of the first problems faced when delegating tasks to machines.

There is, however, an even subtler problem, which has to do with the social standards underlying the evaluation of the output. Returning to the previous example, it is possible that the use of algorithms based on *biased* knowledge (such as the particular weight assigned to the race or ethnicity variable) might be successful in reducing pre-trial and probationary recidivism rates. If public security (i.e., preventing recidivism) is a strongly cherished and shared social value, the implicit risk of bias would nonetheless be highly accepted by the society at large. This has two implications: (1) the social value of public security produced by the output may prevail over concerns about discrimination at an individual level; (2) the resulting output is incorporated into the knowledge base (or training dataset) as new statistical data (*input*), thus reinforcing the bias in its original design.

Procedure

A major problem with the use of algorithms can be found at the procedural level, where inputs are processed and transformed into outputs. In some cases, the procedure is logical and straightforward enough for programmers and even users to follow and understand. But there are other cases in which this procedure turns out to be so complex that not only the end users but also the programmers find it difficult to explain[14]. In such cases, the algorithm or, rather, the logic of the decision[15] based on the algorithm is opaque. Franck Pasquale coined the now well-known expression "black box society" to describe the overall issue of opacity or lack of transparency in the functioning of algorithms[16] in a society that is increasingly reliant on the invisible logic ruling its functioning. The algorithmic procedure seems to hide the key to understanding how many decisions and predictions based on algorithms are made. Moreover, this lack of transparency is not only a technical issue, but a legal one as well.

From a technical standpoint, certain algorithmic procedures, such as neural networks[17], are made up of systems capable of independently establishing, updating and developing the rules of their future functioning, making autonomous decisions or carrying out actions to maximize the chances of obtaining results, in ways that can be unpredictable even for the programmers. These systems are capable of learning dynamically from experience and of evolving, modifying and adapting their internal structure. Unlike simple algorithms based on decision trees, for example, whose decisions can be traced logically from initial question to answer, more complex algorithms based on neural networks are characterized by non-linear decisions. This means that each information input node (representing the processing unit) is connected to various internal nodes of the network which are in turn organized at multiple levels. This allows each single node to process the signals received before passing the results of its elaborations to the next level. This is why it can be so difficult to guarantee transparency in the decision-making process or to pinpoint the factors that determined the decision ultimately made.

Apart from the issues of technical opacity, access to the underlying logic of algorithmic procedures can also be limited due to legislation regulating intellectual property rights and trade secrets to protect the economic interests of the creators. Without going into the complex issue of the application of this regulation to the case of algorithms, a few general observations can be made. On the one hand, intellectual property rights mainly seem to protect the source code, which the owner is not required to disclose. On the other hand, the law provides only slim margins of protection to algorithms through copyright or patent law. Furthermore, even if the algorithms benefited from this form of protection, the filing of the patent itself would imply disclosure of the algorithm's functioning. Nonetheless, disclosure of how a process works in order to patent it seems rather different from explaining how a screening algorithm makes its decisions. Finally, a further obstacle to accessing the logic of a screening algorithm can be found in the legislation on trade secrets, which protects strategic information contributing to a company's economic value. While such legislation does not apply to the legal acquisition of secret information (deduced, for example, through reverse engineering techniques), the technical obstacles based on the opacity of algorithms makes this unlikely to happen.

As will be discussed in Chapter 8, the technical and legal inaccessibility to the logic of algorithmic decision-making raises the overarching question of how these algorithms logically process information and produce their outputs. The question is important given the ever-growing encroachment of algorithmic decisions in all areas of everyday life, their potential impact on individual rights and freedoms, and their frequently incontestable and unverifiable nature. Because of this opaqueness and the problematic nature of justifying outputs (which have prompted a number of different strategies for attribution, responsibility and explanation[18]), we must be increasingly attentive to evaluating the results produced by algorithmic decision-making. This is certainly a complex task, and one which this book hopes to shed light on through its examination of the different but intertwining perspectives of legal legitimacy, social acceptability and ethical preference[19].

Output

Output refers to the concrete result of an algorithmic procedure. The main problem with output is the risk for producing discriminatory effects. This can occur because of problems with the construction of the knowledge base or selection of the training dataset (input), or because of errors of logic in the decision-making mechanism (procedure). In either case, the discriminatory effect can easily be the natural consequence of a previous bias or error embedded within the algorithm, and is hence difficult to detect and contest[20]. The discriminatory effect lurks in the nooks and crannies of the ostensible neutrality and infallibility of the algorithmic procedure in producing the anticipated results.

There is a significant gap in anti-discrimination law that can and must be addressed in order to contrast discrimination stemming from algorithmic procedures. This legal lacuna derives from the fact that the main European directives on anti-discrimination law date from the beginning of 2000[21], when it was still difficult to foresee the full development of artificial intelligence systems and machine learning that underlie algorithmic decision-making procedures[22]. Although there is no explicit provision in these directives relating to what is now known as algorithmic discrimination, one can exploit the distinction between *direct* and *indirect discrimination*[23] to contrast a number of relevant cases:

> Importantly, in machine learning contexts, indirect discrimination is the most relevant type of discrimination, even if one qualifies implicit bias as direct discrimination. The algorithmic score itself, or the criteria that drive it, will often be a neutral criterion that may put protected groups at a specific disadvantage. This finding is complicated by the fact that a number of machine learning techniques, such as deep neural networks, do not necessarily allow for the recovery of the relevant factors used by the model to generate the output. It may be tempting to conclude that, if an adverse impact on a protected group can be proven and if it cannot be linked to a specific neutral factor (e.g., ownership of red cars), this may constitute direct discrimination. However, indirect discrimination can also be triggered by a neutral "practice"; the entire algorithmic decision-making procedure can be seen as such a practice that is neutral as long as protected criteria are not explicitly or implicitly used in the model. Therefore, independent of the type of machine learning procedure used, involuntary forms of sampling bias or incorrect labeling will amount to indirect discrimination if they are not the result of implicit bias, but rather of oversight or sloppiness. If it is unclear whether or not implicit bias was at work, indirect discrimination acts as a default provision for involuntary discrimination. Similarly, indirect proxy discrimination may constitute indirect discrimination if the relevant factors for or simply the outcome of the decision-making model closely

correlate with group membership so that, again, one protected group is put at a specific disadvantage.[24]

The fact remains that, for the aforementioned reasons, European anti-discrimination law does not apply to all possible cases, but only to certain types of interaction in certain areas. These regulations are thus inadequate to fully deal with the scope of algorithmic processes. There are several reasons for this:

> First, algorithmic processes will sometimes bypass the material and personal scope of existing anti-discrimination legislation. Second, while it may multiply instances of indirect discrimination, the purported predictive accuracy of machine learning models provides an easy justification for these effects. Third, to refute these claims, victims would have to prove the model wrong – an almost impossible task in the face of models that are often inscrutable even to their developers, and without access to the training data and the model specifications.[25]

This three-part classification is obviously heuristic, and serves to map out a number of issues that the algorithmic processes are likely to raise; however, it is equally evident that these issues are tightly interconnected and mutually reinforcing. It therefore becomes necessary to consider our subject, the governance of algorithms, in terms that are more complex.

The governance of algorithms

A fundamental tension emerging from the problematic issues just described lies at the center of the governance of algorithms: "On the one hand, algorithms are invoked as powerful entities that govern, judge, sort, regulate, classify, influence or otherwise discipline the world. On the other hand, algorithms are portrayed as strangely elusive and inscrutable, or in fact as virtually unstudiable"[26]. The governance of algorithms raises a twofold issue. While algorithms are claimed to govern reality[27] (that is, they constitute one of the main tools of governance), they themselves must be governed, subjected to discussion, deliberation, verification, control and revision, or in other words, to the whole set of practices that form an essential safeguard for any democratic society[28]. Many have already pointed out that algorithms must be made *accountable*, that is, coupled with an explanation that justifies their use in a responsible way[29]. We will come back to this point in Chapter 8.

For now, it is important to understand just how algorithms come to govern our lives. This implicit agenda, for the most part unplanned and unforeseen, unfolds on two different planes: that of *being* and that of what *ought to be*. It is sometimes difficult to distinguish between the two, as they may overlap; this, in fact, is one of the challenges of governing algorithms. Let us try to explain the distinction in clear terms.

When we entrust a decision to a machine-based algorithm, the decision produces consequences in the real world that alter, more or less profoundly, a certain state of affairs: a mortgage is or is not granted; probation is or is not assigned; a financial transaction is or is not completed; an application is or is not selected, and so on. For the parties involved, the alternatives are tangible and significant, and the changes in the world they entail are crucial. These decisions produce empirical consequences that are situated and grasped at the level of being, especially as their implementation is often directed and incorporated into technological devices or processes.

This is the most tangible result of the implementation of algorithms and their way of governing reality. However, it is certainly not the only one, since the functioning of algorithms at the level of being depends largely on how they function at the level of what ought to be, according to an *algorithmic entanglement*, to which we need to direct our attention. One must thus analyze how algorithms affect the dimension of what ought to be or, in other words, of normativity. This happens in two ways: (1) by identifying *algorithmic threshold values* produced by profiling and prediction machines; (2) through the production of *algorithmic counterfactuals* determined by simulation processes.

Algorithmic threshold values

One of the main tasks assigned to algorithms is that of making predictions. Predicting preferences, behaviors, habits, attitudes or people's voting patterns has become a fruitful and vital science. These predictions are no longer so much the result of imagination, aimed at depicting different and unexpected worlds, but rather the result of analyses based on algorithms aimed at representing expected and desired worlds. They are an extended version of the world we wish to see. These analyses are carried out by what are referred to as "predictive machines"[30]. Thus, prediction lies at the heart of our information societies:

> Prediction is a fundamental input. We may not realize it, but predictions are everywhere. Our business and personal lives are full of predictions. Often our predictions are hidden as input into the decision-making process. Better predictions mean better information, which means better decision-making. The prediction is "intelligence" in the spy sense of "getting useful information". Predictive machines consist of useful information generated artificially. Intelligence counts. [...] As the cost of predictions continues to fall, we are discovering their usefulness for an incredibly wide range of further activities, which make all kinds of things possible in the process.[31]

The systematic collection of data and their aggregation generates gigantic datasets (Big Data) that can be fed into the knowledge bases or training datasets of predictive machines. These machines include any AI or machine learning system that uses algorithmic procedures to infer the unknown (new data) from what is known (collected data) and that constantly refines its predictive abilities in an ever expanding range of areas and activities. The "unknown" supplied by these predictions is less of a descriptive account of new knowledge and scientific discovery and more of a prescriptive and normative account of how it wants to influence and direct our choices and of the assumptions, often imperceptible and inaccessible, about the rights and benefits to be granted or denied. Some examples may help. Predictive algorithms make it possible to analyze and predict consumers' preferences and thus to offer them a wider range of desired goods, thereby influencing and corroborating their choices. At the same time, by creating an ideal customer profile and anticipating customer preferences for specific goods or services, the concrete profile of given consumers can be traced back and compared to the ideal profile; those with the best match can be offered better trading conditions (such as discounts) or other benefits (with the result of differentiating or even discriminating between different consumer profiles[32]). The definition of this ideal profile, which is artificially produced by an algorithm, has a clear normative value, since it involves the granting (or denial) of a certain advantage (benefit, price, etc.) on the basis of evaluation.

This last point is crucial, for it provides a good illustration of what I call the algorithmic threshold value. Predictive algorithms can identify values in relation to what rights, benefits, prerogatives or other opportunities can be granted or denied. I define an *algorithmic threshold value* as the minimum value, generated by an algorithmic procedure, that must be met in order to grant or deny certain rights, benefits, prerogatives or other opportunities. Let us consider someone applying for a loan. An algorithm can use information from a large training dataset to learn or develop an ideal beneficiary profile of those least likely to default on a loan. A credit institution can use a screening algorithm to determine how closely the applicant's profile matches that of the ideal beneficiary, which thus acts as a threshold value for the granting of the loan. Thus, a threshold value can be determined by an abstract profile (a set of relevant characteristics), an evaluative score, a set of factors or predictors, which corresponds to a set of data processed by an algorithm, to which is assigned a normative function of prediction and evaluation of a concrete instance.

This implies an algorithmic proceduralization of normativity that can affect the granting of rights or benefits. It also challenges the procedural fairness (an integral part of the rule of law) of the algorithmic decision-making process, given that its opaqueness and embeddedness within technological processes tend to totally or partly elude the democratic process of discussion, interpretation, scrutiny and revision. This problem is associated with an epistemological problem, which is no less onerous. The predictions generated by algorithmic procedures to identify threshold values are often based on mere statistical correlation. This has raised numerous discussions and concerns. The issue is thorny, so without going into any great detail, we limit ourselves to the following remarks:

> Statisticians have developed many sophisticated methods to reduce large amounts of data and identify associations between variables. A typical association

measure, [...] called "correlation" or "regression", implies drawing the line con-
necting a set of data points and deriving the curve of that line. Some associations
may have a clear causal interpretation; others not. But statistics alone cannot tell us
what the cause is and what the effect is.[33]

Simply put, statistical correlations show that two factors are related, but do not
explain how or why. It may therefore appear incongruous or counterintuitive that
the granting of a benefit, such as a loan or reduced insurance premiums, could be
statistically correlated to factors apparently unrelated to the credit or insurance
sector[34]. The issue is significant enough that computer scientist and philosopher
Judea Pearl devoted an entire book to it[35], emphasizing the need to return to a
stricter consideration of the concept of causality:

> Much of this data-driven story threatens us today. We live in an age that assumes
> that Big Data is the solution to all our problems. Courses in "data science" pro-
> liferate in our universities and positions as "data scientist" are profitable in com-
> panies that participate in the "data economy". But I hope with this book to
> persuade you that the data is profoundly mute. The data can tell us that the
> people who took a medicine recovered more quickly than those who did not,
> but are unable to tell us why. Perhaps those who took the medicine did so
> because they could afford it and would recover just as quickly if they didn't.[36]

Data interpretation is not a problem that is solved in terms of the quantity of data
that can be acquired (the formula greater data = better explanation does not hold)
in technological terms; data interpretation is a problem that must be accounted for
epistemologically[37]. It therefore requires formulation of a model capable of
explaining the process that generated the data:

> In some circles, there is an almost religious faith in the fact that we can find
> answers to these questions in the data themselves, if only we are sufficiently
> good at searching for data. However, the readers of this book have realized
> that this belief can be easily taken apart. The questions I have just asked are all
> causal, and the answer to causal questions can never be provided by the data
> alone. The latter oblige us to formulate a model of the process that generated
> the data or at least some aspect of this process.[38]

In sum, predictive algorithms identify threshold values that exert a normative role
through their decisions: they provide an assessment that affects the granting (or
denial) of rights, benefits, prerogatives or other opportunities, generally without
providing any causal or intuitive explanation for those decisions.

This is not the only normative effect that can be attributed to algorithms.
Another is related to the ability of computers to generate simulations. This implies
an imperceptible but radical conceptual shift from the level of being to that of what
ought to be.

Algorithmic counterfactuals

This idea comes from watching the movie "Sully" by Clint Eastwood. The plot is based on a true story, although it is of no concern to us how faithful the story was to reality. The events are as follows. In January 2009, US Airways airline flight 1549 smashed into a flock of geese, three minutes from New York's La Guardia airport. With both engines out, pilot Chesley "Sully" Sullenberger, assisted by co-pilot Jeffrey Skiles, decided not to try reaching an airport runway. Instead, Sully dead-sticked his Airbus 320 to a landing in the Hudson River, saving the lives of 155 people. Later, the National Transportation Safety Board claimed that several confidential computerized simulations indicated that the plane could have landed safely at the LaGuardia or Teterboro Airports without its engines. In the end, Sully managed to prove that the computerized simulations were wrong, and that there were no real alternatives to what he had done. This, however, is not the point.

The point is that the simulation, generated by means of the algorithms in the on-board software, was used to scrutinize events that had already occurred, and to assess what might have otherwise occurred. The computer simulation was used to produce what we might define as an *algorithmic counterfactual*, or in other words, a representation of reality in a virtual world that allows us to assess and judge what happened in the real world[39]. The algorithmic counterfactual actually works to tell us how the agent should have behaved in reality.

This idea is not completely new. We have always liked to think of alternative and ideal worlds as a valid criterion for counterfactual judgment. At the same time, however, the notion has undergone substantial changes. For instance, the virtual reality of an algorithmic counterfactual is profoundly different from a Kantian regulative ideal of reason. While the former tells us how things could or should have been in the proximate alternative world, the latter only expresses archetypal standards, which can be approximated but never fully attained. Those regulative ideals or archetypal standards assign a direction to a practice, but do not rule out practices.

In Judea Pearl's work as well, one can find a similar expression, although used with a slightly different meaning. Pearl has referred to the "algorithmization of counterfactuals" in the following sense:

> When the scientific question of interest involves retrospective thinking, we resort to an expression proper to causal reasoning called the counterfactual. [...] As in the case of the prediction of the effect of interventions (already mentioned), in many cases we can emulate human retrospective thinking with an algorithm that assumes what we know of the observed world and produces a relative response to the counterfactual world. This "algorithmization of counterfactuals" is another germ of the Causal Revolution.[40]

While in this book I have expressed concern about the whole chain of problems associated with the use of algorithms (ranging from potential cognitive biases that affect the formation of the knowledge base or training dataset, the lack of transparency of the black box of an inference engine, up to the possible discriminatory effect of algorithmic output), Pearl believes that the outsourcing of algorithmic counterfactuals to thinking machines has a decisive and beneficial impact:

> Counterfactuals are the constitutive element of moral behavior as well as of scientific thought. The ability to reflect on one's past actions and to imagine alternative scenarios is the basis of moral freedom and social responsibility. The algorithmization of counterfactuals invites thinking machines to benefit from this capacity and to participate in this (so far) exclusively human way of thinking about the world.[41]

Actually, Pearl is perfectly aware of what we define as the meta-problem of delegation ("This raises an obvious question: to what extent can we trust a computer simulation?"[42]). What puzzles us about the normative function of algorithmic counterfactuals is that their ability to predict alternative worlds is mainly based, ultimately, on a static training dataset that describes the world as it is ("assuming what we know about the observed world"[43]). Algorithmic counterfactuals (the what-if of the proximate worlds) tend to reaffirm the primacy of the existent in a more or less surreptitious manner. In this way, the virtual that is generated by an algorithmic procedure is not instrumental to the imagination of new and different worlds, but rather to the prediction of expected and desired worlds.

In other words, algorithms perform another normative function in their ability to generate simulated representations of the course of actions, which can then serve as a criterion for the evaluation and counterfactual judgment of the course of actions that has actually occurred. They can thus claim to tell us retrospectively how we should have behaved, based on the projection of what we know of the observed world. Despite the undisputed heuristic value of counterfactual simulation[44], we believe that this normative dimension deserves careful scrutiny as well as public and critical discussion, as does any circumstance in which the norms are created or enforced outside a deliberative process[45].

Having shed some light on the chain of problems arising from the use of algorithms and the overlap between their empirical and normative dimension, it is time to turn our attention to two closely related meta-problems that will serve as the backdrop against which the issue of algorithm governance should be addressed in the future. We refer to them as meta-problems because they can affect all the problems stemming from the algorithmic process. They are: (1) the meta-problem of delegation; and (2) the meta-problem of standards.

Meta-problems in the governance of algorithms

The meta-problem of delegation

One of the main reasons that is invoked to justify the outsourcing of tasks to machines is their alleged reliability. However, the relative reliability of machines in performing tasks and in providing solutions does not rule out the potential risks deriving from: (1) the complexity of the functioning of machines; (2) the relative degree of autonomy with which they perform the tasks delegated to them; (3) the inherent problems concerning all phases of their decision-making process. Anyone who uses these machines, and decides to depend on them, is not merely relying on the correct functioning of a machine, process or device, but is trusting them in a way that always involves an element of risk. In fact, where there is delegation there is trust and, where there is trust, there is also necessarily risk, as Niklas Luhmann has taught us[46].

Those who decide to depend on machines to perform complex tasks, whose performance and outcome are not always entirely predetermined, are doing so in a state of incomplete information. Thus, they run the risk that something could escape from control. The expression *trusted-computer* is misleading: if the functioning of a machine is entirely predetermined and predictable (so as not to normally lead to deviations or a choice between alternatives), there is no need to talk about trust; one could refer to mere reliance. If, on the other hand, the functioning of a machine is not entirely predetermined and predictable (so as to entail some form of autonomy resulting from the choice between alternatives or the machine's ability to change its internal state[47]), it is possible, in our opinion, to talk about trust[48] as we would do with any human agent. However, it is precisely the presence of trust that raises the meta-problem of delegation.

What, in fact, does trust mean when it refers to machines whose actions are based on algorithms? Is it possible to talk about trusting a machine the same way we would talk about trusting human agents? In other words, does trust in this case concern the artificial agents or their programmers? Furthermore, is it a form of intersubjective trust (which occurs between agents) or of systemic trust (which occurs when an agent has to decide whether or not to rely on a particular system in order to operate within it[49])? These questions concern the issue of trust, which is increasingly evoked with reference to the Internet and more generally to the digital environment, where it is a matter of strengthening a climate of trust between network users and Big Tech, which constantly acquire, manage and process our data through algorithmic processes.

Although I have elsewhere admitted the conceptual possibility of trust towards artificial agents[50] and while noting that we deal with the delegation of tasks to agents operating on the basis of algorithms, the pervasiveness and systematic manner in which algorithms are used in the digital context makes us believe that we are dealing with a case of systemic rather than intersubjective trust. In other words, as users, we are not called on to choose which specific algorithmic procedure deserves our trust. It would be difficult if not impossible for users to evaluate each and every algorithmic agent's trustworthiness. We are instead dealing with the overall functioning of a complex algorithmic system. After all, the delegation of decisions to algorithmic procedures is, from this point of view, an impersonal and wholesale delegation, rather than a personal or individualized one. Or, to put it more precisely, there is in this regard an *ex ante* and an *ex post* viewpoint.

On the one hand, each of us is *ex ante* an integral part of a system that is increasingly built on algorithms, which we may have a greater or lesser degree of systemic trust in, but which is difficult to challenge as a whole. On the other hand, when an algorithmic process creates problems or turns out to be inefficient, we can raise an *ex post* question as to the degree of intersubjective trust given to the algorithmic process in question. With systemic trust, when we decide to behave within a system, we are guided by consideration of the general objectives concerning how the system works: in this case, it is necessary to refer to general standards to evaluate the overall objectives of the system. In the case of intersubjective trust, when we decide to delegate a task to others, we are guided by consideration of the specific goals we want to achieve through the delegated act: this is a classic case of conditional trust, in which specific standards of evaluation of the individual's goals come into play. Both cases raise the meta-problem of standards.

The meta-problem of standards

What standards or indicators are used to evaluate the relevance or urgency of the problems entrusted to algorithms and the efficiency or correctness of their solutions? This, in our opinion, is the key aspect of reflection on the governance of algorithms. In fact, it is not enough to refer to the reliability or effectiveness with which the algorithms perform and solve the tasks as the exclusive or main evaluation criterion for their functioning. The evaluation must necessarily be broader and involve all phases of the algorithmic process, with particular reference to the examination of the outcomes produced through standards adopted based on a public discussion as open, transparent and as widely-shared as possible. In other words, we cannot evaluate the outcomes of an algorithmic process based only on a *performance* without questioning the ethical, social and legal consequences which the outsourcing of tasks to machines involves.

The evaluation of algorithmic processes, inasmuch as it involves people's rights, freedoms and other important values, must invest a broad sphere of normativity in at least three possible directions, taking into account legal legitimacy, social acceptability and ethical preference[51]. Making sure that a procedure has achieved its purpose is not enough: investigation must be based on standards through which this purpose can be evaluated in more general terms. These standards can thus be legal, social and ethical. This raises an extremely delicate and complex issue: that of understanding the type of society we are now as well as the type of society we wish to build. There is another aspect, which shall be taken up again in Chapter 8, that deeply characterizes the technological revolution of contemporary societies, perhaps even capturing its essence: we have traditionally sought first to understand and explain the world, and only then to build on it; now, instead, we build machines that can decide and act before we are called on to understand and explain their functioning and underlying logic. Let us return to the question of standards or normative indicators.

To the extent that decisions and tasks are entrusted to automated systems operating on the basis of algorithms, those systems incorporate the rules or criteria that guide those decisions or actions. Once incorporated into the automated functioning of these systems, the rules and criteria become less visible and controllable, so that they are substantially removed from public scrutiny and verification. From a legal standpoint, these automated systems embody rules and criteria[52] that are directly applied. This leads to outcomes that gain in terms of effectiveness what they lose in terms of legal legitimacy. The automated enforcement of rules and criteria is likely to eliminate or limit that sphere of reflexivity (concerning the deliberation, discussion, interpretation and public revision of rules and criteria), which is essential for the correct, fair and democratic production, understanding and enforcement of legal rules and criteria.

The delegation of decisions and tasks to algorithmic processes creates outcomes that need to be evaluated also and perhaps above all on the basis of standards of social acceptability. We need to investigate the extent to which the ends these processes pursue through their output are socially shared. This is relevant from two standpoints: the first related to trust and the other to law. Any delegation, as already seen, presupposes a specific form of trust that involves some kind of risk. Trust can be either intersubjective or systemic but, in either case, it raises some uncertainty, some more or less calculable risk. If the aim pursued through the algorithm has wide social approval, with strong social cohesion backing achievement of that aim, the risk, too, will be all the more socially acceptable[53]. This demonstrates once again how the acceptance of risks deriving from delegated decisions and tasks is closely related to the individuation of standards that measure the extent of shared social acceptability of the purposes pursued through the algorithmic process.

We can briefly reconsider the case where a defendant's recidivism risk is evaluated by a software program. This pits two conflicting values against one another: protection of the defendant's individual rights and improvement of public security through crime prevention. The proper balance is hard to strike. Both involve a risk. On the one hand, there is the risk of harming or discriminating against the defendant, perhaps as the result of a biased knowledge base or training dataset. On the other hand, there is the risk that the crime might recur if the evaluation is too lenient. In both cases, the risk assessment and its social acceptance are closely related to the degree of social preference for the goals pursued by the algorithmic process (individual rights or public security). The higher the preference for protecting public security, the higher the degree of social acceptance of the score produced by the algorithmic process in terms of crime prevention. This, of course, is likely to conflict with protection of the defendant's rights. This raises the second aspect of relevance of the social acceptability standards, in terms of the law, which emerges from the example just outlined.

Decisions or tasks delegated to algorithms do not always follow legally recognized procedures. More often, the procedure actually followed is merely an algorithmic process, whose compliance with the law is not always easy to measure *ex ante*[54]. In such cases, the more a procedure achieves a socially shared purpose, the more likely it will be deemed to be compliant with the law[55], at least where the input or logic of its functioning is not easily verifiable or comprehensible. In other words, the more the output of an algorithm is socially accepted and shared, the less its input or procedure is likely to be critically evaluated (including from the viewpoint of its legal legitimacy). Therefore, if the consideration of social standards is relevant for evaluating the output of algorithms regardless of their efficiency, the social acceptance or sharing of these outputs can hide and hence contribute to propagating cognitive *bias* or other forms of opaqueness in the functioning of the algorithmic process.

Finally, evaluation of the delegation of decisions and tasks to machines driven by algorithms should also consider the standards that measure the ethical preference of the outputs achieved. In other words, it is not only a question of whether certain outcomes comply with the law or involve acceptable risks for society. We also have to ask whether we are building the society we desire, when we embody values in devices and machines that convey more or less transparent forms of *nudging*[56] or when algorithms produce outputs that are relevant from an axiological standpoint. With this in mind, a number of expert groups[57] have recently been set up to study the ethical impact of AI. Their primary aim is to bring back into the public sphere the debate on norms, principles and values that their progressive incorporation into devices and machines has totally or partially silenced. This is a crucial point that we will return to again and again, since the governance of algorithms is not a purely technological, legal or epistemological issue, even though these three factors play an essential role in this regard. The governance of algorithms mainly involves our judgement, that is, our ability to evaluate the overall outcome of a procedure in a sphere of reflexivity that, through the reconsideration of a system, is able to better understand and transform the system in question.

We do not build our world following a cognizant and deliberate plan. On the contrary, things are evolving against the backdrop we have thus far outlined and which characterizes our world and its knowledge: (1) action is no longer the exclusive prerogative of human agents; (2) we outsource an increasing number of decisions and tasks to artificial agents: this does not necessarily increase the level of human or artificial intelligence, but implies that action overtakes intelligence; (3) we do not build on what we have understood and are able to explain but try to understand and explain what we have already built. To the extent that we are able to analyze and reinterpret the world we build, we are still able to make use of what has been defined as semantic capital[58], meaning the patrimony of value and meaning that makes sense of our actions and gives us a direction. We should not forget, in conclusion, that algorithmic processes do not affect just the level of being, transforming how we decide and act, but also and above all that of what ought to be, in terms of normativity, affecting how we should decide and act in comparison with the decisions and actions of artificial agents.

Notes

1 On this matter, see R. MIRANDA, *Chi è Dmitry Kaminskiy? La mente dietro il primo robot consigliere d'amministrazione*, accessible online: https://formiche.net/2014/05/chi-che-dmitry-kaminskiy-la-mente-dietro-al-primo-robot-consigliere-damministrazione/.

2 See, on this point, N. BURRIDGE, *Artificial Intelligence Gets a Seat in the Bboardroom*, accessible online: https://asia.nikkei.com/Business/Artificial-intelligence-gets-a-seat-in-the-boardroom.

3 See, *supra*, chap. 1.

4 See A. CURIAT, *Mit, un algoritmo per operatori finanziari*, accessible online: http://money. wired.it/finanza/2013/05/08/mit-privacy-trasparenza-5728752.html, which points out that "the criticalities of international finance, in fact, are more evident precisely when they are inserted in the context of computerized securities trading operations. Errors in *trading* software can quickly propagate into the system with potentially catastrophic repercussions. This is what happened in 2010, the year of the famous 'Flash Crash': the algorithms used by *high-frequency* traders, operators who use the speed of computer calculation to operate in financial markets in time intervals that can be measured in fractions of a second, have misinterpreted the conditions of the US stock exchange. A small original miscalculation turned into a negative spiral of sales that burned billions of dollars in capitalization within a few hours". On this subject, see R.K. NARANG, *The Truth About the High-Frequency Trading: What Is It, How Does It Work, and Why Is It a Problem?* Wiley, Hoboken, 2014; ID., *Inside the Black Box: A Simple Guide to Quantitative and High-Frequency Trading*, Wiley, Hoboken, 2013; S. PATTERSON, *Dark Pools: The Rise of the Machine Traders and the Rigging of the US Stock Market*, Crown Business, NY, 2013; I. ALDRIDGE, *High-Frequency Trading: A Practical Guide to Algorithmic Strategies and Trading Systems*, Wiley, Hoboken, 2013.

5 Google's Web page indexing system is based on the *most popular rule*, that is, on an analysis algorithm (*PageRank*) that assigns a numerical weight (measurable and therefore monetizable) to a site based on its links, and thus allows calculation of the degree of popularity, giving it a higher order value within the search system: the more links a site has, the higher its number of *PageRanks* and the greater the probability of being visited. In this regard, see S. BRIN, L. PAGE, *The Anatomy of a Large-Scale Hypertextual Web Search Engine*, in "Seventh International World-Wide-Web Conference", Brisbane, Australia, April 14–18, 1998, accessible online: http://ilpubs.stanford.edu:8090/361/. For a critique of the effects of the most popular rule for democracy, see L.M. BARTELS, *Is the "Popular Rule" Possible? Polls, Political Psychology and Democracy*, in "The Brookings Review", vol. 21, issue 3, 2003, pp. 12–15.

6 F. PASQUALE, *The Black Box Society: The Secret Algorithms That Control Money and Information*, Harvard University Press, Cambridge Mass., 2015, p. 97. On this issue, see also C. O'NEILL, *Weapons of Math Destruction, op. cit.*; P. DOMINGOS, *The Master Algorithm: How the Quest for the Ultimate Learning Machine Will Remake Our World*, Basic Books, NY, 2018; B. CHRISTIAN, T. GRIFFITHS, *Algorithms To Live By: The Computer Science of Human Decisions*, Henry Holt and Co., NY, 2016.

7 In this sense: T. GILLESPIE, "The relevance of algorithms", in T. GILLESPIE, P.J. BOCZKOWSKI, K.A. FOOT (eds.), *Media Technologies: Essays on Communication, Materiality, and Society*, The MIT Press, Cambridge Mass., 2014, pp. 167–193, p. 167. See also S. BAROCAS, S. HOOD, M. ZIEWITZ, *Governing Algorithms: A Provocation Piece*, 2013, pp. 1–12, accessible online: https:// ssrn.com/abstract=2245322.

8 Among others, see, with particular reference to the issue of artificial agents, U. PAGALLO, "*What robots want: Autonomous machines, codes and new frontiers of legal responsibility*", in M. HILDEBRANDT, J. GAAKEER (eds.), *Human Law and Computer Law: Comparative Perspectives*, Springer, Dordrecht, 2013, pp. 47–65; R. CONTE, R. FALCONE, G. SARTOR, *Introduction: Agents and Norms: How to fill the Gap?*, in "Artificial Intelligence and Law", vol. 7, issue 1, 1999, pp. 1–15; M. COECKELBERGH, *Virtual Moral Agency, Virtual Moral Responsibility: on the Moral Significance of the Appearance, Perception, and Performance of Artificial Agents*, in "AI & Society", vol. 24, issue 2, 2009, pp. 181–189.

9 For a more detailed reconstruction of the debate, see B.D. MITTELSTADT, P. ALLO, M. TADDEO, S. WACHTER, L. FLORIDI, *The Ethics of Algorithms. Mapping the Debate*, in "Big Data & Society", vol. 3, issue 2, 2016, pp. 1–21; M. D'AGOSTINO, M. DURANTE, *Introduction: The Governance of Algorithms, op. cit.*; M. HILDEBRANDT, *Algorithmic Regulation and the Rule of Law*, in S. OLHEDE, P. WOLFE (eds.), "The Growing Ubiquity of Algorithms in Society:

Implications, Impacts and Innovation", special issue of "Philosophical Transactions of The Royal Society A: Mathematical Physical and Engineering Sciences", vol. 376, 2018, pp. 1–11; ID., *Law As Computation in the Era of Artificial Legal Intelligence. Speaking Law to the Power of Statistics*, 2017, accessible online: https://ssrn.com/abstract=2983045; R. BROWNSWORD, *Technological Management and the Rule of Law*, in "Law Innovation Technology", issue 8, 2016, pp. 100–140.

10 Of course, this poses further relevant problems, such as those concerning the *quality of data* or the production of *synthetic data*, which cannot be addressed in this context.

11 It is interesting to remark that a machine can be affected by a problem that Yochai Benkler attributed not long ago to human beings: "The filtering and information accreditation functions suffers from an agency problem. To the extent that the values of the editor diverge from those of the users, an editor who selects relevant information based on her values and plans for the users does not facilitate user autonomy, but rather imposes her own preferences regarding what should be relevant to users given her decision about their life choices". See on this, Y. BENKLER, *The Wealth of Networks, op. cit.*, p. 216.

12 In this sense, see the paradigmatic case "State v. Loomis", 130 Harvard Law Review (2016), 1530–1537. For a critical comment, see H.W. LIU, C.F. LIN, Y.J. CHEN, *Beyond State v Loomis: Artificial Intelligence, Government Algorithmization and Accountability*, in "International Journal of Law and Information Technology", vol. 27, issue 22, 2019, pp. 122–141; S. QUAT-TROCOLO, *Intelligenza artificiale e giustizia: nella cornice della Carta Etica Europea. Gli spunti per una urgente discussione tra scienze penali e informatiche*, in "La Legislazione penale", 18 December 2018, accessible online: http://www.lalegislazionepenale.eu/intelligenza-artificiale-e-giustizia-nella-cornice-della-carta-etica-europea-gli-spunti-per-unurgente-discussione-tra-scienze-penali-e-informatiche-serena-quattrocolo/; ID., *New Questions and Ancient Solutions? Consolidated Regulatory Paradigms vs Risks and Fears of "Predictive" Justice*, in "Criminal Cassation", vol. 4, issue LIX, 2019, pp. 1748–1765.

13 Among others, M. CASTELLI, *et al., Predicting Per Capita Violent Crimes in Urban Areas: An Artificial Intelligence Approach*, in "Journal of Ambient Intelligence and Humanized Computing", vol. 8, issue 1, 2017, pp. 29–36; A. EDWARDS, "Big data, predictive machines and security", in M.-R. MCGUIRE, T.-J. HOLT (eds.), *The Routledge Handbook of Technology, Crime and Justice*, Routledge, Abingdon, 2017, pp. 451–461.

14 F. PASQUALE, *The Black Box Society, op. cit.*, p. 145.

15 On this point, see, among others, T. ZARSKY, *The Trouble with Algorithmic Decisions: An Analytical Road Map to Examine Efficiency and Fairness in Automated and Opaque Decision Making*, in "Science, Technology & Human Values", vol. 41, issue 1, 2016, pp. 118–132.

16 F. PASQUALE, *The Black Box Society, op. cit.*, p. 3.

17 On this point, see, among others, R. ROJAS, *Neural Networks: a Systematic Introduction*, Springer Science & Business Media, Heidelberg, 2013.

18 See, *infra*, chap. 8.

19 On the relations between these issues, but with reference to the broader topic of legal design, see U. PAGALLO, *Il diritto nell'età dell'informazione, op. cit.*, chap. V, in particular pp. 151–160.

20 For a reconstruction of this propagation effect, see P. HACKER, *Teaching Fairness to Artificial Intelligence: Existing and Novel Strategies Against Algorithmic Discrimination under EU law*, in "Common Market Law Review", vol. 55, 2018, pp. 1–35, in particular pp. 5–8; S.U. NOBLE, *Algorithms of Oppression: How Search Engines Reinforce Racism*, NYU Press, NY, 2018. On the subject of algorithmic discrimination, see also V. EUBANKS, *Automating Inequality: How High-Tech Tools Profile, Police, and Punish the Poor*, St. Martin's Press, NY, 2018; S. BORNSTEIN, *Antidiscriminatory Algorithms*, in "Alabama Law Review", vol. 70, issue 2, 2018, pp. 519–572; I. ŽLIOBAITĖ, *Measuring Discrimination in Algorithmic Decision Making*, in "Data Mining & Knowledge Discovery", vol. 31, 2017, pp. 1060–1089; S. BAROCAS, A.D. SELBST, *Big Data's Disparate Impact* in "California Law Review", vol. 104, issue 3, 2016, pp. 671–732; B. CUSTERS, T. CALDERS, B. SCHERMER, T. ZARSKY (eds.), *Discrimination and Privacy in the Information Society*, Springer, Dordrecht,

2013; F. KAMIRAN, I. ŽLIOBAITÉ, T. CALDERS, *Quantifying Explainable Discrimination and Removing Illegal Discrimination in Automated Decision Making*, in "Knowledge & Information Systems", vol. 35, 2013, pp. 613–644.

21 It is possible to refer to the following four directives: Directive 2000/43/EC which implements the principle of equal treatment between persons irrespective of racial or ethnic origin; Directive 2000/78/EC which establishes a general framework for equal treatment in employment and working conditions; Directive 2004/113/EC which implements the principle of equal treatment between men and women with regard to access to goods and services and their provision; Directive 2006/54/EC concerning the implementation of the principle of equal opportunities and equal treatment of men and women in matters of employment and occupation.

22 There is now a different appreciation and awareness of the subject, as can be seen from R. BINNS, "Algorithimic accountability and public reason", in M. D'AGOSTINO, M. DURANTE (eds.), *The Governance of Algorithms, op. cit.*, pp. 543–556, in particular p. 546: "The emerging areas of 'discrimination aware data mining' (DADM), and 'fairness, accountability and transparency in machine learning' (FAT-ML) explore various techniques with which organizations can identify such damage and incorporate ethical limitations, such as loyalty, in their systems". On this topic, see also J. BURREL, *How the Machine "Thinks": Understanding Opacity in Machine Learning Algorithms*, in "Big Data & Society", 2016, pp. 1–12, accessible online: https://journals.sagepub.com/doi/10.1177/2053951715622512; for a critical view, see M. LEESE, *The New Profiling: Algorithms, Black Boxes, and the Failure of Anti-discriminatory Safeguards in the European Union*, in "Security Dialogue", vol. 45, issue 5, 2014, pp. 494–511.

23 Article 2, para. 2 of Directive 2000/43/EC for direct and indirect discrimination means respectively the following: "a) direct discrimination shall be taken to occur where one person is treated less favourably than another is, has been or would be treated in a comparable situation on grounds of racial or ethnic origin; b) indirect discrimination shall be taken to occur where an apparently neutral provision, criterion or practice would put persons of a racial or ethnic origin at a particular disadvantage compared with other persons, unless this provision, criterion or practice is objectively justified by a legitimate aim and the means of achieving it are appropriate and necessary". The other directives on the subject adopt the same distinction.

24 P. HACKER, *Teaching Fairness to Artificial Intelligence, op. cit.*, p. 11. On this subject, see also J. KLEINBERG, J. LUDWIG, S. MULLAINATHAN, C.R. SUNSTEIN, *Discrimination in the Age of Algorithms*, "NBER Working Paper No. w25548", February 2019, accessible online: https://ssrn.com/abstract=3332296; A. PRINCE, D.B. SCHWARCZ, *Proxy Discrimination in the Age of Artificial Intelligence and Big Data*, in "Iowa Law Review", March 2019, accessible online: https://ssrn.com/abstract=3347959. This also raises the related issue of protecting group privacy, which constitutes a further significant limitation to the individual profiling process. On this, see, among others, L. FLORIDI, *Open Data, Data Protection, and Group Privacy*, in "Philosophy & Technology", vol. 27, issue 1, 2014, pp. 1–3; L. TAYLOR, L. FLORIDI, B. VAN DER SLOOT (eds.), *Group Privacy: New Challenges of Data Technologies*, Philosophical Studies, Springer, NY, 2017; B.D. MITTELSTADT, *From Individual to Group Privacy in Big Data Analytics*, in "Philosophy & Technology", vol. 30, issue 4, 2017, pp. 475–494.

25 P. HACKER, *Teaching Fairness to Artificial Intelligence, op. cit.*, pp. 11–12. Interestingly, Hacker suggests integrating the protection offered by anti-discrimination legislation with that provided by the GDPR for the protection of personal data, since discriminatory results can be achieved with automated processing of personal data, including the hypothesis of profiling. We will return to this point in the next chapter, to point out how the GDPR system, while containing important provisions in this regard, leaves open some gray areas that stem from the limits of application of the Regulation just to personal data.

26 S. BAROCAS, S. HOOD, M. ZIEWITZ, *Governing Algorithms: A Provocation Piece, op. cit.*, p. 3.

27 Ted Striphas spoke in an evocative way of "algorithmic culture", to signal that the massive recourse to algorithms not only affects numerous decision-making processes, but also conditions and shapes our own culture, generating forms of reliance on new ways of representing reality. In this sense, see T. STRIPHAS, *Algorithmic Culture*, in "European Journal of Cultural Studies", vol. 18, issue 4–5, 2015, pp. 395–412.

28 In this sense, it should be remembered that the very process of interpretation, discussion and deliberation is a process that requires knowledge and competence, and therefore it is never reducible to a mere question of decision. In this perspective, see G. BONIOLO, *The Art of Deliberating. Democracy, Deliberation and the Life Sciences between History and Theory*, Studies in Applied Philosophy, Epistemology and Rational Ethics, Springer, Dordrecht, 2014.

29 Among others, see J.-A. KROLL, *et al., Accountable Algorithms*, in "University of Pennsylvania Law Review", vol. 165, 2017, pp. 633–705, accessible online: https://ssrn.com/abstract= 2765268.

30 A. AGRAWAL, J. GANS, A. GOLDFARB, *Prediction Machines: The Simple Economics of Artificial Intelligence*, Harvard Business Review Press, Boston, 2018, p. 29.

31 *Ibid.*

32 On consumer discrimination due to predictive algorithms, see among others, S. ATHEY, *Beyond Prediction: Using Big Data for Policy Problems*, in "Science", vol. 355, issue 6324, 2017, pp. 483–485; M. SHAW, *et al.* (eds.), *Handbook on Electronic Commerce*, Springer Science & Business Media, Heidelberg, 2012.

33 J. PEARL, D. MACKENZIE, *The Book of Why, op. cit.*, p. 9.

34 F. PASQUALE, *The Black Box Society, op. cit.*, p. 97.

35 J. PEARL, D. MACKENZIE, *The Book of Why, op. cit.*

36 J. PEARL, D. MACKENZIE, *The Book of Why, op. cit.*, p. 6.

37 See in this sense L. FLORIDI, *The Fourth Rev., op. cit.*, p. 16.

38 J. PEARL, D. MACKENZIE, *The Book of Why, op. cit.*, p. 351.

39 We have addressed this problem in greater depth in the following text: M. DURANTE, "Technology and the ontology of the virtual", in S. VALLOR (ed.), *Oxford Handbook of Philosophy of Technology*, Oxford University Press, Oxford, forthcoming.

40 J. PEARL, D. MACKENZIE, *The Book of Why, op. cit.*, p. 9.

41 J. PEARL, D. MACKENZIE, *The Book of Why, op. cit.*, p. 10

42 J. PEARL, D. MACKENZIE, *The Book of Why, op. cit.*, p. 295.

43 J. PEARL, D. MACKENZIE, *The Book of Why, op. cit.*, p. 9.

44 *Ibid.*

45 M. DURANTE, *Il futuro del web, op. cit.*, p. 82. On this point, see again G. BONIOLO, *The Art of Deliberating, op. cit.*

46 N. LUHMANN, *Familiarity, Confidence, Trust: Problems and Alternatives, op. cit.*

47 *Ibid.*

48 M. DURANTE, "Safety and security in the digital age. Trust, algorithms, standards, and risks", in D. BERKICH, M.V. D'ALFONSO (eds.), *On the Cognitive, Ethical, and Scientific Dimension of Artificial Intelligence*, Philosophical Studies Series, Springer, Dordrecht, 2019, pp. 371–383.

49 See, *supra*, chap. 3. On this point, see L. FLORIDI, *The Fourth Rev., op. cit.*, p. 165 *et seq.*

50 On this point, see M. DURANTE, *What is the Model of Trust for Multi-Agent Systems?, op. cit.*

51 On this subject, see U. PAGALLO, M. DURANTE, *The Pros and Cons of Legal Automation and its Governance*, in "European Journal of Risk Regulation", vol. 7, issue, 2, June 2016, pp. 323–334. On this topic, see also B.D. MITTELSTADT, *et al., The Ethics of Algorithms: Mapping the Debate, op. cit.*

52 Sometimes they constitute real forms of technological normativity, that is, they embody legally relevant norms in automated devices or systems. There is a vast literature on the subject, including in particular: K. YEUNG, "Towards an understanding of regulation by design", in R. BROWNSWORD, K. YEUNG (eds.), *Regulating Technologies: Legal Futures, Regulatory Frames and Technological Fixes*, Hart, London, 2007, pp. 79–108; M.H. SCHWARTZ,

Teaching Law by Design: How Learning Theory and Instructional Design Can Inform and Reform Law Teaching, in "San Diego L. Rev.", vol. 38, 2001, pp. 347–451.

53 See, *supra*, chap. 7.
54 F. PASQUALE, *The Black Box Society, op. cit.*, p. 202.
55 M. DURANTE, *Il futuro del web, op. cit.*, p. 82.
56 R.H. THALER, C.R. SUNSTEIN, *Nudge, op. cit.*
57 See L. FLORIDI, *et al.*, *AI4 People – An Ethical Framework for Good AI Society: Opportunities, Risks, Principles, and Recommendations, op. cit.*
58 L. FLORIDI, *Semantic Capital, op. cit.*, p. 483.

8

THE ASYMMETRIC DISTRIBUTION OF DATA AND RIGHTS

Our data

A key feature of information societies – and a recurring theme throughout this book – is that we are constantly producing and disseminating our personal data. Whenever we act online or in the infosphere, we are creating data whose fate is unclear. Ultimately, we do not know where our data ends up: Who is collecting it, who is it being transferred to, what is it being used for, and why? Even more importantly, do existing data rights regulations protect our personal data for its entire life cycle? Our data is distributed on as wide a scale as possible, and we are constantly being urged to share more. Even so, our rights to this data are not always distributed in an as effective (or even adequate) manner. In other words, today's information societies are characterized by an asymmetric distribution of data and rights.

Let us step back for a moment to examine how our rights follow and accompany us. Imagine that I own a watch, which I therefore refer to as "my" watch. Note that the expression "my" encompasses a number of rights, subsumed in the right of ownership of the watch. Based on this right, as I am its owner, I can exclude any other person from having any relationship with it (*ius excludendi alios*); I can use it (*ius utendi*), and I can reap benefit from it (*ius fruendi*), for example, by selling it to a third party (*ius alienandi*). As the owner, I can even decide to destroy it (*ius abutendi*). This set of rights follows and accompanies me even if I distance myself from my watch, interrupting the immediate relationship I have with it. For example, I may leave it in a drawer, lend it to a friend, or even lose it. In any case, the rights I have over my watch will follow along the entire course of its life cycle, and even allow me to dispose of the watch after my death. Even if I lose sight of the watch itself, I do not lose sight of the rights that are inherent to it, which I can exercise at any time, sometimes merely as a result of the fact that our immediate relationship has been interrupted; for example, I can ask my friend to give back the watch he borrowed. Because of the physical nature of the watch, the relationship between its life cycle and the distribution of rights that concern it is relatively strict, observable and enforceable.

We traditionally consider the relationship with what is ours to be based on a given power of control. The situation is radically different when our personal data is at stake. For one thing, it is hard to describe the data as being ours using the normal language of ownership[1]. Without getting into the complexities of data regulation laws, we can say that several typical characteristics of property law do not apply straightforwardly to data. Just consider, for example, how hard it is to exclude others from accessing or using our data, or the challenges of expunging records of personal data in the information society. Yet despite the considerable efforts being made to provide individuals with better control over their personal data, referring to the relationship we have with our data as a strict relationship of control is problematic in itself precisely because of the ease with which data can be shared, reproduced and de-contextualized. This can happen to the point that data can even be reclassified: personal data, for instance, can be anonymized or pseudo-anonymized, and temporarily classified as non-personal rather than personal data.

Legal epistemology has the tendency to represent the world and reality based on traditional legal notions, which are largely dependent on the analogical world and thus mainly concern physical objects and stable and observable concrete relations. The law is therefore designed to provide individuals with rights and forms of control over their data that reflect a past version of the world[2]. However, the massive production and circulation of data, particularly in contexts governed by algorithms as discussed in Chapter 7, is gradually being automated. Not all data are equal, since their characteristics can change according to how they are processed.

Below, we intend to propose a taxonomy of data showing how the dissemination of different types of data is not necessarily accompanied by an equal distribution of rights. This idea is certainly not new, since the law itself provides for different modes and degrees of protection with regard to different types of data. For example, the law distinguishes between non-personal data, personal data and particular categories of data (previously referred to as sensitive data), and provides different modes and degrees of protection for each[3].

We would also like to propose a categorization that the law does not explicitly take into account, but which implicitly underlies the recognition of certain rights and forms of protection. Once again, we will avoid getting into the legal technicalities of data protection and focus on how a given representation of the world affects the protection of our rights and the understanding of the technological context in which we are embedded. We distinguish between three types of data with different potential legal relevance: (1) data as constituent elements; (2) data as economic resources; and (3) data as a prerequisite.

Types of data

Data as constituent elements

This is the meaning of data that figures strongly in Luciano Floridi's considerations. It encompasses a far broader meaning than that of personal data, which only refers to information related to an identified or identifiable natural person. In Floridi's sense of the concept, human beings can be described as a coherent and well-structured set of data: we are our data[4]. This means that in many important circumstances, when it comes to our data, we ourselves are at stake, meaning our individual personality, dignity and autonomy. This, for example, is how Floridi conceives of the concept of informational privacy: privacy is not so much something that presides over the sphere of confidentiality or gives us control over our personal information as something that concerns the very nature of who we are:

> Looking at the nature of a person as being constituted by that person's information enables one to understand the right to privacy as a right to personal immunity from unknown, undesired, or unintentional changes in one's own identity as an informational entity, both *actively* and *passively*. Actively, because collecting, storing, reproducing, manipulating, etc. Alice's information amounts now to stages in stealing or cloning her personal identity. Passively, because breaching Alice's privacy may now consist in forcing her to acquire unwanted data, thus altering her nature as an informational entity without consent.[5]

Starting from the recognition of the principle of *informational self-determination*[6], this idea has achieved increasingly widespread consensus. When it comes to the matter of protecting data understood as constituent elements of the person, it is necessary to establish rights of personality, which have been conceived as fundamental rights that lie at the legal foundation in the construction of a natural person in her essential dignity and autonomy. Thanks to recognition of the constituent nature of data, personal rights meant to protect such data have been understood and construed as instruments of legal protection that shall accompany data subjects throughout the entire life cycle of their data. In a modern information society, this means that the distribution of data considered to be constituent elements of a person must be accompanied by provisions that protect fundamental personality rights.

Data as economic resources

This is what we mean when we say "data is the new oil"[7], as the data economy has long been aware[8]. In this sense, data represent a fundamental economic resource, on which a large part of current economic growth depends. In this perspective, it is not surprising that the most highly capitalized companies in the world today have a data-driven core business or that major political institutions are seeking ways to encourage the free flow of data as the fundamental lever for developing the digital single market. In this sense, data require legal protection because they have considerable economic value. Where there is (economic) value, there is a right to protect it. This is expressed in two different, but closely related perspectives. On the one hand, individuals are entitled to subjective rights for the economic use of data: to this end, traditional legal tools (property, licenses, patents and other intellectual property rights) are often used. On the other hand, it has been recognized, as just remarked, that the economic exploitation of data requires the creation of a digital single market that provides the best conditions for the free circulation of data, allowing their collection, dissemination, aggregation, and so on. The creation of this market in turn requires establishment of a framework providing legal certainty, as a prerequisite for economic investment, innovation and development of business. In this perspective, the distribution of rights is not correlative to the data distributed but rather to the distribution itself of data, which implies their free circulation. An example can be seen in Article 1 of the GDPR, which establishes the subject–matter and objectives of the Regulation:

1.   This Regulation lays down the rules concerning the protection of natural persons with regard to the processing of personal data, and rules relating to the free movement of personal data.
2.   This Regulation protects the fundamental rights and freedoms of natural persons and in particular their right to the protection of personal data.
3.   The free movement of personal data within the Union shall be neither limited nor prohibited for reasons connected with the protection of natural persons with regard to the processing of personal data.

Article 1, paragraph 1 of the GDPR identifies its subject–matter, putting on the same footing: (1) the protection of natural persons with regard to the processing of their personal data (mainly involving data understood as constituent elements); and (2) the free circulation of personal data (mainly involving data understood as economic resources). Paragraphs 2 and 3 define the purposes of the Regulation. Paragraph 2 explicitly identifies, as an objective of the Regulation, the protection of the fundamental rights and freedoms of natural persons, with particular reference to the right to protection of personal data. This paragraph conveys a conception of law as a means to affirm and protect a human person in some fundamental respect, that is, with regard to what is situated at the foundation of the construction of personality. Paragraph 3 states that the free circulation of personal data cannot be limited or prohibited for reasons relating to the protection of natural persons with regard to the processing of their personal data. This paragraph conveys a different conception of the law: here the law is intended to build a framework of legal certainty within which to develop economic investments, innovations and business, or in other words, the digital single market. Article 1 of the GDPR shows the stubborn, dialectical tension between natural persons and the free market. This means that the rights accompanying the life cycle of data are themselves in a delicate balance and require constant adjustment, since they belong to different legal perspectives according to the type of data they are meant to protect. The situation is complicated by the fact that these types of data are not ontologically different from one another, but rather overlap. In fact, the data are often the same. What changes is the perspective from which one observes it: i.e., what makes it legally relevant. There is a third aspect that complicates things even further: data as a prerequisite.

Data as a prerequisite

This is the sense in which data are relevant as a prerequisite for the recognition (or denial) of rights, benefits, privileges or other opportunities, already touched on in Chapter 7. In this perspective, data are not so relevant as such, but rather in that their aggregation and processing makes it possible to set normative threshold values, particularly for profiling purposes[9].

Another example will help to illustrate the legal relevance of this type of data. Reference in the GDPR (both in its articles and in a series of recitals[10]) is often made to the fact that the processing of personal data may in some cases pose a "high risk" for the data subject's rights and freedoms. The whole system of the GDPR rests on a *risk-based approach*, that is, on the idea that the data processor and controller in charge of the data processing should always take adequate organizational and technical measures aimed at preventing harmful events ("data breaches") with regard to the likelihood and seriousness of the risks that the processing of personal data may involve.

When dealing with a high risk, the GDPR establishes that special precautions must be taken. There is no need to dwell here on the precise nature of these precautions, but we would like to emphasize that at no point does the Regulation define what exactly is meant by high risk, although it does offer, notably within its recitals, some interesting clues in this regard. The Article 29 Working Party[11] has taken charge of providing an interpretation of what is meant by high risk. To this end, it has developed nine criteria for assessment. A risk is considered high according to the rule of two, that is, when two criteria occur simultaneously, or when an instance of data processing is deemed, for its intensity and severity, capable of independently causing a high risk[12]. If we group the nine criteria into three macro-categories, we can obtain the following taxonomy:

1.   *Processing methods* (criteria 3, 5 and 8);
2.   *Nature of the data* (criteria 4, 6 and 7);
3.   *Prerequisite for the exercise of a right or the enjoyment of a service* (criteria 1, 2 and 9)

This third group is of special interest to us, for it says that "personal data are processed to make decisions concerning certain natural persons following a systematic and global assessment of personal aspects relating to natural persons, based on the profiling of such individuals' data, or following the treatment of special categories of personal data", with the effect that such processing "may present a high risk for the rights and freedoms of the persons concerned, especially because they prevent the latter from exercising a right or making use of a service or a contract" (Recital 91 of the GDPR).

This category is an excellent example of data as a *prerequisite*. However, the technical language of the Regulation may prevent us from fully understanding what is at stake and where the major problems relating to the protection of individual rights reside. The concrete example used in Chapter 7 concerning the granting of a loan by a credit institution should help to clarify this point.

A data analytics company can collect large amounts of data in order to model the likelihood of different classes of borrower to repay their loans. In compliance with the GDPR, the company may adopt adequate measures to process this data, perhaps, for example, by anonymizing or pseudo-anonymizing it. After all, the company is only interested in finding statistical correlations that will help to associate certain relevant factors (i.e., data as predictors) with the likelihood to repay loans, and to come up with an abstract profile of a reliable borrower. For this purpose, it is not really important for the company to associate the relevant factors (from which the abstract profiles are derived) with the identity of the people who implicitly provide such data[13]. The guarantees the GDPR sets for the protection of personal data do not apply to anonymized or pseudo-anonymized data. The data analytics company can hence elaborate abstract profiles that correspond to normative threshold values, by using Big Data, statistical correlations or other inference methodologies (that do not necessarily impinge on people's personal data, even if it has been shown that data analytics easily allows the de-anonymization of non-personal data). In our example, the data analytics company provides the credit institution with the outcome of the profiling attributes to be used to process loan application requests – often completely automatically.

At this point, it is in the applicants' best interest to provide their personal data and any other data that will help them fit the abstract profile of the ideal borrower. These data are thus a prerequisite for the stipulation of the contract. On the one hand, everyone who applies for the loan is interested in demonstrating that they possess the relevant factors matching the predictors; on the other hand, applicants have almost no control (or very limited control[14]) over the aggregated data processed to come up with the predictors and create the abstract profile. Anyone who is denied the loan through an automated processing of personal data will have a hard time contesting the decision, even though it is based on the alleged right to explanation. Before turning to this issue, which is set to become central in the current legal and epistemological debate, we would like to return once more to the theme of the asymmetric distribution of data and rights illustrated by this example.

If we look at this case from a more general standpoint, which considers not only the point of view of the individual but also of societies in the era of data-driven economies, on the one hand, we see an increasing number of individuals who for a variety of reasons are sharing data that enjoy the protection of certain rights (whether personal or economic); on the other hand, we see a growing quantity of (pseudo-anonymized or anonymized) collected and aggregated data from which predictors, abstract profiles or other normative threshold values can be derived, and which are covered by no form of rights, control or other form of protection. There is, for instance, a misalignment between the elaboration of an abstract profile and the possible subsuming of the subject (i.e., of its concrete profile) within that abstract profile. When subjects provide their data as a *prerequisite* for being assessed against an abstract profile in order to obtain a right, a benefit, a prerogative or any other opportunity, it is in fact already too late to challenge how the abstract profile or threshold value was derived. The subject can only challenge the decision based on the automated processing (including profiling) of their personal data after the profile has already been developed. We must therefore take a closer look at what the power to contest such decisions actually means.

Explaining and contesting

Once again, we find ourselves confronted with an issue that goes beyond strictly legal considerations to encompass a much larger problem involving the construction of our world, which increasingly results from automated decisions and actions governed by algorithmic procedures and AI systems whose logic and functioning tend to escape the understanding of individuals. This problem affects the formation of knowledge and therefore the ability of individuals to foresee and anticipate the consequences of decisions and actions which used to be the exclusive prerogative of human beings and are now progressively being outsourced to machines that, as a rule, are not accountable for those decisions and actions.

In this context, a fierce and important debate has been waged in Europe concerning the existence of the right to *explanation*. If the existence of a right to explanation has now been postulated, it is not only to understand whether such a right may be recognized within the legal framework developed by the aforementioned GDPR, but for another more crucial reason. For while the GDPR carries out an essential function, dictating the principles and rules that govern the free circulation of data and the protection of rights and freedoms of natural persons with regard to the processing of personal data, it nonetheless represents merely the platform facilitating this debate, which is destined to continue and acquire growing centrality elsewhere.

If the existence of a right to explanation has now been postulated, it is because behind the formation of knowledge, the freedom of individuals is at stake. It is not just a question of providing a legal remedy, as we will see, for those who intend to challenge decisions based exclusively on the automated processing of their personal data. The stakes are higher and involve the very rethinking of the idea of freedom in a context in which predicting, deciding and acting are no longer the exclusive prerogative of human beings. The issue of explanation calls into question, far beyond the strictly legal framework, the very meaning of freedom. We are free, so to speak, not so much because we are able to freely determine the course of actions (with respect to which we could have decided and acted differently) but because, as human beings and in transcendental terms, we are free because and to the extent that we are able to explain what happens to us. It is this reflective capacity to take a distance from the world, through explanation, which allows us not to be passively subjected to what happens to us in the world and to project certain courses of action in it. To the extent that we are subject to the consequences of decisions and actions, whose logic and functioning we cannot explain, we feel that we are losing touch with our own freedom, with its language and its grounds.

Let us take a step back and see how this question started from the legal scope of application of Article 22 of the GDPR[15]. First, Article 22, paragraph 1 of the GDPR established that the data subject has "the right not to be subjected to a decision based solely on automated processing, including profiling, which produces legal effects concerning him or her or similarly significantly affects him or her". The Article 29 Working Party specified[16] that the meaning of "decision based solely on automated processing" was to be understood as "the ability to make decisions using technological tools without human intervention". In turn, the latter expression ("without human intervention") must be interpreted as the absence of "any effective influence on the result" by humans. This means, in other words, that we cannot speak of an automated decision where there is "significant control over the decision [...] made by someone who has the authority and the competence to change the decision".

Apart from any interpretation concerning the scope of the provision set in paragraph 1 and the potential distinction between an automated decision and profiling, it is important to note that the GDPR seems to establish the following general principle in the digital governance of current information societies: individuals should not be subject to decisions that have been made without any human involvement, at least in the sense of being able to adjust the course of the decision. We can interpret this principle in one of two ways. It can be seen as a basic tenet of civilization that intercedes to limit the process of automating decisions and to offer individuals a significant measure of protection aimed at strengthening a climate of trust between network users or, more generally, between the members of the information society. Otherwise, following Hegel, we can see it as a sort of "owl of Minerva", which takes flight as dusk is falling (that is, *post-factum*), when understanding collides with a reality that has already been set in motion and is virtually unstoppable. The law stands alone as the last bulwark against an inevitable tide: the growing delegation of decisions and actions to automated systems, which we can only partly understand and control. Such a provision seems to be best understood in its essential epistemic function as a powerful filter through which to observe, carefully and critically, the reality we are building. In other words, the law reveals the existence of a problem that it helps us to envisage and understand; however, it would be unreasonable and unrealistic to expect the law to be the only or primary solution. We will discuss this problem more fully in the next chapter. For now, let us return to Article 22 of the GDPR.

Article 22, paragraph 3 of the GDPR provides that in cases where a decision is necessary for entering into, or for the performance of, a contract between the data subject and a data controller or is based on the data subject's explicit consent, "the data controller shall implement suitable measures to safeguard the data subject's rights, freedoms and legitimate interests", providing "at least the right to obtain human intervention on the part of the controller, to express his or her point of view and to contest the decision". Paragraph 3 therefore provides, in given cases, a series of rights for the protection of the data subject: the right to obtain human intervention in the automated decision-making process; the right to express his or her point of view; the right to contest the decision. This has led to debate about whether the provision of these forms of protection implies the existence of a right to explanation, which is not otherwise expressly specified by the GDPR.

Actually, the term "explanation" is used once in the GDPR, but only in recital 71[17], which provides an interesting summary of the set of measures that should be put in place to protect the data subject:

> The data subject should have the right not to be subject to a decision, which may include a measure evaluating personal aspects relating to him or her and which is based solely on automated processing and which produces legal effects concerning him or her or similarly significantly affects him or her [...]. In any case, such processing should be subject to suitable safeguards, which should include:
>
> 1. specific information about the data subject,
> 2. the right to obtain human intervention,
> 3. to express his or her point of view,
> 4. to obtain an *explanation* of the decision reached after such assessment,
> 5. and to challenge the decision.

However, Articles 13 and 14 of the GDPR, which establish the controller's reporting requirements, expressly state that the controller is required to inform in clear language the data subject prior to processing: (1) the existence of automated decision-making (including profiling); (2) meaningful information about the logic involved in the decision; and (3) information about the significance and potential consequences of such processing for the data subject. In this case, although explanation is not explicitly mentioned, reference is plainly made to the *logic* involved in automated decision-making. This set of regulatory provisions has been interpreted in different ways, sparking an ongoing debate about whether the GDPR establishes a right to explanation. For our purposes, it is not necessary to enter the fray[18]. Suffice it here to highlight the main positions on the subject.

On the one hand, there are those who hold that a right to explanation of automated decision-making is not guaranteed by the GDPR. Thorough analysis by such scholars leads them to conclude that it is impossible to gather indisputable evidence of such a right from the fragmentary norms of the Regulation[19]. On the other hand, there are those claim that such a right does exist, albeit for different reasons. One must therefore pay close attention to the arguments underlying these sorts of interpretation. Bryce Goodman and Seth Flaxman have argued, for example, that a right to explanation can be substantially inferred from the requirement for providing the data subject with a meaningful explanation of the logic involved in making a decision[20]. Explanation is understood here as being the logic behind the decision, and it is a fundamental part of the more general requirement to inform the data subject of any automated decision-making procedure based on the processing of personal data. Ugo Pagallo has, instead, argued that the existence of a right to explanation can be inferred, from a procedural standpoint, from the general right to defense, i.e., from the inalienable need to provide the data subject with the right to fully challenge the decision[21]. In other words, how can people actually defend themselves from the consequences of decisions that significantly affect them without knowing how that decision was made?

Even if recognized, application of a right to explanation could be limited by a variety of factors. This ties in with what was discussed in Chapter 7. Because the logic of decisions is based on algorithmic processes that are often protected by intellectual property rights or trade secret law, it is difficult to imagine the right to explanation being enforced to the point that full disclosure would be required of the controller. In addition, there are technical obstacles that may stand in the way of a complete explanation. These obstacles may stem from the fact that: (1) the algorithmic decision-making is vitiated at the source by the presence of cognitive biases in the formation of its knowledge base or training dataset; and (2) the complexity of the algorithmic process itself makes the logic of the decision opaque or inscrutable.

While the presence of these obstacles has raised doubts about the actual usefulness of a right to explanation if it is so difficult to enforce[22], it has at the same time generated serious reflection on the core meaning of explanation and on how to guarantee opportunities for understanding the logic of automated decisions we want to challenge. Outlined below are some of the main strategies that have been developed in this regard, with particular reference to the epistemological considerations they raise.

The logic of automated decisions

There are three general strategies for outlining and clarifying the logic of an automated decision: (1) the first stresses the accountability requirement that must necessarily accompany the decision, by identifying those who must account for the logic of the decision; (2) the second focuses on the possibility of providing an alternative solution to the explanation as a means of safeguarding the data subject's rights; (3) the third and most radical strategy is that of setting up an automated process of explanation to track the automated decision-making process.

Accountability

Many scholars have argued for the need to provide mechanisms of accountability[23] for those who make use of (or otherwise profit from) systems, devices or other agents making decisions or acting based on algorithms. Amongst these, we may refer, in particular, to a recent paper by Frank Pasquale, who proposed a fourth law of robotics[24] that takes up and expands on the three laws of robotics for an algorithmic society proposed by Jack Balkin[25]. Here is how Pasquale sums up Balkin's laws:

> Balkin argues that algorithms "(a) construct identity and reputation through (b) classification and risk assessment, creating the opportunity for (c) discrimination, normalization, and manipulation, without (d) adequate transparency, monitoring, or due process." In response to these and other problems caused by algorithmic processing of data, he proposes three laws for an algorithmic society:
>
> 1. With respect to clients, customers, and end-users, algorithm users are information fiduciaries.
> 2. With respect to those who are not clients, customers, and end-users, algorithm users have public duties. If they are governments, this follows immediately. If they are private actors, their businesses are affected with a public interest, as constitutional lawyers would have said during the 1930s.
> 3. The central public duties of algorithm users are not to externalize the costs and harms of their operations. The best analogy for the harms of algorithmic decision-making is not intentional discrimination but socially unjustified pollution.[26]

Pasquale suggests adding a fourth law of robotics, which is meant to address the issues of attribution, responsibility and explanation raised by the outsourcing of decisions and tasks to machines, because "we may need to ensure that robots and algorithmic agents are traceable to and identified with their creators"[27]. Pasquale suggests the following law: "A robot must always indicate the identity of its creator, controller, or owner"[28]. In advancing this hypothesis, he is motivated by the following reasoning:

> In this case, the foundational status of a law of provenance arises out of its presumption that any given robot or algorithmic system has a creator, controller, or owner. The cutting edge of the AI, machine learning, and robotics fields emphasizes autonomy, whether of smart contracts, high-frequency trading algorithms (at least in time spans undetectable by humans), or future robots. There is a nebulous notion of "out of control" robots, which escape their creator's control—and even ideas that creators of such robots should escape responsibility once that "escape" has occurred. A requirement that any AI or robotics system has some designated party responsible for its action would help squelch such ideas.[29]

Pasquale is fully aware of the intrinsic difficulty in implementing his proposal, which depends, for example, on the fact that robots and algorithms evolve beyond their original programming due to interactions with other agents and machines[30]. However, it is important to observe how he implicitly addresses the problem of explanation. To Pasquale, explanation remains a purely human matter, which requires the identification of a subject who can be called upon to account for the machine. It is this mechanism of identification that can and must be automated, that is, designed *ex ante*, through a system of programmed traceability of operations to a responsible subject. Significantly, Pasquale defines this mechanism as a form of "responsibility-by-design"[31].

In sum, it is necessary to identify an accountable person, in order to explain or to account for a decision; it is thus necessary to implement a criterion allowing identification of the accountable person by design. Obviously, this solution raises many problems not only related to the technical and legal complexity that its implementation requires, but also to the possibility of conveying implicit value choices in the design of the system itself[32]. It is no coincidence that the issue of legal design – in its bifurcated meaning as the incorporation of norms into devices and as the process of elaboration of normative solutions – has recently acquired and is destined to acquire even further significance in the context of legal and moral thought[33]. The next solution is rather different, since it offers a sort of way out from the traditional issue of explanation by providing a conceptual alternative to it.

The counterfactual explanation

Some scholars have taken a different path in order to skirt the problem of explanation[34], arguing that an autonomous right to explanation cannot be found in the GDPR, and even if it were, it would only apply to very limited cases. In addition, explaining the logic of algorithmic decision-making is often thwarted by a series of concrete technical (related to the opaqueness of decisions) and legal (related to the legal limits imposed by intellectual property rights or trade secrets) challenges. However, the ethical and social value of explanation is indispensable. Therefore, in order to create the atmosphere of trust required for the social acceptance of algorithmic decision-making[35], data subjects should be provided with a different type of explanation that allows them to attain their objectives, rather than mere clarification of how a decision was taken.

A possible solution is that of providing the data subject with a *counterfactual* explanation, meaning an explanation that shows subjects how they *should have behaved* in order to have achieved their aims. More precisely:

> This approach provides the data subject with significant explanations to understand a given decision, the bases to challenge it and indications about how the owner can change his behavior or his situation in order to obtain the desired decision in the future, without clashing with the strict application limits imposed by the definition of automated individual decision-making process of the GDPR.[36]

In this perspective, which focuses on counterfactuals, the subjects would be equipped with a heuristic tool that would allow them to: (1) understand; (2) challenge; and (3) change the decision. In fact, a counterfactual explanation would be able, first of all, to offer key information about the logic involved in the automated decision-making process, as it allows us to understand and evaluate the influence of certain factors on a specific decision, showing which minimum variation of these factors would have resulted in a different decision. Secondly, a counterfactual explanation would give us the grounds to contest the decision, because evaluation of the relevant factors would allow us to challenge a specific decision as opposed to a generic class of possible decisions[37]. Finally, this method of explanation would be able to show hypothetical modifications of a course of action that would allow subjects to achieve their purpose, in the closest possible world.

It is not the goal here to examine and discuss the set of assumptions and arguments that support the idea of a counterfactual explanation. However, a careful but critical analysis of this idea would be likely to suggest that while this form of explanation is fairly good at modifying future decisional outcomes, it is not necessarily good at helping subjects to understand and challenge present decisions. A counterfactual explanation, in fact, does not necessarily reveal the specific reasons why a decision was made, as the authors seem to believe[38], but rather, in our view, only a hint of its possible reasons, and this does not always provide a sufficient legal basis for challenging the decision made[39].

What is interesting to note, however, is that among the various ways in which the counterfactual explanations can be implemented a rather suggestive hypothesis is being made: namely, that such explanations should be accounted for and provided automatically, so as to minimize the data subject's and controller's burden of proof and the time required for the automated decision-making to be challenged. All of this falls within the more general framework of the automation of explanation that constitutes, as we shall see below, the third hypothesis under consideration.

The automation of explanation

The Berkman Klein Center Working Group on Explanation and Law explored in a recent paper[40] a different and intriguing hypothesis: that of delegating explanation to automated systems of AI. The basic idea is simple: both the decision and its explanation should be automated. The authors of the paper believe that the best way to make AI systems accountable for their automated decisions is still that of offering an explanation, but they also estimate that the costs and methods of explanation should be internalized through an automated explanation system. This implies carrying out an extremely important task from an epistemological viewpoint: parsing the notion of explanation in terms that allow it to be implemented by an automated AI system. This is the starting point of the Working Group:

> When we talk about an explanation for a decision […], we generally mean the reasons or justifications for that particular outcome, rather than a description of

the decision-making process in general. In this paper, when we use the term explanation, we shall mean a human-interpretable description of the process by which a decision-maker took a particular set of inputs and reached a particular conclusion. In addition to this formal definition of an explanation, an explanation must also have the correct type of content in order for it to be useful. As a governing principle for the content an explanation should contain, we offer the following: an explanation should permit an observer to determine the extent to which a particular input was determinative or influential on the output.[41]

Based on this definition, the Working Group considers it technically feasible to obtain from AI systems legally operative explanations that are claimed by human beings. This does not mean that explanations provided by machines are totally similar to those of human beings, but rather that when called on to justify their decisions, machines could offer explanations based on standards that are comparable to those required by the law from human beings.

Their technical feasibility largely depends on the fact that "the explanation is *distinct* from transparency. Explaining does not require knowing the flow of bits through an AI system, any more than explanation from humans requires knowing the flow of signals through neurons (neither of which would be interpretable to a human!)"[42]. More specifically, the authors believe that two technical properties can make the elaboration of explanations by AI systems possible: (1) *local explanation*; and (2) *counterfactual credibility*.

> *Local Explanation.* In the AI world, explanation for a specific decision, rather than an explanation of the system's behavior overall, is known as local explanation. AI systems are naturally designed to have their inputs varied, differentiated, and passed through many other kinds of computations—all in a reproducible and robust fashion. It is already the case that AI systems are trained to have relatively simple decision boundaries to improve prediction accuracy, as we do not want tiny perturbations of the input changing the output in large and chaotic ways. Thus, we can readily expect to answer the first question [...] —what were the important factors in a decision—by systematically probing the inputs to determine which have the greatest effect on the outcome. This explanation is local in the sense that the important factors may be different for different instances. For example, for one person, payment history may be the reason behind their loan denial, for another, insufficient income.
>
> *Counterfactual Faithfulness.* The second property, counterfactual faithfulness, encodes the fact that we expect the explanation to be causal. Counterfactual faithfulness allows us to answer the remaining questions [...]: whether a certain factor determined the outcome, and related, what factor caused a difference in outcomes. For example, if a person was told that their income was the determining factor for their loan denial, and then their income increases, they might reasonably expect that the system would now deem them worthy of getting the loan. Importantly, however, we only expect that counterfactual

faithfulness apply for related situations—we would not expect an explanation in a medical malpractice case regarding an elderly, frail patient to apply to a young oncology patient. However, we may expect it to still hold for a similar elderly, less frail patient.[43]

The authors point out that the automated explanation system can be kept logically distinct from the automated decision system. This consideration is fraught with significant consequences that are not immediately obvious. But let us proceed by degrees. Those who program a decision system wish for:

the predictions ($\hat{y}$) to match the real world (y). The designer of the explanation system must output a human-interpretable rule e_x () that takes in the same input x and outputs a prediction $\breve{y}$. To be locally faithful under counterfactual reasoning formally means that the predictions $\breve{y}$ and $\hat{y}$ are the same under small perturbations of the input x. This framework renders concepts such as local explanation and local counterfactual faithfulness readily quantifiable. For any input x, we can check whether the prediction made by the local explanation ($\breve{y}$) is the same as the prediction made by the AI system ($\hat{y}$). We can also check whether these predictions remain consistent over small perturbations of x (e.g. changing the race).[44]

This long, complex passage means that the predictions, $\breve{y}$ and $\hat{y}$, of the two distinct systems are both based on a common mode of representation of the world, that is, the formation of the knowledge base (the same input x), which allows them to produce quantifiable and more easily comparable outputs. Difficulties arise when it comes to "converting the inputs to AI systems–presumably some large collections of variables [...]–into human-interpretable terms, such as age or gender"[45].

This brings up once again one of the fundamental epistemological problems of automated processes we have already pointed out: Who is going to adapt to the representation of whom? Which epistemic agent's world are we gradually adapting ourselves to? If we are entrusting decisions and tasks to machines and expect them to provide explanations of how they perform their tasks, does it not therefore make sense to adapt our representation of the world to theirs? In a certain sense, is it not better for us to facilitate their tasks? Are we perhaps creating a multi-agent system in which we increasingly adapt our representation of the world to the one we wish to implement inside and through machines?

Significantly, the authors of the paper remark in the context of the question under consideration that "explanations from AI systems will be most straightforward if the relevant terms are known in advance. [...] There will be some technical innovation required, but by and large we see relatively few difficulties for AI systems to provide the kinds of explanation that are currently required in the case where legislation or regulation makes it clear what terms may be asked for *ex ante*"[46]. Behind this obvious consideration lies the equally obvious idea that a system can better account for how it works and adapt itself to the required standards if it is able to implement a representation of the world that is instrumental and conforms to its way of functioning:

> The challenges increase if the relevant terms cannot be determined in advance. For example, in litigation scenarios, the list of relevant terms is generally only determined ex post. In such cases, AI systems may struggle; unlike humans, they cannot be asked to refine their explanations after the fact without additional training data. [...] In summary, to build AI systems that can provide explanation in terms of human-interpretable terms, we must both list those terms and allow the AI system access to examples to learn them. System designers should design systems to learn these human-interpretable terms, and also store data from each decision so that is possible to reconstruct and probe a decision post-hoc if needed.[47]

Equally significantly, the authors of the paper highlight the relative weaknesses and strengths of human and automated explanation[48]. This is a promising approach, which relies on a balanced assessment of different solutions, on the trade-off between costs and benefits, and on the related possibility of encouraging technological innovation, given that the solution to the issue of automated decision may be found in an automated explanation. Instead of limiting the exercise of computational power, they suggest that an even more intensive use of this power can provide technically feasible solutions:

> We have also argued that it should be technically feasible to create AI systems that provide the level of explanation that is currently required of humans. The question, of course, is whether we *should*.[49]

The Berkman Klein Center Working Group has succinctly captured the essence of the problem: there are, in fact, numerous economic, legal, political and social (both intentional and unintentional) consequences deriving from the increased automation of decisions and tasks that must be taken into account[50] in order to evaluate the appropriateness of delegation to algorithmic processes. The issue becomes even more thorny and complex when we wish to entrust decisions and safeguards that the law provides for the protection of people's rights and freedoms to automated processes. In view of what was observed in Chapter 7, we need to examine whether and to what extent such an intense process of automation (affecting the law) is feasible and desirable. In Chapter 9, the final chapter, we will take up this issue, while also trying to draw some conclusions from what has been said so far in relation to the progressive concentration of power resulting from technological decentralization.

Notes

1 In this sense, see L. FLORIDI, *The Fourth Rev., op. cit.*, p. 121: "[...] one may still argue that an agent 'owns' his or her information, no longer in the metaphorical sense just

seen, but in the precise sense in which an agent is her or his information. 'Your' in 'your information' is not the same 'your' as in 'your car' but rather the same 'your' as in 'your body', 'your feelings', 'your memories', 'your ideas', 'your choices', and so forth. It expresses a sense of constitutive *belonging*, not of external *ownership*, a sense in which your body, your feelings, and your information are part of you but are not your (legal) possessions". On the subject of data property, see J. CIANI, *Property Rights Model v. Contractual Approach: How to Protect Non-personal Data in Cyberspace?*, in "International Trade Law", vol. 4, 2017, pp. 831–854; ID., "Governing data trade in intelligent environments: A taxonomy of possible regulatory regimes between property and access rights", in I. CHATZIGIANNAKIS, Y. TOBE, P. NOVAIS, O. AMFT (eds.), *Intelligent Environments 2018*, vol. 23, Ambient Intelligent and Smart Environments, IOS Press, 2018, pp. 285–297.

2 An example can be seen in the 1981 Strasbourg Convention, known as Convention 108, of the Council of Europe, concerning the protection of personal data: inspired by a proprietary perspective of data, it identified consensus as the main instrument for having control over personal data.

3 Article 4 of the GDPR provides for the definition of "personal data" and identifies the categories of "genetic data", "biometric data" and "data relating to health". Article 9 of the GDPR specifically regulates the processing of "special categories of personal data", i.e., the data that the previous Directive 96/46/EC defined as "sensitive data".

4 Floridi develops in rigorous philosophical terms an idea that has been also expounded in the legal field, for instance, by S. RODOTÀ, *Tecnologie e diritti*, Il Mulino, Bologna, 1995; ID., *Il mondo nella rete. Quali diritti, quail i vincoli*, Laterza, Romea-Bari, 2014.

5 L. FLORIDI, *The Fourth Rev., op. cit.*, p. 120.

6 As an example of the complex process between privacy and the right to protection of personal data, see a long passage of the fundamental ruling of the German Federal Constitutional Court of 1983 (*Bundesverfassunggericht*, decisions vol. 65, 1 *et seq*), which contains a meaningful statement about the principle of informational self-determination: "A social order – and the legal order enabling it – in which the citizens no longer can know who knows what, when, and on what occasion about them, would be incompatible with the right to informational self-determination. [...] If someone is uncertain whether deviant behaviour is noted down and stored permanent as information, or is applied or passed, he will try not to attract attention by such behavior. [...] This would not only impact his chances of development, but would also impact the common good, because self-determination is an elementary functional condition of a free democratic society based on its citizen capacity to act and to cooperate". On this topic, see G.M. REHM, *Just Judicial Activism? Privacy and Informational Self-Determination in U.S. and German Constitutional Law*, in "University of West Los Angeles Law Revue", vol. 32, 2001; G. HORNUNG, C. SCHNABEL, *Data Protection in Germany II: Recent Online Decisions Searching for Computers, Automatic Number Plate Recognition and Data Retention*, in "Computer Law & Security Review", vol. 25, issue 2, 2009, pp. 115–122.

7 This widespread expression, used by journalists and politicians over the last decade, seems to date back to 2006, and is attributed to the English mathematician Clive Humby, founder of the Customer Data Science company "Dunnhumby".

8 The famous analogy between data and oil is not an effective expression: the ranking of the most capitalized companies worldwide show that the top positions, historically occupied by oil companies, are now occupied by companies operating in the ICT world: Apple, Alphabet (Google), Microsoft, Amazon, Facebook.

9 There is a wide literature on the topic. See, among others, S. DELACROIX, M. VEALE, "Smart technologies and our sense of self: Going beyond epistemic counter-profiling", in M. HILDEBRANDT, K. O'HARA (eds.), *Law and Life in the Era of Data-Driven Agency*, Edward Elgar, Cheltenham, 2019, pp. 80–99; S. WACHTER, *Normative Challenges of Identification in the Internet of Things: Privacy, Profiling, Discrimination, and the GDPR*, in "Computer Law & Security Review", vol. 34, issue 3, pp. 436–449, 2018; E. BAYAMLIOĞLU, I. BARALIUC, L. JANSSENS, M. HILDEBRANDT (eds.), *Being Profiled: Cogitas Ergo Sum. 10 Years of Profiling the European Citizen*, Amsterdam University Press, Amsterdam, 2018; I. MENDOZA, L.A. BYGRAVE,

"The right not to be subject to automated decisions based on profiling", in T. SYNODINOU, P. JOUGLEUX, C. MARKOU, T. PRASTITOU (eds.), *EU Internet Law: Regulation and Enforcement*, Springer, Dordrecht, 2017, pp. 77–98; M. HILDEBRANDT, *The Dawn of a Critical Transparency Right for the Profiling Era*, in "Digital Enlightenment Yearbook", 2012, pp. 41–56; ID., *Profiling and the Law of Law*, in "Identity in Information Society (IDIS)", vol. 1, 2008, pp. 1–16, accessible online: https://ssrn.com/abstract=1332076; ID., "Defining profiling: A new type of knowledge?" in M. HILDEBRANDT, S. GUTWIRTH (eds.), *Profiling the European Citizen*, Springer, Dordrecht, 2008, pp. 17–45; I. RUBINSTEIN, R.D. LEE, P.M. SCHWARTZ, *Data Mining and Internet Profiling: Emerging Regulatory and Technological Approaches*, UC Berkeley Public Law Research Paper No. 1116728, in "University of Chicago Law Review", vol. 75, 2008, pp. 261–285.

10 In particular, the GDPR expressly makes reference to "high risk" in recital 76, where it recalls the need to implement an objective assessment for identifying the likelihood and gravity of the risk; in art. 34 and in recitals 86 and 89 in relation to the obligation to communicate a data breach to the data subject; in art. 35 and in recitals 84 and 91 with reference to the impact assessment on data protection (the so-called DPIA); in art. 36 and in recital 94 concerning the prior consultation of the supervisory authority; and, finally, in art. 70 and in recital 77, where it includes among the tasks of the European Data Protection Board (EDPB) the publication of guidelines, recommendations and best practices concerning the circumstances in which a violation of personal data is likely to present a high risk for the rights of the interested parties.

11 The reference is to the opinion adopted on 4 April 2017, entitled "Guidelines on impact assessment on data protection and determination of the possibility that the treatment may present a high risk for the purposes of Regulation (EU) 2016/679", issued by the "Article 29 Working Group on Data Protection" (WP29), replaced today by the EDPB.

12 In sum, these are the nine criteria developed by the WP29: (1) Evaluation or assignment of a score; (2) automated decision-making process; (3) Systematic monitoring; (4) Sensitive data or highly personal data; (5) Large-scale data processing; (6) Creation of correspondences or combination of data sets; (7) Data relating to vulnerable stakeholders; (8) Innovative use or application of new technological or organizational solutions; (9) Treatment that in itself prevents the interested parties from exercising a right or from making use of a service or a contract.

13 With the warning (which it is not possible to address here) that, through pseudo-anonymized data, it is often possible to trace back to the original data subjects. On this point, see P. OHM, *Broken Promises of Privacy: Responding to the Surprising Failure of Anonymization*, in "UCLA Law Review", vol. 57, 2010, pp. 1701–1777.

14 As in the case of the protection of *group privacy*.

15 Article 22. "Automated decision-making relating to natural persons, including profiling".

16 Guidelines on automated decision-making processes and profiling – WP251, defined on the basis of the provisions of Regulation (EU) 2016/679, adopted by the Working Group Art. 29 on 3 October 2017 (amended and adopted on 6 February 2018).

17 Recital 71 of the GDPR.

18 Article 22 of the GDPR, and the so-called *right to explanation* have been broadly investigated. On this point, see among others, A.D. SELBST, J. POWLES, *Meaningful Information and the Right to Explanation*, in "International Data Privacy Law" vol. 7, issue 4, 2017, pp. 233–242; J. MAZUR, *Right to Access Information as a Collective-Based Approach to the GDPR's Right to Explanation in European Law*, in "Erasmus Law Review," vol. 11, issue 3, 2018, pp. 178–189. On the topic of automated decision making, see in general the Working Party Article 29, WP251rev.01, "Guidelines on Automated individual decision-making and Profiling for the purposes of Regulation 2016/679 – As last Revised and Adopted on 6 February 2018", as well as WP260, "Guidelines on transparency under Regulation 2016/679".

19 S. WACHTER, B.D. MITTELSTADT, L. FLORIDI, *Why a Right to Explanation of Automated Decision-Making Does Not Exist in the General Data Protection Regulation*, in "International Data Privacy Law", vol. 7, issue 2, 2017, pp. 76–99.

20 B. GOODMAN, S. FLAXMAN, *European Union Regulations on Algorithmic Decision-making and The Right to Explanation*, in "AI Magazine", vol. 38, issue 3, 2017, pp. 50–57.

21 U. PAGALLO, "Algo-rhythms and the beat of the legal drum", in M. D'AGOSTINO, M. DURANTE (eds.), *The Governance of Algorithms, op. cit.*, pp. 507–524.

22 M.E. KAMINSKI, *The Right to Explanation, Explained*, in "Berkeley Technology Law Journal", vol. 34, issue 1, 2019, pp. 18–24.

23 The notion of *accountability* includes the idea of accounting for one's action and hence of taking the necessary measures beforehand to prevent the occurrence of damage as a result of one's action, based on the assumption that the acting person is in the best position to know, and bear, the consequences of their actions. When decisions and actions are delegated to machines, which cannot be held *accountable* for their own operations, *accountability* tends to be attributed to those who make use of such machines (or gain profit from them). On this point, see, among others, R. BINNS, *Algorithmic Accountability and Public Reason, op. cit.*; N. DIAKOPOULOS, *Accountability in Algorithmic Decision-making*, in "Communications of the ACM", vol. 59, issue 2, 2016, pp. 56–62; M. BOVENS, RE GOODIN, T. SCHILLEMANS (eds.), *The Oxford Handbook of Public Accountability*, Oxford University Press, Oxford, 2014.

24 F. PASQUALE, *Toward a Fourth Law of Robotics: Preserving Attribution, Responsibility, and Explainability in an Algorithmic Society*, in "Ohio State Law Journal", vol. 78, issue 5, 2017, pp. 1243–1255.

25 J. BALKIN, *The Three Laws of Robotics in the Age of Big Data*, in "Ohio State Law Journal," vol. 78, issue 5, 2017, pp. 1217–1241.

26 F. PASQUALE, *Toward a Fourth Law, op. cit.*, p. 1244.

27 F. PASQUALE, *Toward a Fourth Law, op. cit.*, p. 1253.

28 *Ibid.*

29 F. PASQUALE, *Toward a Fourth Law, op. cit.*, p. 1254.

30 *Ibid.* This would make it necessary to identify "multiple *'potentially responsible parties'*".

31 *Ibid.*

32 On this subject, see among others, A. CAVOUKIAN, *Privacy by Design: The Definitive Workshop*, in "Identity in Information Society", vol. 3, issue 2, 2010, pp. 247–251; U. PAGALLO, *Il diritto nell'età dell'informazione, op. cit.*, pp. 129–161; P. BREY, "Values in technology and disclosive computer ethics", in L. FLORIDI (ed.), *Information and Computer Ethics*, Cambridge University Press, Cambridge, 2010, pp. 41–58; M. HILDEBRANDT, *Legal Protection by Design: Objections and Refutations*, in "Legisprudence", vol. 5, 2011, pp. 223–248.

33 See H. HAAPIO, *et al., Legal Design Patterns for Privacy*, in "Data Protection/LegalTech – Proceedings of the 21st International Legal Informatics Symposium IRIS ", 2018, pp. 445–450; A. ROSSI, M. PALMIRANI, *A Visualization Approach for Adaptive Consent in the European Data Protection Framework*, in "2017 Conference for E-Democracy and Open Government (CeDEM) IEEE", 2017, pp. 159–170.

34 On this point, see S. WACHTER, B.D. MITTELSTADT, C. RUSSEL, *Counterfactual Explanations Without Opening the Black Box: Automated Decisions and the GDPR*, in "Harvard Journal of Law & Technology", vol. 31, issue 2, 2018, pp. 841–887.

35 S. WACHTER, B.D. MITTELSTADT, C. RUSSEL, *Counterfactual, op. cit.*, p. 843.

36 S. WACHTER, B.D. MITTELSTADT, C. RUSSEL, *Counterfactual, op. cit.*, p. 844.

37 S. WACHTER, B.D. MITTELSTADT, C. RUSSEL, *Counterfactual, op. cit.*, p. 872 *et seq.* Notably: "Although art. 13, co. 2, lett. f, the art. 14, co. 2, lett. g, and the art. 15, co. 1, lett. h, do not request information regarding specific decisions, counterfactuals represent a minimal form of disclosure to inform the data subject with respect to the 'logic involved' in specific decisions".

38 S. WACHTER, B.D. MITTELSTADT, C. RUSSEL, *Counterfactual, op. cit.*, p. 882: "Counterfactual explanations provide reasons why a particular decision was received (e.g., low income), offer grounds to contest it (e.g. if the data controller used inaccurate data about the income of the applicant), and provide limited 'advice' on how to receive the desired result in the future (eg an increase of 4,000 pounds/year would have resulted in a positive application)".

39 As the authors tend to recognize very correctly. See, in this sense, S. WACHTER, B.D. MITTELSTADT, C. RUSSEL, *Counterfactual, op. cit.*, p. 883: "As a minimal form of explanation,

counterfactuals are not appropriate in all scenarios. In particular, where it is important to understand system functionality, or the rationale of an automated decision, counterfactual may be insufficient in themselves. Further, counterfactuals do not provide the statistical evidence needed to assess algorithms for fairness or racial bias".

40   F. DOSHI-VELEZ, M. KORTZ, *Accountability of AI Under the Law: The Role of Explanation*, in "Berkman Klein Center Working Group on Explanation and the Law, Berkman Klein Center for Internet and Society working paper", 2017, accessible online: https://dash. harvard.edu/handle/1/34372584.

41   F. DOSHI-VELEZ, M. KORTZ, *Accountability, op. cit.*, pp. 2–3. Furthermore, p. 3: "Another way of formulating this principle is to say that an explanation should be able to answer at least one of these questions: what are the main factors of a decision? [...] Would changing a certain factor have changed the decision? [...] Why did two similar cases receive different decisions, or vice versa?"

42   F. DOSHI-VELEZ, M. KORTZ, *Accountability, op. cit.*, pp. 6–7.

43   F. DOSHI-VELEZ, M. KORTZ, *Accountability, op. cit.*, p. 7.

44   *Ibid.*

45   F. DOSHI-VELEZ, M. KORTZ, *Accountability, op. cit.*, p. 8.

46   *Ibid.*

47   F. DOSHI-VELEZ, M. KORTZ, *Accountability, op. cit.*, p. 9.

48   See on this point F. DOSHI-VELEZ, M. KORTZ, *Accountability, op. cit.*, pp. 9–10. In sum, the authors make the intriguing point that the strength of human explanation lies in the ability to offer *post hoc* explanations of the decision, that is, after the fact has happened, where the machine, in order to offer an *ex ante* or *ex post* explanation, must be explicitly designed for this purpose (requiring an explicit taxonomy or the ability to learn from similar cases). The weak point of human explanation lies in its potential lack of accuracy or unreliability, particularly where explanation is used to mask the social pressure that has influenced human decision. On the contrary, machines are not exposed to social pressure and, if programmed in this sense, will keep track of their decision-making process, subjecting this process to validation as part of the explanation.

49   F. DOSHI-VELEZ, M. KORTZ, *Accountability, op. cit.*, p. 12.

50   *Ibid.*: "The fact of the matter is that AI systems are increasing in capability at an astounding rate, with optimization methods of black-box predictors that far exceed human capabilities. Making such quickly-evolving systems be able to provide explanation, while feasible, adds an additional amount of engineering effort that might disadvantage less-resourced companies because of the additional personnel hours and computational resources required; these barriers may in turn result in companies employing suboptimal but easily-explained models".

9

EXIT, VOICE AND LOYALTY

Designing possible solutions

There are great classics which are useful and fruitful to rediscover when the timing is right. In his 1970 work *Exit, Voice and Loyalty: Responses to Decline in Firms, Organizations and States*,[1] the great economist and social scientist Albert O. Hirschman posed an extremely important question: How can individuals react to a crisis of a company, an organization or the state itself, or to the deteriorating quality of goods or services such entities provide?

Hirschman's approach was interesting in that he related the hypothesis of a crisis or a temporary decline (considered remediable) to the role that each individual could play in helping to find a solution to the crisis and in remedying the deteriorating quality of goods or services. Hirschman identified two possible strategies: exit and voice. Without delving into the details of his analysis, we can briefly examine how the two strategies work.

Exit is the classic economic strategy of abandoning one good or service for another which is deemed to be of equal or better quality, and therefore a perfectly good substitute for the first. This traditional mechanism based on competition may weaken the supplier of the good or service in the short term, but it may improve performance in the medium or long term by creating pressure on the company to restore the previous level of quality. Hirschman also considers the case in which a consumer's exit threat constitutes a form of voice and a last step before actually exiting.

From an economic standpoint, the strategy of voice may be considered as a complement to the hypothesis of exit, even though it precedes it. Voice means just that: making one's voice heard. A consumer complains about the deteriorating quality of a good or service so that the company will redress the problem. Consumers may choose voice over exit for several reasons. Firstly, they may believe that no other supplier can provide the same quality good or service, or they may be driven by ideological (regarding a political party, for example) or legal motivations (because opportunities for exiting and accessing another market are restricted). Secondly, consumers may prefer voice over exit because they have developed a particular attachment to (the supplier offering) that particular good or service. In this case, consumers avoid exiting because they wish to maintain a relationship with the supplier (which has become an integral part of their lives) or out of concern that their exit might ultimately damage the supplier's business. Finally, consumers may value the very availability of the good or service itself, and be prepared to contest any deterioration in its quality (such as with a public good or service).

In this context, loyalty plays a very special role, reflecting the special bond or feeling of allegiance the consumer has towards the supplier. The stronger the connection, the more likely it is that a consumer will prefer voice over exit. In other words, consumers will try to make their voices heard because of their deep bond with the supplier, whom they are reluctant to abandon. The strength of the bond can vary, and consumers tend to be more loyal towards a supplier if gaining access to the supplied good or service was particularly difficult or onerous. For an individual who worked hard to get into a particular school, for example, seeing the school lose its reputation or declare bankruptcy will be an extremely unpleasant experience. This individual will thus be committed to supporting the school's reputation, either out of a sense of nostalgia or as a question of identity, even though it might be easier just to send his or her own child to a different school.

Consumer loyalty to a supplier also increases as a measure of the extent to which a good or service has become ingrained in the consumer's life, making exit tantamount to relinquishing their own habits or part of themselves; these consumers are heavily invested in the supplier. Consumer loyalty may also grow according to their perception of how seriously the supplier takes them and if they believe their suggestions might be used by the supplier to improve the quality of the good or service.

In this sense, a supplier (company, organization, party or state) will benefit from creating a spirit of loyalty and allegiance, since it helps to promote consumer commitment even in times of crisis and decline. Loyalty can also have a cost, of course, if it leads to acceptance or tolerance of remediable errors, dictated by blind attachment to the existing reality or by the belief that exiting would be a leap in the dark. In such cases, loyalty ceases to be a drive for change. Loyalty plays a positive role, instead, when it is combined with the intent to make one's own voice heard or when combined with the threat of exit.

More generally, the concrete possibility for reacting to deterioration in business firms, organizations and states relies on an appropriate combination of both strategies. In most cases, it is thus better or even necessary to keep both channels open. Reducing the chances for exit or voice implies a diminished ability to respond to decline. The importance of this model derives not only from the heuristic and practical value of the two strategies, but from considering that underlying both exit and voice is the need to combine economics with politics: exiting from the organization and having a voice within the organization. This raises an important aspect concerning voice: the power of voice springs from the joining together of many voices more than from that of a single individual[2]. In fact, individuals are isolated not only in conditions of monopoly, but also when dealing with information or power asymmetries[3]. In this sense, when defining voice, Hirschman reminds us of its individual or collective dimension, which consists in:

> any attempt to change, instead of evading, a reprehensible state of affairs, either by soliciting the directly responsible management individually or collectively, either by appealing to a higher authority with the intention of imposing a change in management, or through various types of actions and protests, including those aimed at mobilizing public opinion.[4]

For voice to be a valid alternative to exit, it is therefore necessary for the management of an organization to be sensitive to voice, or at least for there to be some room for public opinion. Another option is that of appealing to the power of a higher authority for a change in management. The value of Hirschman's model is that it invites us to consider the options open to individuals or groups when faced with deterioration in the quality of a good or service normally expected from the supplier in question.

It is from precisely this critical perspective that Hirschman's model has recently been taken up by Jack Balkin and applied fruitfully to the world of online information[5]. When dealing with Big Tech, it is hard to see how much space is left for exit or voice by network users. Even though they are an integral part of the digital environment – which exists in large part thanks to their contributions and efforts – network users have very limited power over the Net. We are therefore faced not only with the question of the quasi-monopolistic position of Big Tech, which limits network users' strategic options, but also with the fact that users have invested countless hours and significant energy into the construction of the digital world residing on online platforms.

When examining this issue, it is again important to recall the two salient characteristics of the impact of ICTs we have focused on in this book. Firstly, we observed that ICTs are not so much tools in the hands of users as they are devices that shape and structure the environment in which users operate and live. Secondly, we remarked that it is precisely the decentralized nature of these technologies and notably of the Internet that has allowed the phenomenon of power concentration in the acquisition, management and analysis of data by Big Tech capable of extracting value from the large amounts of data produced and shared by users, particularly through online platforms. Often the two phenomena – the decentralization of the network and the concentration of power – are unjustifiably equated or superimposed, without understanding instead that one is rather the condition that makes the other possible. It is exactly with regard to the environment and the practices developed on online platforms that Balkin observes the following:

> Exit from online platforms is normally not the dominant strategy. First, exit from a platform may be costly because of network effects. Second, Klonick

points out that many end-users already belong to more than one platform and may view platforms as complementary, rather than as substitute goods. Thus, leaving Facebook is not like leaving Russia for the United States. One can inhabit multiple platforms simultaneously. Exit may not be the favored option because participation in one platform may make participation in others more valuable.[6]

Balkin highlights two factors: the advantage for users to exploit network effects, namely, the decentralized and capillary system of connections of social networks created through platforms, which the user is reluctant to give up. And then the possibility for users to inhabit and establish links on more than one platform at a time. Consequently, personalization of the platforms (both in the sense of users personalization developed by the platform and personalization of the platform *brand*) does not result in them being perceived as substitute goods, but rather as complementary goods. However, these factors are probably not the key to explaining why exit is not the main strategy when it comes to online platforms. There are two, more subtle, reasons:

> Social media companies, in turn, encourage the idea that end-users are part of a larger community and encourage participants to continue to check in—and post—as much as possible. Companies work hard to design their sites so as to attract—and capture—their end-users' time and attention. In addition, companies may have compiled significant databases of end-users' preferences, interests, and behaviors. Although one can exit in the sense of no longer visiting the site, this by itself does not erase data about end-users or prevent later use of the data by the company—or by others to whom the data is later sold. Unless the company has promised to erase all data collected—or has been required to erase it by law—personal data remains with the company for its later use. In this specific sense, exit is not possible.[7]

This passage highlights two extremely delicate and important points. Firstly, users are encouraged to invest significant amounts of the scarce resources of time and attention participating in online communities, which thus become a constitutive dimension of their lives. Not only do users build part of their identity and life online, but they also contribute to building the digital context in which this part of their identity and life is interpreted and acquires meaning[8]. In light of this consideration, it is understandable that users are unwilling to abandon a context they have helped build and feel a part of: exit would amount to cutting off a part of their life. Secondly, even if users decide to exit from a platform, they cannot necessarily take everything with them. It would rather be like leaving home and abandoning your most precious possession: your personal data. This is the key aspect of the case under examination. Exit from a platform does not necessarily mean you get to take your data with you or that it will be automatically cancelled (especially if it has been transferred to third parties).

This would require a fiduciary commitment (or legal obligation) on the part of social media companies, which appears to be in contrast with their business model. When a company is in possession of the user's personal data, we can say that exit in this sense is impossible (or useless). As such, other strategies must be followed:

> Hence, when end-users feel badly treated on online platforms, the dominant strategies are likely to be loyalty—bearing with the situation and hoping for improvement—or voice—complaining about bad treatment and demanding accountability and/or reform. Note that when, as often happens, people are kicked off a platform, they are not choosing exit—they would like to stay and complain. [...] In addition to calls for reform, perhaps the most important form of voice in online platforms occurs when end-users tag or identify content that they consider inappropriate. Not only is this kind of voice ubiquitous, it is constitutive of the online community and its norms. The moderation systems of online companies actually depend on this kind of voice. Moderation systems, like many opensource projects, employ end-users as a kind of unpaid workforce that polices the platform, drawing attention to potential violations of community norms, and, in the process, shaping their evolution.[9]

For the above reasons, exit is only rarely[10] a truly viable option. Users, faced with no real alternatives[11], tend to remain part of the community they have helped to create and try to protest from within, especially since they do not generally want to be excluded. But Balkin also points out another extremely interesting fact. Because users' voices are channeled by the platforms themselves, the amount of attention they receive reflects how well they serve the interests of social media companies and the development of online communities. In the absence of any real possibility for exit, voice can hopefully generate pressure and demands for greater participation or transparency in how online communities and platforms work, but it does not have any real impact on the private digital governance or business models adopted by social media companies:

> Because voice tends to dominate exit in online speech platforms, system operators face continual pressure from end-users (as well as from non-members who regard the platform as socially important). The exercise of voice leads naturally to a demand for due process. We should not confuse the influence of end-users on social media companies with genuine democracy.[12]

Balkin does not believe that the digital governance carried out by private companies can really be shaped or directed by users' pressure from within in the absence of a more structured institutional process[13]. Concerns advanced by Balkin in this context have found an echo in a far more radical request for exit recently promoted by Jaron Lanier[14].

Radical exit: abandoning social networks

Jaron Lanier's work is interesting not only because it is an example of radical exit (Lanier does not recommend leaving one platform for another, but immediately cancelling accounts on all social networks) but also because it allows us to sum up some of the main issues dealt with throughout this book. Lanier lists ten main reasons supporting his recommendation[15]. I examine them togheter below, to highlight only a few points of interest.

Reduced freedom of choice

Social media that collect and process huge amounts of their users' data use mechanisms that tend to reinforce or even induce behaviors, without users being fully aware of the effect of this form of manipulation. Lanier describes all of this as "algorithmic behavioral manipulation"[16]. Social media often adopt "adaptive [...] algorithms that continually make small changes to try to get better results"[17]. These changes consist of personalized and constantly recalibrated stimuli that bring to the users' attention a set of opinions, goods and services, which was once the object of a more general and open communication (promotion and advertising), whereas now it is addressed in a more personal and hidden way to each user. Lanier's thesis is that the best results induced by adaptive algorithms are the most profitable results for social media companies, which exploit, as already observed by Balkin, the *network effect* or *lock in*:

> The unfortunate fact is that once an application starts working, everyone gets caught up in it. It is difficult to abandon a social network to switch to another, because those you know are on the first. It is practically impossible for the individuals of an entire society to back up all the data, move them simultaneously and restore the memory at the same time. This type of effect is called "network" or *lock in*. And on digital networks it is difficult to avoid it. Originally, many of us who worked to bring the Internet to a giant scale hoped that it would bring people together – that it would bring a network effect and *lock in* – it would be the Internet itself. [...] We have not taken into consideration the fact that fundamental digital needs [...] would have led to new types of monopolies, precisely because of the network effects and the lock in. To be precise, since you are the product – and not the customer – of social media, the correct term is "monopsony".[18]

Thus, algorithmic behavioral manipulation creates forms of dependency and reduces our freedom of choice. This happens in a systematic but less visible way, because in the end the automated personalization to which we are constantly subject tends to form bubbles (the so-called *filter bubbles*)[19] that represent authentic traps of desire, in which we are continuously referred to ourselves and to our actual or induced preferences. Our freedom of choice is diminished not only because we are manipulated but also because we are driven to always choose the same thing: ourselves.

Large-scale predicting and the amplification effect

Social media not only uses adaptive algorithms, but also predictive algorithms. The personalization process (which we mentioned in the previous point) actually follows a large-scale depersonalization or predicting process:

> The maximum that algorithms can do [...] is to calculate the *possibility* that a person acts in a certain way. But what for a single person is perhaps only a possibility, inserted *in the average* of multitudes of people is approaching a certainty. A population can be affected with greater predictability than a single person.[20]

The ability to predict depends on the possibility of collecting and processing large amounts of data, which are distributed in a decentralized way. Quantity affects quality at some point and changes our point of view on things, not only in an epistemological, but also in a normative way. Luciano Floridi has spoken about *distributed morality*[21], to point out phenomena that become morally relevant only when they assume certain proportions. Many of the most troublesome phenomena of social media (from *fake news* to *trolls*, from perturbations of electoral campaigns to online hate speeches, from fake accounts to clustering and user profiling mechanisms) depend on the network's ability to amplify certain effects or behaviors or to offer a capital of attention for phenomena that otherwise would not be equally relevant:

> If you see flames coming out of the hood of a car and shout: "Fire!", you could save the lives of those inside that car. If you shout the same sentence in a crowded club, you instead risk causing a general stampede and getting someone crushed and killed by the crowd, regardless of whether there really is a fire.[22]

This also implies that certain phenomena appear to be different from what they actually are. A huge number of users participate in the construction of the online environment, but no one is really in a position to perceive exactly the boundaries of the digital context. What we say or do online is likely to be continuously decontextualized. Furthermore, as noted above, what we say or do online is also likely to be shown (re-contextualized) to others through a filter bubble that can reshape or modify the original meaning[23]. This reduces shared knowledge (the fact of knowing *p* and knowing that others know *p*), which lies at the foundation of authentic intersubjective communication, and generates, in contrast to the promise of transparency, a high degree of opacity in online communication:

> What is happening is that today more than ever we see so little of what others see. [...] The difference between what is shown to someone else and what I imagine could be shown to him cannot be known. The opacity of our times is terrible, and things could not have gone worse, because the degree of opacity

is itself opaque. I remember when we thought that the Internet would create a transparent society. The opposite happened.[24]

The judgment machine

Let me return to a point I have already addressed in Chapter 7, as I want to highlight another aspect here. Many scholars have stressed the importance of this point, since it concerns the normative impact of the use of algorithms: the algorithms used to categorize and classify the behaviors and preferences at the basis of *ranking systems* involve an implicit evaluation of such behaviors and preferences that works as a constant judgment machine:

> Algorithm ranking systems may not be significant or reliable from a scientific point of view, but in real life they are important. They determine the news you see, the people to whom you are proposed as a possible partner, the products that are offered to you. The judgments based on social media could determine which loans will be granted to you, which countries you can visit, if you will be chosen for a job, what education you can receive, the result of your car insurance claim and your freedom to gather with other people. [...] The inability to carve out a space in which to reinvent oneself without being constantly judged: this is what makes me unhappy. How can you have self-esteem if esteem is now calculated in another way?[25]

Thus, despite the usual emphasis with which Lanier proposes his thesis, there is a relevant aspect in the passage just cited. What we do and the preferences we show online are likely to turn into data that are processed to assess our behaviors and preferences. Not only does this have a normative impact, but it also makes sense of our world because it constantly interprets and judges it and therefore it also interprets and judges the expectations we have about it. This aspect refers to the aforementioned issue of semantic capital[26]. In Floridi's view, semantic capital is something fundamentally different from economic capital and refers precisely to our ability to reinterpret and make sense of our world[27]. It is not easy to reinterpret and make sense of our world when the very relationship we have with it is increasingly mediated by the fact that we are constantly subject to categorizations, classifications and evaluations that concretely affect our expectations and our lives and that are mostly motivated by economic and commercial needs.

Ultimately, Lanier's is an example of radical exit based on the belief that exiting from social networks is the only way to question (and eventually push to change) the business model on which social media companies are based, that is, free access to social media in exchange for user data transfer. This is also its limit. It is not easy to rethink such a deep-rooted business model, even if it is becoming increasingly urgent and necessary to address the issue of the dominant position of Big Tech[28]. There is a further aspect that, although remarked by Balkin and Lanier, constitutes a limit to the proposal of radical exit. The idea of exit still assumes a representation of the online world as a place you can enter and exit from, you are either connected or disconnected to, as you wish. This representation is outdated. The image of an *onlife* reality, in which digital and analogue converge, makes us understand that we can transmigrate from one platform to another, determining its success or failure, but we can hardly stop participating in the construction of a world based on ICT, in which a consistent part of our identity and life takes place.

Although exit makes us understand important aspects of the problem (such as, primarily, that of the power asymmetry between users and Big Tech), it can hardly represent a winning strategy, for the reasons just considered. We must thus investigate the possibility of resorting to forms of voice. The latter can take two different forms. It can be understood traditionally as the attempt to make one's voice heard by public or private organizations that affect digital governance. It can also be understood more broadly as an attempt to reflect on the limits of automation processes and on the role of human beings within them, in order to start a public, open and shared discussion on this troublesome issue.

Voice: algorithmic news recommendation systems

A recent example of voice has been described in an interesting paper[29] exploring online personalization in the supply of information through algorithmic systems of news recommendation (*algorithmic news recommenders*). The authors start from consideration of what, in the light of what has already been observed, we know to be a significant issue:

> The deployment of various forms of AI, most notably of machine learning algorithms, radically transforms many domains of social life. [...] different algorithms are used to customize news offerings to increasingly specific audience preferences. While this personalization of news enables media organizations to be more receptive to their audience, it can be questioned whether current deployments of *algorithmic news recommenders* (ANR) live up to their emancipatory promise. Like in various other domains, people have little knowledge of what personal data is used and how such algorithmic curation comes about, let alone that they have any concrete ways to influence these data-driven processes.[30]

The authors believe that it might be programmatically more useful to figure out how to make it possible for people to influence the algorithmic systems of news recommendation through expression of their voice rather than taking on the Herculean task of trying to make such systems more transparent. In this perspective, referring to the work of Albert Hirschman, they define "voice as the possibility to exert control over the algorithms that curate people's own news provision"[31]. This is a broader interpretation that refers to all the concrete ways in which people can influence algorithmic news recommenders, in order to make them more receptive and responsive to the people's interests rather than to those of the communication companies. In order to enable people to express their voices, the authors suggest introducing personal algorithmic recommendation systems (*algorithmic recommender personae*):

> These are pre-configured and anthropomorphized *types of recommendation algorithms* from which people can choose when browsing (news) sites. Not to be mistaken with idealized (or stereotyped) user types (and their alleged reading behaviour) to which people need to conform, algorithmic recommender personae allow people instead to demand from technologies, such as ANR, to behave in ways that align with their own specific (news) interests at each single moment.[32]

Such systems would respond better than others to people's need to exert control over the algorithmic news feed. This response could be measured with regard to what is required by four ideal-typical models to express voice: (1) alternation; (2) awareness; (3) adjustment; (4) obfuscation. Let us take a brief look at what they consist of.

Alternation

The first way to control algorithmic news feeds simply lies in the possibility of alternating different outlets and forms of communication, including the use of a variety of different recommendation systems. As the authors correctly remark, the possibility of alternating different ways of aggregating news (therefore accessing different sources and perspectives) reduces users' exposure to a single or main recommendation mechanism but does not provide them with the identification of cognitive biases or an understanding of the logic of algorithmic recommendation systems. Furthermore, it should be emphasized that the alternation mechanism more closely resembles a form of exit than of voice, to refer again to Hirschman's categories.

Awareness

Another way to influence news recommendation systems is to be more aware of how they work, that is, how news feeds are personalized. Greater awareness also gives users more choice of recommendation systems, outlets and forms of communication. Information duties relating to the processing of personal data, provided for example by the GDPR, or transparency practices in the privacy policies of the main social networks, are certainly useful tools in providing information to users about the purposes for which their data is collected and used; however, they say little about how this specifically affects the selection of the news that users receive[33].

Adjustment

A third way in which we can influence news recommendation systems consists in letting them gradually adapt to our preferences and interests. As the authors correctly observe, there are already many ways in which users can interact with technologies and adjust them to their needs. This is not only made possible by how certain platforms work, but is also a desired outcome as it further reveals individual preferences[34]. However, to date, the number of communication outlets that allow users to adjust recommendation algorithms to their own needs is limited, since it is difficult for companies to balance their business interests with the users' concern for stronger forms of control over the process of selection, aggregation and supply of news[35].

Obfuscation

News feed personalization systems work better the more user data they can process. Therefore, the last and probably most counterintuitive way of influencing algorithmic recommendation systems, as observed by the authors, is that of obfuscating one's own data. This strategy has been proposed by, among others, Helen Nissenbaum, and consists of "deliberate addition of ambiguous, confusing or misleading information to interfere with surveillance or data collection"[36]. This strategy aims at strengthening individual privacy and constitutes a form of resistance against the process of *datification* and profiling of individual behaviors. However, it is a strategy that appears counterintuitive even with respect to the issue of news personalization, as the authors point out: "But what if this exactly is what news readers need in order to benefit from news personalization? Obfuscation may therefore be a great form of resistance against large-scale surveillance systems, but it disavows and disables the possibilities for algorithmically defined personal news recommendations"[37]. In light of this consideration, the authors therefore believe that obfuscation may be rather a selective practice, through which readers only partially implement this form of resistance, giving it a more strategic sense, aimed at preserving some benefits of personalized news feed.

These four ideal-typical models of expression of voice have pros and cons. The authors therefore suggest resorting to a further model, provided by the personal algorithmic recommendation systems, that is, by systems constructed according to five different types of readers (*personae*): "the Explorer (news from unexplored territory), the Diplomatic (news from the other side), the Wizard (surprising news), the Moral Vacationer (guilty pleasures), or the Expert (specialized news based on previous consumption)"[38]. These types are not inspired by stereotypes, but by a value underlying the acquisition of information: (respectively) diversity; intellectual diplomacy; serendipity; escape from reality; and competence. By clicking each time on the corresponding icons, readers would constantly be able to configure their preferred recommendation system. In the authors' words:

> These pre-configured and anthropomorphized types of recommendation algorithms enable people to intuitively express their wishes of different sortings of news articles depending on their specific (news) mood and purpose. The crucial and defining characteristic of these recommender personae is that they

do not ask people to identify with certain stereotypical news reader types (as is sometimes done). Instead, the user is given the opportunity to demand from algorithmic systems to behave in a certain desired way.[39]

The interest in this proposal lies in the idea that the expression of voice (the possibility to exert control over that particular flow of data that is the selection, aggregation and feed of news) is made possible by a design choice, that is, through the configuration of the computational model (i.e., the personal algorithmic recommendation system). It is a design or architectural (or rather counter-architectural) solution that is configured as a choice of *pro-ethical design* rather than of *ethics by design*, to put it in Floridi's terms[40]. In fact, it is aimed at making the user's choice more aware of the news feed, but it does not intend to incorporate an implicit value choice in the functioning of the personal algorithmic recommendation system. The critical aspect of this proposal lies elsewhere. It resides precisely in the purpose of the system, which is to reinforce the online readers' tendency to obtain the desired news and, by doing so, to lock themselves into a trap of desire, that is, into a bubble or echo chamber, in which the representation of reality, built on selected information, is increasingly consistent with a set of already formed and engrained interests, expectations and desires. The fact that this is the result of a more autonomous choice of the reader rather than of how an algorithm works is only slightly reassuring.

If the delegation of a task to an algorithmic process raises a problem, entrusting it to a human being does not necessarily solve the problem, if the result remains largely the same. If the question is to follow the correct "information diet"[41], it does not matter too much who the dietician is. The issue is rather to decide which decisions and tasks to entrust to automated processes and for what purposes. The next and last section focuses on this question, once again highlighting the need to express one's own voice, albeit in a different sense from that seen thus far. In the following paragraph, voice is not understood in strictly individual terms but as an unavoidable collective sphere of reflection, which acts as a critical interface between the identification of a problem and its possible solution.

Voice: the limits to automation

Many of the problems we have dealt with so far (from the governance of algorithms to the possible limitation of autonomy and freedom; from the asymmetric distribution of data and rights to the need to explain the choices made based on computational models) have a common conceptual and problematic core: What is the role of humans before the progressive automation of decisions and tasks? What are the limits of the automation process? How does automation limit or put human autonomy and freedom at risk?

We tried to answer this set of questions with Ugo Pagallo in a text that focused on the problem in a specific and particularly delicate context: that of legal automation[42] – a context that is all the more significant the more assiduously the law is asked to settle controversial issues affecting digital governance. However, many of the remarks made in that context can easily be generalized and provide useful ideas for the present field of analysis.

In the debate on automation, there are two recurring considerations that are worth questioning from the beginning: the first concerns the sharp contrast between the human sphere and that of automation; the second involves the relationship between the syntactic and the semantic dimension.

Firstly, it is important to note that automation (the ability to decide or perform tasks automatically) has always been an integral part of humankind. It is a constituent element, which in some respects represents a strength of human beings, and an important resource from an evolutionary point of view. The automatic cuts across the human. There are innumerable situations in which human beings act or react in a completely automatic way, for example, because this is part of their biological functioning or because they are pressed by the circumstances of the case or by the threat of danger or again because this automatism corresponds to a more or less conscious defense mechanism. Human beings did not need to outsource decisions or tasks to experience automation, because they have always had direct experience of it. It would have been really problematic from an evolutionary point of view if humanity had not been able to constantly rely on its ability to act or react automatically without having to submit every decision or behavior to deliberation. It is not surprising, in this view, that human beings choose to outsource decisions and tasks and to depend on this sort of delegation. It is mostly a winning strategy that is difficult to renounce, in relation to which we cannot speak of a sharp contrast between what is human and what is automation.

Secondly, the difficulty of welding the syntactic with the semantic dimension is the argument invoked to expose the limits of the progressive delegation of decisions and tasks to automated systems: the risk inherent in the delegation process would consist in the machine's inability to understand what it does and to have access to the meaning of the decisions and tasks carried out. This aspect certainly represents a difficult facet of the question but, without going into the details of this complex issue, suffice it here to observe that the question of semantic limits is ill-framed, since it largely conceals the real issue which must be addressed: that of controversial cases. If from an epistemological point of view, the current trend is to face and try to solve the semantic problems of automation at a syntactic level, gradually adapting the world to the representational model of machines[43], or to exploit human beings as a semantic engine (such as in the case of human-based computation[44]), from the normative (i.e., legal, ethical and social) standpoint, the real problem is to us the investigation of controversial cases.

Human beings have always been confronted with controversial cases. This consideration is perhaps evident in the legal sphere, but also has a wider scope. In fact, it has never been merely a matter of settling legally relevant questions, but of tackling, through the filter of a legal controversy, decisive issues for the entire society. Issues that orientate the fundamental choices of a society and allow it to deal with the emergence of the new, notably where the novelty is determined by the technological evolution and its challenging impact on society. Legal controversies have always been the institutionalized and hence socially recognized opportunity for a public forum of discussion, interpretation and comprehension of debated issues and problems. This does not concern all legal controversies, nor even the majority of them.

There is a distinction, made famous in the legal field by Herbert Hart's work, which is useful to recall in the present context: the difference between plain and hard cases. Hart noted that plain cases, meaning cases in which the debated legal question can be considered easy to solve, are those "in which the general terms do not seem to require any interpretation and in which the recognition of the claims appears to be uncontroversial or *automatic* [...], in which there is a general agreement on the judgments concerning the application of the classification terms"[45]. In this sense, the parallel drawn by Hart between plain cases and automation has three main characteristics that can equally be applied to the more general issue of delegation of decisions and tasks to automated systems. Firstly, there are cases that do not require particular recourse to human intelligence for their interpretation and application, so that they appear directly and openly available to an automation process. Secondly, these cases are not so infrequent; on the contrary, they are the most common and recurrent cases, since the law is only rarely confronted, if at all, by something absolutely new. Thirdly, the automatic nature of plain cases derives from the generally shared opinion regarding the terms of their application. In less formalistic terms, this means that a case is all the plainer the closer the connection is between the decision of the case and the normative context, constituted and permeated by a set of shared values and principles, in which the case is applied.

This point is important, because it means that the existence of a common conceptual and axiological core, which assesses the social acceptability of decisions, is not an accidental characteristic of law, but the condition of possibility of its normal functioning. This aspect was illustrated by Brian Bix who observed:

> Hart was interested in the problem of social control through law: not in questions of strategy or political theory, relating to how social control could be better achieved, but to the preliminary question of how social control was even possible. How can a government guide the actions of the population through laws and precedents and to what extent do these tools necessarily require integration? Hart replied: "If it were not possible to communicate general standards of conduct, which a large number of individuals can understand, without needing further guidance, where they are required to maintain behavior when the situation arises, nothing we recognize as a right could exist."[46]

This means that a system can function normally only if a rather high degree of automaticity is assured. In this sense, it is necessary that a considerable number of individuals and, we might add, of machines are able to follow general standards of conduct and to maintain the proper behavior in the required setting, with no need for further guidance. Of course, this concerns the plain or routine cases.

From there, it is not difficult to state what a hard case is in general terms. A case can be defined as such when there is likely to be general disagreement concerning: (1) the meaning of the terms of the legal question; (2) how these terms are related in legal reasoning; (c) the role of the principles at stake in the case at hand.

This progression, from interpretation of terms to the role of principles through legal reasoning, makes it clear that the disagreement can relate not only to the meaning of the text, but also and primarily to the understanding of the values and principles constituting its normative context of interpretation and application. This also means that the different types of disagreements that make a case difficult bring into play and illustrate what the law is, that is to say the very concept of the law, to use Herbert Hart's expression. Indeed, hard cases shed light and allow us to reflect publicly on all the relevant standards of conduct, whether they be rules, principles or values, which can be adopted as the legal basis of a decision and that require additional understanding and direction in terms of human intelligence not only in a semantic, but also in an axiological sense. If we apply this consideration to the broader case of delegation of decisions and tasks to automated systems, we can derive some useful considerations.

First of all, we can understand that the issue of automation concerns not only the semantic level, but also more broadly the question of the set of values and principles that constitute the normative context in which decisions and tasks are carried out by machines. As remarked[47], the delegation process cannot be evaluated merely on the basis of technical standards of efficiency, but also and above all on normative standards of opportunity that assess the consequences of delegated decisions and tasks more comprehensively: For what interests, for what socially relevant purposes is the delegation process taking place? What risks are we willing to take to achieve those purposes or interests?

Secondly, it must be remarked that the interpretation of a hard case never takes place within a normative vacuum, but always within an already structured context. If the delegation of decisions and tasks involves risks – inherent to the consequences produced by an automated process and to their level of irreversibility – we must first ask ourselves about the degree of social acceptance of these risks, which is commensurate with the desirability of the ends and interests to be achieved through the automation process, and thus with the degree of social cohesion that accompanies the pursuit of these ends and interests. We must therefore ask ourselves how shared the values and principles involved in hard cases and underlying the interests and aims pursued are. As we have already observed, the higher the degree of social cohesion in the normative context of interpretation and application of the hard case, the higher the degree of social acceptance of the risk inherent to the delegation process will be, that is, the unintended consequences of decisions and tasks outsourced to machines.

This leads to a final and crucial remark. The response to the issue of delegation of decisions and tasks to automated systems is eminently axiological. It is oriented by normative consideration of the values and principles underlying the aims and social interests pursued. It concerns not only the possibility of exit from an economic viewpoint or the possibility of protest from a political viewpoint, but more generally the possibility of *having a voice*, either *ex ante*, in the sphere of design of the solutions to be adopted, or *ex post*, in the sphere of reflexivity related to the assessment of the consequences of the solutions adopted. Just as the interpretation of legal hard cases has always been a fundamental interface between the understanding of the law and its concrete application, in the same way it is necessary – not necessarily through the law – to identify a forum for debate aimed at clarifying the existing but not always visible connection between the delegation of decisions and tasks to automated systems and the normative context in which we need to assess the consequences of such delegation.

In other words, we cannot examine, for example, the efficiency or the legitimacy of a decision taken by a computational system without taking into account (from an ethical, legal, economic or political standpoint) the risks we are willing to take. Furthermore, this risk assessment should be carried out in relation to the ends pursued and to the degree of social cohesion underlying these ends. The discussion is about ends. It is not a question of replacing the discussion of means with the discussion of ends. In fact, there is no discussion about ends without a careful, preliminary consideration of how the instruments work; however, such consideration is not only technological, but also and primarily epistemological, since today's computational systems require their own representation or model of the world (with the result of the gradual adaptation of the world to the functioning of machines). Yet there is no discussion about means without a discussion about ends: ends which do not belong to the means themselves, but to the society in which these means are called upon to be deployed.

For an avalanche of snow it is, certainly, a good thing to fall (it is its only condition of existence), but not so good for those living downhill from the avalanche itself. As with a lawsuit, we must never cease asking ourselves whether we are dealing with a plain case or a hard case. When we realize that we are facing a hard case, we must summon or take into consideration everyone who is involved, everyone who should have a voice, as well as those who absent but will nonetheless be affected[48] by the outcomes of our decisions. Hard cases are a lens through which we can see ourselves for who we are and ask ourselves who we want to be. They guide our choices and allow us to be open to innovation; they force us to renegotiate the relationship we have with what already exists and with what appears to us to be stable and familiar.

We have a task and a decision that cannot be delegated. The task is to examine and deal with hard cases. Finding the solution cannot be delegated. The ancient wisdom of the law makes us realize not only that are we called upon to decide, but also that we cannot but decide. This is the true hallmark of decision: it cannot be renounced or deferred. In the context of digital technology, the decision that we cannot entrust to others is that of tracing the shifting line between plain and hard cases.

It is here – and not elsewhere – that the essence of humanity lies.

Notes

1 A.O. HIRSCHMAN, *Exit, Voice, and Loyalty: Responses to Decline in Firms, Organizations, and States*, Harvard University Press, Cambridge, Mass., 1970.

2 A.O. HIRSCHMAN, *Exit, Voice, and Loyalty, op. cit.*, p. 57.

3 On the relationship between information asymmetries and power in information societies, see M. DURANTE, *The Democratic Governance of Information Societies, op. cit.*

4 A.O. HIRSCHMAN, *Exit, Voice, and Loyalty, op. cit.*, p. 47.

5 J. BALKIN, *Free Speech, op. cit.*, pp. 1149–1210.

6 J. BALKIN, *Free Speech, op. cit.*, p. 1199.

7 J. BALKIN, *Free Speech, op. cit.*, pp. 1199–1200.

8 On this point, see M. DURANTE, *The Online Construction of Personal Identity through Trust and Privacy*, in "Information", vol. 2, issue 4, 2011, pp. 594–620. On this subject, see also J. BALKIN, *Free Speech, op. cit.*, pp. 1200–1201.

9 J. BALKIN, *Free Speech, op. cit.*, p. 1200.

10 A.O. HIRSCHMAN, *Exit, Voice, and Loyalty, op. cit.*, p. 39. This refers to the hypothesis analyzed by Hirschman, in which the exit option becomes a particularly effective solution, in the system of free enterprise, as an expression of the principle of free competition.

11 A.O. HIRSCHMAN, *Exit, Voice, and Loyalty, op. cit.*, p. 50.

12 J. BALKIN, *Free Speech, op. cit.*, pp. 1200–1201.

13 *Ibid.*

14 J. LANIER, *Ten Arguments for Deleting Your Social Media Accounts Right Now*, Henry Holt & Co., NY, 2018.

15 *Ibid.*

16 J. LANIER, *Ten Arguments, op. cit.*, p. 15.

17 J. LANIER, *Ten Arguments, op. cit.*, p. 26.

18 J. LANIER, *Ten Arguments, op. cit.*, p. 36. This leads to the idea of radical exit, p. 37: "One of the main reasons to delete your social media accounts is that there isn't a real choice to move to different social media accounts. Quitting entirely is the only option for change".

19 On this subject, see E. PARISER, *The Filter Bubble, op. cit.*; and C.R. SUNSTEIN, *Republic.com*, Princeton University Press, Princeton, 2002.

20 J. LANIER, *Ten Arguments, op. cit.*, pp. 44–45.

21 L. FLORIDI, *Distributed Morality in an Information Society*, in "Science and Engineering Ethics", vol. 19, issue 3, 2013, pp. 727–743.

22 J. LANIER, *Ten Arguments, op. cit.*, p. 63.

23 In this sense J. LANIER, *Ten Arguments, op. cit.*, pp. 63–64, and also, p. 65: "Speaking through social media isn't really speaking at all. Context is applied to what you say after you say it, for someone else's purposes and profit".

24 J. LANIER, *Ten Arguments, op. cit.*, p. 110.

25 J. LANIER, *Ten Arguments, op. cit.*, p. 118.

26 L. FLORIDI, *Semantic Capital, op. cit.*

27 L. FLORIDI, *Semantic Capital, op. cit.*, p. 481.

28 On this subject, see also M. MOORE, *Tech Giants and Civic Power*, Centre for the Study of Media, Communication and Power, King's College London, London, 2016.

29 J. HARAMBAM, N. HELBERGER, J. VAN HOBOKEN, *Democratising Algorithmic News Recommenders: How to Materialize Voice in a Technologically Saturated System*, in "Philosophical Transactions of The Royal Society", vol. 376, 2018, pp. 1–21.

30 J. HARAMBAM, *et al.*, *Democratising, op. cit.*, p. 1.

31 J. HARAMBAM, *et al.*, *Democratising, op. cit.*, p. 4.

32 *Ibid.*

33 J. HARAMBAM, *et al.*, *Democratising, op. cit.*, p. 10.

34 *Ibid.*

35 J. HARAMBAM, *et al.*, *Democratising, op. cit.*, p. 12.

36 H. NISSENBAUM, F. BRUNTON, *Obfuscation: A User's Guide to Privacy and Protest*, The MIT Press, Cambridge Mass., 2015, p. 1.

37 J. HARAMBAM, *et al., Democratising, op. cit.*, pp. 12–13.

38 J. HARAMBAM, *et al., Democratising, op. cit.*, p. 14.

39 J. HARAMBAM, *et al., Democratising, op. cit.*, pp. 17–18.

40 L. FLORIDI, *The Fourth Rev., op. cit.*, p. 218.

41 C.A. JOHNSON, *The Information Diet. A Case for Conscious Consumption*, O'Reilly Media, Boston, 2015.

42 U. PAGALLO, M. DURANTE, *The Pros and Cons of Legal Automation and its Governance, op. cit.*

43 See, *supra*, chap. 2 and chap. 3. See also, on this point, L. FLORIDI, *The Fourth Rev., op. cit.*, pp. 165–191.

44 L. FLORIDI, *The Fourth Rev., op. cit.*, p. 167.

45 H.L.A. HART, *The Concept of Law*, ed. 2, Clarendon Press, Oxford, 1994, p. 123 (our italics).

46 B.H. BIX, *Jurisprudence: Theory and Context*, Sweet & Maxwell, London, 2019, p. 51.

47 See, *supra*, chap. 7.

48 H.L.A. HART, *The Concept of Law, op. cit.*, p. 123.

CONCLUSION

The shelf of the world

The meditation on the impact of ICTs on law, society and knowledge does not and cannot properly have a conclusion, because this impact and consequently the meditation that arises from it are still ongoing. Here lies one of the main lessons we have learned about this area of investigation and analysis: it is a dynamic area, in continuous transformation, in which the actors involved are changing their strategies and repositioning themselves in relation to the changes of perspective, to the disruptive effects of technological innovation, and to the emergence of complex issues and real struggles for power, which affect and reshape the sphere of digital governance and the current information societies.

We have seen how the decentralization of the Internet, the production of online content and the dissemination of data and information have helped to strengthen the position of Big Tech, giving rise to the phenomena of concentration of power and accumulation of data (*information silos*) in the hands of a few large companies. We have remarked how the rise of platform owners and network service providers has created new forms of intermediation between public actors and private individuals that change the institutional arrangement of traditional forms of government, soliciting the development of novel forms of digital governance. We do not yet fully comprehend the structure, organization and criteria of political legitimacy of such forms of digital governance. This has a consequence we have underlined several times, for which some decisions or policy choices, for instance in the field of fake news, oblivion or explanation, are likely to create side-effects, raise new issues or reinforce the dominant position of actors that we wished to submit to greater control and regulation.

We pointed out that the delegation of decisions and tasks to artificial agents, algorithms, AI systems or other computational models reduces the sphere of human control over such decisions and tasks. This has raised an immediate and increasing claim for further control, evaluation and scrutiny over the activities performed by such systems, which have been fully or partially removed from human direction and control. More generally, we have hypothesized that computational power, which is the *engine* of the development of societies dependent on digital ICTs, gradually adapts not only the world but also the representation of reality to how the technologies that it promotes work. Data are the *fuel* of this engine. But if we stop at the consideration that this engine works on its own and in such a way that only a few can use and avail of, we would limit our analysis to the practical, albeit important, level of politics, law and economics. In fact, the power to process data and turn them into output, according to different models and representations of reality, produces new forms of knowledge, new points of view, and new levels of abstraction.

Hence the key question: Who will adapt to the representation of whom? This is not a question with a general scope, and has different implications in the specific contexts and regional epistemologies in which computational power will be exerted and applied. Because computational power is above all the heading of a complex and structured relationship between the empirical and the epistemological dimension of reality, between the government (or governance) and the knowledge of society. The circularity between power and knowledge has never been so pressing, strong and full of nuance and different perspectives on the world as today.

We can spend many hours playing chess with a friend: it would be a realistic contest, in which two agents share the same rules and logic of the game. We can describe the strategic confrontation between two generals at war as if it were a chess game: it would be a metaphorical contest, in which two agents draw on the strategic resources made available by the virtual representation of a real game. We can play chess against a computer capable of defeating the greatest champions: it would be a contest, in which two agents share the same rules but not the same logic of the game (how the relevant data and strategies making up the game are processed). We can design an AI program (*adverse AI*) that simulates the competition with a fraudster or a disease as if it were a chess game: in this case it would be a contest in which an artificial agent is programmed to compete with an agent and learn from its mistakes. Thus, the points of view from which reality can be represented proliferate.

Computational power basically produces new forms of knowledge, while raising fundamental issues of governance, because we can regulate the modes, contexts and tools with which computational power is exerted but we cannot or should not regulate the production of knowledge as such. We must learn to live in a world we have helped to create, where there is a proliferation of agents and systems that decide and function based on models and representations of the world that are not necessarily ours. The attempt to anthropomorphize the different manifestations of digital reality and reduce them to a common human measure is not only vain but also blind to the opportunities of learning from the proliferation of points of view different from ours and from the rise of levels of abstraction from which to observe reality. Tom Gruber remarked, during a workshop[1], that cooperation between human beings and computers has significantly increased medical diagnostic capacity, since human beings and computers have a *different* ability to recognize errors (false positives and false negatives).

This does not mean that we have to passively accept the technological evolution of digital technology. As a matter of fact, the outputs of this evolution are not always distributed or redistributed in a fair and equitable manner. This raises a problem for democracy. What emerged from our investigation is that this chess game – the *digital* chess game – does not leave things unchanged, but alters, shifts and turns them upside down. Often, however, this transformation does not change the starting conditions, but reinforces them. It makes the intelligent more intelligent and the stupid more stupid. It makes more developed and modern countries even richer in information and less developed and backward countries still poorer in information. It makes technologically advanced societies more suited to current transformations and technologically less structured societies more resistant to change. It enhances trust in the digital world where the delegation of decisions and tasks to digital technologies and computational systems becomes the norm and socially shared purpose, sometimes to the detriment of the ability to assess, discuss and criticize these results within the public sphere. It produces *bubbles* that act as filters in the selection of information and *echo chambers* that act as filters in their evaluation. It mixes information with misinformation for the benefit of some and to the detriment of many others. It distributes or denies opportunities and rewards, it grants or refuses rights and privileges, in a word, it discriminates based on inferences that it draws from our own preferences, from our repeated behaviors, from what we pay attention to. It even remembers things we want to forget or have canceled. It knows more about us than we know ourselves. It allows some actors to exploit the information or power asymmetries that it has helped to create.

I do not want to delve into the question of the interpretation of Martin Heidegger's conception of technology, but there is something, in that conception, which has always struck me. The German philosopher was well aware of the fact that technology was not reducible to a mere sum of technological tools but constituted a model of knowledge through which to govern reality. Heidegger summarized the ability of technology to manipulate the world and to subject it to its own purposes through the word *Gestell*. Some of his examples are not unlike those of Norbert Wiener and often have to do, as I have already pointed out[2], with the ability to extract energy from the world[3], to accumulate and store it, in order to later attribute it to a purpose other than that for which it was originally given. *Gestellen* indicates precisely this ability to bring order and put together, store and collocate things, in order to eventually find them where they have been stored and collocated. *Stelle* indicates the place, the position. In English, *shelf* has probably the same origin as *Stellen*, placing or storing, in German. For Heidegger, technology produces an order, in that it places and stores things where we can retrieve them: there is a shelf of the world that makes the world itself infinitely available and manipulable.

The shelf of the world has not disappeared and is not empty. And yet, it seems to me sometimes that the impact of digital technologies, in their ever more rapid and incessant pace, obeys a further law, that of *heterotopia*, to borrow a term from Michel Foucault[4], according to which things are not where they appear to be, where we thought we have stored them and we were sure to be able to retrieve them. Floridi himself spoke of a "power to cleave of the digital"[5], by which:

> The digital "cuts and pastes" reality, in the sense that it couples, decouples, recouples features of the world—and therefore our corresponding assumptions about them—which we never thought could be anything but indivisible and unchangeable. It splits apart and fuses the "atoms" of our experience and culture, so to speak. It changes the bed of the river, to use a Wittgensteinian metaphor.[6]

Perhaps this sense of continuous transformation, dislocation and displacement derives from the fact that we are only at the beginning of the digital revolution and of its technological impact on our world. It is the reflection of a stage that is not fully mature in our relationship with current technological processes. Or maybe it is really a constituent character of the digitalization of reality. The impact of digital ICTs is such that it does not leave things as they are: it changes the nature of agents, habits, objects and institutions and therefore it subverts the existing order, without necessarily generating a new one. It opens up new possibilities that, when implemented and exploited, turn into powers and resources which are often not distributed in an egalitarian manner but, on the contrary, are likely to result in concentrations of wealth, in dominant positions or more simply in competitive advantages. It is a struggle, with respect to which the task of reaffirming the fundamental values, the guiding principles, the priorities and the rules of the game, which can transform – or attempt to transform – a fierce confrontation between enemies in a fair competition between opponents rests on us.

Notes

1 *Workshop on the Normative Challenges of Converging Technologies: AI, Big Data, and the Internet of Everything*, which I organized with Ugo Pagallo, as part of the *International Association for Computing and Philosophy* (IACAP Meeting 2017), at the McCoy Family Center for Ethics in Society at Stanford University. Tom Gruber, one of the leading experts on the development of sharing knowledge and collective intelligence systems, is, together with Dag Kittlaus and Adam Cheyer, the creator of Siri, the virtual assistant, purchased and produced by Apple.

2 In this sense, see *supra*, chap. 2. And, more broadly, M. DURANTE, *Il futuro del web, op. cit.*, p. 48 *et seq.*

3 Both Wiener's and Heidegger's reflections on technology imply, more or less explicitly, reference to the idea of *energy*, which is the subject of multiple references and examples. See M. HEIDEGGER, *The Question Concerning Technology, op. cit.*, p. 5: "The revealing that holds sway throughout modern technology does not unfold into a bringing-forth in the sense of *poiesis*. The revealing that rules in modern technology is a challenging, which puts to nature the unreasonable demand to supply *energy* that can be extracted and stored as such" (we underline energy). See N. WIENER, *The Human Use of Human Beings, op. cit.*, p. 30: "I want this book to be understood as a protest against this inhuman use of human

beings, since I am convinced that employing a man by asking and attributing it less than his human condition entails, means to defeat this condition and waste his energies. It is a degradation of the human condition to tie a man to an oar and use it as a *source of energy*" (our italics).

4 M. FOUCAULT, *Of Other Spaces: Utopias and Heterotopias*, in "Diacritics", vol. 16, issue 1, 1986, pp. 22–27. The term heterotopia indicates, for Foucault, those spaces (p. 24) "that have the curious property of being in relation with all the other sites, but in such a way as to suspect, neutralize, or invent the set of relations that they happen to designate, mirror, or reflect".

5 See L. FLORIDI, *Digital's Cleaving Power and Its Consequences*, in "Philosophy & Technology", vol. 30, issue 2, 2017, pp. 123–129. Ugo Pagallo spoke of "technological repositioning" of legal systems. In this sense, see U. PAGALLO, *Il diritto nell'età dell'informazione, op. cit.*, pp. 1–3.

6 L. FLORIDI, *Digital's Cleaving Power, op. cit.*, p. 123.

BIBLIOGRAPHY

Agar N., *Truly Human Enhancement. A Philosophical Defense of Limits*, The MIT Press, Cambridge, Mass. 2013.

Agrawal A., Gans J., Goldfarb A., *Prediction Machines: The Simple Economics of Artificial Intelligence*, Harvard Business Review Press, Boston 2018.

Aldridge I., *High-Frequency Trading: A Practical Guide to Algorithmic Strategies and Trading Systems*, Wiley, Hoboken 2013.

Anders G., *Die Antiquiertheit des Menschen*, Beck, Munich 1956.

Anderson C., The End of Theory: The Data Deluge Makes the Scientific Method Obsolete, in "*Wired Magazine*", 2008, pp. 1–3.

Arendt H., *The Origins of Totalitarianism*, Penguin, London, 2017.

Arendt H., Lying in Politics. Reflections on the 'Pentagon Papers', first published in "*The New Yorker*", November 18, 1971, and reprinted in H. Arendt, *Crises of the Republic: Lying in Politics*, Mariner Books, Orlando, FL 1972.

Arendt H., Truth and Politics, first published in "*The New Yorker*", February 25, 1967, and reprinted with minor changes in H. Arendt, *Between Past and Future*, Viking Press, New York 1968.

Athey S., Beyond Prediction: Using Big Data for Policy Problems, in "*Science*", vol. 355, issue 6324, 2017, pp. 483–485.

Aurucci P., Applications and Security Risks of Artificial Intelligence for Cyber Security in Digital Environment, in "*Journal of Ambient Intelligence and Smart Environments*", vol. 23: Intelligent Environments, 2018, pp. 308–317.

Austin J.-L., *How to Do Things with Words*, Harvard University Press, Cambridge Mass. 1962.

Baier A.-C., "Trust and its vulnerabilities" and "Sustaining trust", in *Tanner Lectures on Human Values*, vol. 13, University of Utah Press, Salt Lake City 1991, pp. 109–174.

Balkin J.M., Free Speech in the Algorithmic Society: Big Data, Private Governance, and New School of Regulation, in "*UCDL Rev.*", 2017, pp. 1149–1210.

Balkin J.M., The Three Laws of Robotics in the Age of Big Data, in "*Ohio State Law Journal*", vol. 78, issue 5, 2017, pp. 1217–1241.

Barabási A-L., *Linked. The New Science of Networks*, Perseus Books, New York 2002.

Barocas S., Hood S., Ziewitz M., Governing Algorithms: A Provocation Piece, 2013, pp. 1–12, accessible online: https://ssrn.com/abstract=2245322.

Barocas S., Selbst A.D., Big Data's Disparate Impact, in *"California Law Review"*, vol. 104, issue 3, 2016, pp. 671–732.

Bartels L.M., Is the "Popular Rule" Possible? Polls, Political Psychology and Democracy, in *"The Brookings Review"*, vol. 21, issue 3, 2003, pp. 12–15.

Bayamlıoğlu S., Baraliuc I., Janssens L., Hildebrandt M. (eds.), *Being Profiled: Cogitas Ergo Sum. 10 Years of Profiling the European Citizen*, Amsterdam University Press, Amsterdam 2018.

Benkler Y., *The Wealth of Networks: How Social Production Transforms Markets and Freedom*, Yale University Press, New Haven 2006.

Benkler Y., Faris R., Roberts H., *Network Propaganda. Manipulation, Disinformation, and Radicalization in American Politics*, Oxford University Press, Oxford 2018.

Bertram T., et al., Three Years of the Right to be Forgotten, 2018, accessible online: https://blog.acolyer.org/2018/03/22/three-years-of-the-right-to-be-forgotten/.

Binns R., Algorithimic Accountability and Public Reason, in M. D'Agostino, M. Durante (eds.), *The Governance of Algorithms*, special issue of *"Philosophy & Technology"*, vol. 31, issue 4, 2018, pp. 543–556.

Bix B.H., *Jurisprudence: Theory and Context*, Sweet & Maxwell, London 2019.

Bobbio N., *Democracy and Dictatorship: The Nature and Limits of State Power*, Polity Press, New York 2017.

Boniolo G., *The Art of Deliberating. Democracy, Deliberation and the Life Sciences between History and Theory*, Studies in Applied Philosophy, Epistemology and Rational Ethics, Springer, Dordrecht 2014.

Borgman C.L., *Big Data, Little Data, No Data*, The MIT Press, Cambridge, Mass. 2015.

Bornstein S., Antidiscriminatory Algorithms, in *"Alabama Law Review"*, vol. 70, issue 2, 2018, pp. 519–572.

Bostrom N., *Superintelligence. Paths, Dangers, Strategies*, Oxford University Press, Oxford 2016.

Bovens M., Goodin R.E., Schillemans T. (eds.), *The Oxford Handbook of Public Accountability*, Oxford University Press, Oxford 2014.

Boy G.A., *The Handbook of Human–Machine Interaction. A Human Centered Approach*, CRC Press, Boca Raton 2017.

Brey P., Values in technology and disclosive computer ethics, in L. Floridi (ed.), *Information and Computer Ethics*, Cambridge University Press, Cambridge 2010, pp. 41–58.

Brin S., Page L., *The Anatomy of a Large-Scale Hypertextual Web Search Engine*, in "Seventh International World-Wide-Web Conference", Brisbane, Australia, April 14–18, 1998, accessible online: http://ilpubs.stanford.edu:8090/361/.

Brown I., Marsden C.T., *Regulating Code: Good Governance and Better Regulation in the Information Age*, The MIT Press, Cambridge, Mass. 2013.

Brownsword R., Technological Management and the Rule of Law, in *"Law Innovation Technology"*, issue 8, 2016, pp. 100–140.

Buechner J., Tavani H., Trust and Multi-agent Systems: Applying the "Diffuse, Default Model" of Trust to Experiments Involving Artificial Agents, in *"Ethics and Information Technology"*, vol. 13, issue 1, 2011, pp. 39–51.

Burrel J., How the Machine "Thinks": Understanding Opacity in Machine Learning Algorithms, in *"Big Data & Society"*, 2016, pp. 1–12, accessible online: https://journals.sagepub.com/doi/10.1177/2053951715622512.

Burridge N., Artificial Intelligence Gets a Seat in the Boardroom, accessible online: https://asia.nikkei.com/Business/Artificial-intelligence-gets-a-seat-in-the-boardroom.

Bygrave L.A., *Internet Governance by Contract*, Oxford University Press, Oxford 2015.

Byrum K., *The European Right to Be Forgotten. The First Amendment Enemy*, Lexington Books, New York 2018.

Carr N., *The Shallows: What the Internet Is Doing to Our Brains*, Norton & Co., New York 2011.

Castelli M., et al., Predicting Per Capita Violent Crimes in Urban Areas: An Artificial Intelligence Approach, in *"Journal of Ambient Intelligence and Humanized Computing"*, vol. 8, issue 1, 2017, pp. 29–36.

Castells M., *Communication Power*, Oxford University Press, Oxford 2009.

Cavoukian A., Privacy by Design: The Definitive Workshop, in *"Identity in Information Society"*, vol. 3, issue 2, 2010, pp. 247–251.

Chen S.H. (ed.), *Big Data in Computational Social Science and Humanities*, Springer, Dordrecht 2018.

Christian B., Griffiths T., *Algorithms to Live By: The Computer Science of Human Decisions*, Henry Holt and Co., New York 2016.

Ciani J., Governing Data Trade in Intelligent Environments: A Taxonomy of Possible Regulatory Regimes between Property and Access Rights, in I. Chatzigiannakis, Y. Tobe, P. Novais, O. Amft (eds.), *Intelligent Environments 2018*, vol. 23, Ambient Intelligent and Smart Environments, IOS Press, Amsterdam 2018, pp. 285–297.

Ciani J., Property Rights Model v. Contractual Approach: How Protecting Non-personal Data in Cyberspace?, in *"Diritto del Commercio Internazionale"*, vol. 4, 2017, pp. 831–854.

Clegg S., *Frameworks of Power*, Sage, London 1989.

Coeckelbergh M., Can We Trust Robots?, in *"Ethics and Information Technology"*, vol. 14, issue 1, 2012, pp. 53–60.

Coeckelbergh M., Virtual Moral Agency, Virtual Moral Responsibility: On the Moral Significance of the Appearance, Perception, and Performance of Artificial Agents, in *"AI & Society"*, vol. 24, issue 2, 2009, pp. 181–189.

Conte R., Falcone R., Sartor G., Introduction: Agents and Norms: How to Fill the Gap?, in *"Artificial Intelligence and Law"*, vol. 7, issue 1, 1999, pp. 1–15.

Corrales M., Fenwick M., Forgó N. (eds.), *New Technology, Big Data and the Law*, Springer, Dordrecht 2018.

Curiat A., Mit, un algoritmo per gli operatori finanziari, accessible online: http://money.wired.it/finan-za/2013/05/08/mit-privacy-trasparenza-5728752.html.

Custers B., Calders T., Schermer B., Zarsky T. (eds.), *Discrimination and Privacy in the Information Society*, Springer, Dordrecht 2013.

D'Agostino M., Durante M., Introduction: The Governance of Algorithms, in M. D'Agostino, M. Durante (eds.), *The Governance of Algorithms*, special issue of *"Philosophy & Technology"*, vol. 31, issue 4, 2018, pp. 499–505.

D'Agostino M., Durante M. (eds.), *The Governance of Algorithms*, special issue of *"Philosophy & Technology"*, vol. 31, issue 4, 2018.

De La Boétie É., *The Politics of Obedience: The Discourse on Voluntary Servitude*, Free Life Editions, New York 1975.

Delacroix S., Veale M., Smart Technologies and Our Sense of Self: Going Beyond Epistemic Counter-Profiling, in M. Hildebrandt, K. O'Hara (eds.), *Law and Life in the Era of Data-Driven Agency*, Edward Elgar, Cheltenham 2019, pp. 80–99.

Diakopoulos N., Accountability in Algorithmic Decision Making, in *Communications of the ACM*, vol. 59, issue 2, 2016, pp. 56–62.

Domingos P., *The Master Algorithm: How the Quest for the Ultimate Learning Machine Will Remake Our World*, Basic Books, New York 2018.

Doshi-Velez F., Kortz M., Accountability of AI Under the Law: The Role of Explanation, *"Berkman Klein Center Working Group on Explanation and the Law, Berkman Klein Center for*

Internet & Society working paper", 2017, accessible online: https://dash.harvard.edu/handle/1/34372584.

Durante M., Dealing with Legal Conflicts in the Information Society. An Informational Understanding of Balancing Competing Rights, in *"Philosophy & Technology"*, vol. 26, issue 4, 2013, pp. 437–457.

Durante M., *Ethics, Law and the Politics of Information. A Guide to the Philosophy of Luciano Floridi*, Springer, Dordrecht 2017.

Durante M., *Il futuro del web. Etica, diritto, decentramento. Dalla sussidiarietà digitale all'economia dell'informazione in rete*, Giappichelli Editore, Torino 2007.

Durante M., *Intelligenza artificiale. Applicazioni giuridiche*, vol. 2, Utet, Torino 2007, pp. 714–724.

Durante M., Rethinking human identity in the age of autonomic computing: The philosophical idea of trace, in M. Hildebrandt, A. Rouvroy (eds.), *Law, Human Agency and Autonomic Computing. The Philosophy of Law meets the Philosophy of Technology*, Routledge, London, New York 2011, pp. 85–103.

Durante M., Safety and security in the digital age. Trust, algorithms, standards, and risks, in D. Berkich, M.V. d'Alfonso (eds.), *On the Cognitive, Ethical, and Scientific Dimension of Artificial Intelligence*, Philosophical Studies Series, Springer, Dordrecht 2019, pp. 371–383.

Durante M., Sicurezza e fiducia nell'età della tecnologia, in *"Filosofia politica"*, vol. 29, issue 3, 2015, pp. 439–458.

Durante M., Technology and the ontology of the virtual, in S. Vallor (ed.), *Oxford Handbook of Philosophy of Technology*, Oxford University Press, Oxford forthcoming.

Durante M., The Democratic Governance of Information Societies. A Critique to the Theory of Stakeholders, in *"Philosophy & Technology"*, vol. 28, issue 1, 2015, pp. 11–32.

Durante M., The Online Construction of Personal Identity through Trust and Privacy, in *"Information"*, vol. 2, issue 4, 2011, pp. 594–620.

Durante M., What is the Model of Trust for Multi-Agent Systems? Whether or not E-trust Applies to Autonomous Agents, in *"Knowledge, Technology & Policy"*, vol. 23, issue 3–4, 2010, pp. 347–366.

Edwards A., Big data, predictive machines and security, in M.R. McGuire, T.J. Holt (eds.), *The Routledge Handbook of Technology, Crime and Justice*, Routledge, London 2017, pp. 451–461.

Ellul J., *The Technological Society*, A. Knopf, New York 1964.

Ellul J., *The Technological System*, Seabury Press 1980.

Eubanks V., *Automating Inequality: How High-Tech Tools Profile, Police, and Punish the Poor*, St. Martin's Press, New York 2018.

Farkas J., Schou J., *Post-Truth, Fake News and Democracy. Mapping the Politics of Falsehood*, Studies in Global Information, Politics and Society, Routledge, London 2019.

Ferguson A.G., *The Rise of Big Data Policing. Surveillance, Race, and the Future of Law Enforcement*, New York University Press, New York 2017.

Feyerabend P., *Conquest of Abundance: A Tale of Abstraction versus the Richness of Being*, University of Chicago Press, Chicago 2001.

Floridi L., A Proxy Culture, in *"Philosophy & Technology"*, vol. 28, issue 4, 2015, pp. 487–490.

Floridi L., Big Data and Their Epistemological Challenge, in *"Philosophy & Technology"*, vol. 25, issue 4, 2012, pp. 435–437.

Floridi L., Digital's Cleaving Power and Its Consequences, in *"Philosophy & Technology"*, vol. 30, issue 2, 2017, pp. 123–129.

Floridi L., Distributed Morality in an Information Society, in *"Science and Engineering Ethics"*, vol. 19, issue 3, 2013, pp. 727–743.

Floridi L., *Information: A Very Short Introduction*, Oxford University Press, Oxford 2010.

Floridi L., Infraethics, in *"The Philosophers' Magazine"*, issue 60, 2013, pp. 26–27.

Floridi L., Is Semantic Information Meaningful Data?, in *"Philosophy and Phenomenological Research"*, vol. 70, issue 2, 2005, pp. 351–370.

Floridi L., Open Data, Data Protection, and Group Privacy, in *"Philosophy & Technology"*, vol. 27, issue 1, 2014, pp. 1–3.

Floridi L., Outline of a Theory of Strongly Semantic Information, in *"Minds and Machines"*, vol. 14, issue 2, 2004, pp. 197–221.

Floridi L., Semantic Capital: Its Nature, Value, and Curation, in *"Philosophy & Technology"*, vol. 31, issue 4, 2018, pp. 481–497.

Floridi L. (ed.), *The Onlife Manifesto: Being Human in a Hyperconnected Era*, Springer, Dordrecht 2015.

Floridi L., *The Fourth Revolution. How the Infosphere is Reshaping the Human Reality*, Oxford University Press, Oxford 2014.

Floridi L., The Logic of Being Informed, in *"Logique et analyse"*, vol. 49, issue 196, 2006, pp. 433–460.

Floridi L., *The Philosophy of Information*, Oxford University Press, Oxford 2011.

Floridi L., What is the Philosophy of Information?, in *"Metaphilosophy"*, vol. 33, issue 1–2, 2002, pp. 123–145.

Floridi L., et al., AI4 People – An Ethical Framework for a Good AI Society: Opportunities, Risks, Principles, and Recommendations, in *"Minds and Machines"*, vol. 28, issue 4, 2018, pp. 689–707.

Foer F., *World Without Mind. The Existential Threat of Big Tech*, Penguin Books, London 2017.

Foster J.-K., *Memory: A Very Short Introduction*, Oxford University Press, Oxford 2008.

Foucault M., *Discipline and Punish: The Birth of the Prison*, Penguin, London 1991.

Foucault M., Of Other Spaces: Utopias and Heterotopias, in *"Diacritics"*, vol. 16, issue 1, 1986, pp. 22–27.

Foucault M., *Power: The Essential Works of Michel Foucault 1954–1986*, Penguin, London 2012.

Foucault M., *The History of Sexuality*, vols. 1–3, Penguin, London 1998.

Fricker M., *Epistemic Injustice: Power and the Ethics of Knowledge*, Oxford University Press, Oxford 2007.

Fukuyama F., *Our Posthuman Future. Consequences of the Biotechnology Revolution*, Farrar, Straus & Giroux, New York 2000.

Furner J., Information Studies Without Information, in *"Library trends"*, vol. 52, issue 3, 2004, pp. 427–446.

Gambetta D., Can we trust trust?, in D. Gambetta (ed.), *Trust: Making and Breaking Cooperative Relation*, Basil Blackwell, Oxford 1990, pp. 213–237.

Gehlen A., *Man: His Nature and Place in the World*, Columbia University Press, New York 1987.

Gillespie T., The relevance of algorithms, in T. Gillespie, P.J. Boczkowski, K.A. Foot (eds.), *Media Technologies: Essays on Communication, Materiality, and Society*, The MIT Press, Cambridge, Mass. 2014, pp. 167–193.

Goethe J.W., *Faust*, Anchor, New York 1990.

Goodman B., Flaxman S., European Union Regulations on Algorithmic Decision-making and a Right to Explanation, in *"AI Magazine"*, vol. 38, issue 3, 2017, pp. 50–57.

Gould C., *Globalizing Democracy and Human Rights*, Cambridge University Press, Cambridge 2004.

Green L., *Silicon States. The Power and the Politics of Big Tech and What It Means for Our Future*, Counterpoint, Berkeley 2019.

Grusky D., Digital Na(t)ives? Variations in Internet Skills and Uses Among Members of the "Net Generations", in *"Sociological Inquiry"*, vol. 80, issue 1, 2010, pp. 92–113.

Grusky D., *Social Stratification*, Westview Press, Boulder, Colorado 2008.

Guardini R., *Letters from Lake Como: Explorations on Technology and the Human Race*, Eerdamans Publishing, Grand Rapids, Michigan 1994.

Gur N., Bjørnskov C., Trust and Delegation: Theory and Evidence, in *"Journal of Comparative Economics"*, vol. 45, issue 3, 2017, pp. 644–657.

Haapio H., et al., Legal Design Patterns for Privacy, in *"Data Protection/LegalTech – Proceedings of the 21th International Legal Informatics Symposium IRIS"*, 2018, pp. 445–450.

Habermas J., *The Future of Human Nature*, Polity Press, New York 2003.

Hacker P., Teaching Fairness to Artificial Intelligence: Existing and Novel Strategies Against Algorithmic Discrimination Under EU Law, in *"Common Market Law Review"*, vol. 55, 2018, pp. 1–35.

Harambam J., Helberger N., van Hoboken J., Democratising Algorithmic News Recommenders: How to Materialize Voice in a Technologically Saturated System, in *"Philosophical Transactions of The Royal Society"*, vol. 376, 2018, pp. 1–21.

Hardin R., *Trust and Trustworthiness*, Russell Sage Foundation, New York 2002.

Hargittai E., *The Digital Reproduction of Inequality*, Routledge, London, New York 2018.

Harris J., *Enhancing Evolution. The Ethical case for Making Better People*, Princeton University Press, Princeton 2007.

Hart H.L.A., *The Concept of Law*, ed. 2, Clarendon Press, Oxford 1994.

Heidegger M., Letter on Humanism, in M. Heidegger, *Basic Writings*, Routledge, London 1993.

Heidegger M., *The Question Concerning Technology*, Harper, New York 1977.

Hildebrandt M., Algorithmic Regulation and the Rule of Law, in S. Olhede, P. Wolfe (eds.), *The Growing Ubiquity of Algorithms in Society: Implications, Impacts and Innovations*, special issue of *"Philosophical Transactions of The Royal Society A: Mathematical Physical and Engineering Sciences"*, vol. 376, 2018, pp. 1–11.

Hildebrandt M., Defining profiling: A new type of knowledge? in M. Hildebrandt, S. Gutwirth (eds.), *Profiling the European Citizen*, Springer, Dordrecht 2008, pp. 17–45.

Hildebrandt M., Law As Computation in the Era of Artificial Legal Intelligence. Speaking Law to the Power of Statistics, 2017, accessible online: https://ssrn.com/abstract=2983045.

Hildebrandt M., Learning as a Machine: Crossovers Between Humans and Machines, in *"Journal of Learning Analytics"*, vol. 4, issue 1, 2017, pp. 6–23.

Hildebrandt M., Legal Protection by Design: Objections and Refutations, in *"Legisprudence"*, vol. 5, 2011, pp. 223–248.

Hildebrandt M., Profiling and the Rule of Law, in *"Identity in Information Society (IDIS)"*, vol. 1, 2008, pp. 1–16, accessible online: https://ssrn.com/abstract=1332076.

Hildebrandt M., The Dawn of a Critical Transparency Right for the Profiling Era, in *"Digital Enlightenment Yearbook"*, 2012, pp. 41–56.

Hirschman A.O., *Exit, Voice, and Loyalty: Responses to Decline in Firms, Organizations, and States*, Harvard University Press, Cambridge, Mass. 1970.

Holmes D.E., *Big Data. A Very Short Introduction*, Oxford University Press, Oxford 2017.

Hornung G., Schnabel C., Data Protection in Germany II: Recent Decisions on Line-Searching of Computers, Automatic Number Plate Recognition and Data Retention, in *"Computer Law & Security Review"*, vol. 25, issue 2, 2009, pp. 115–122.

Johnson C.A., *The Information Diet. A Case for Conscious Consumption*, O'Reilly Media, Boston 2015.

Jonas H., *Philosophical Essays: From Ancient Creed to Technological Man*, University of Chicago Press, Chicago 1974.

Jonas H., *The Imperative of Responsibility; In Search of Ethics for the Technological Age*, University of Chicago Press, Chicago 1979.

Jünger E., *The Worker. Dominion and Form*, Northwestern University Press, Chicago 2017.

Kaminski M.E., The Right to Explanation, Explained, in "*Berkeley Technology Law Journal*", vol. 34, issue 1, 2019, pp. 18–24.

Kamiran F., Žliobaité I., Calders T., Quantifying Explainable Discrimination and Removing Illegal Discrimination in Automated Decision Making, in "*Knowledge & Information Systems*", vol. 35, 2013, pp. 613–644.

Kant I., *Groundwork for the Metaphysics of Morals*, Cambridge University Press, Cambridge 1998.

Kass L., *Life, Liberty and the Defense of Dignity. The Challenge for Bioethics*, Encounter Books, New York 2004.

Keen A., *The Internet Is Not the Answer*, Atlantic Books, London 2015.

Kiss A., Szöke G.L., Evolution or revolution? Steps forward to a new generation of data protection regulation, in S. Gutwirth, R. Leenes, P. de Hert (eds.), *Reforming European Data Protection Law*, Law, Governance and Technology Series, Springer, Dordrecht 2015, pp. 311–331.

Kleinberg J., Ludwig J., Mullainathan S., Sunstein C.R., Discrimination in the Age of Algorithms, "*NBER Working Paper No. w25548*", February 2019, accessible online: https://ssrn.com/abstract=3332296.

Koops B.-J., Leenes R., Privacy Regulation Cannot Be Hardcoded: A Critical Comment on the "Privacy by Design" Provision in Data Protection Law, in "*International Review of Law, Computers & Technology*", vol. 28, 2014, pp. 159–171.

Kroll J.A., et al., Accountable Algorithms, in "*University of Pennsylvania Law Review*", vol. 165, 2017, pp. 633–705, accessible online: https://ssrn.com/abstract=2765268.

Kurzweil R., *The Singularity Is Near. When Humans Transcend Biology*, Viking, New York 2005.

Lanier J., *Ten Arguments for Deleting Your Social Media Accounts Right Now*, Henry Holt & Co., New York 2018.

Lanier J., *Who Owns the Future?*, Simon & Schuster, San José 2014.

Leese M., The New Profiling: Algorithms, Black Boxes, and the Failure of Anti-discriminatory Safeguards in the European Union, in "*Security Dialogue*", vol. 45, issue 5, 2014, pp. 494–511.

Leonelli S., *La ricerca scientifica nell'era dei Big Data*, Meltemi, Milano 2018.

Lessig L., *Code and Other Laws of Cyberspace. Version 2.0*, Basic Books, New York 2006.

Liu H.W., Lin C.F., Chen Y.J., Beyond *State v Loomis*: Artificial Intelligence, Government Algorithmization and Accountability, in "*International Journal of Law and Information Technology*", vol. 27, issue 22, 2019, pp. 122–141.

Luhmann N., Familiarity, confidence, trust: Problems and alternatives, in D. Gambetta (ed.), *Trust: Making and Breaking Cooperative Relation*, Basil Blackwell, Oxford 1990, pp. 94–107.

Luhmann N., *Trust and Power*, ed. 2, Polity Press, New York 2017.

Lynch M., *In Praise of Reason: Why Rationality Matters for Democracy*, The MIT Press, Cambridge, Mass. 2012.

Lynch M., *The Internet of Us. Knowing More and Understanding Less in the Age of Big Data*, Liveright, London, New York 2016.

Lynch M., *True to Life: Why Truth Matters*, The MIT Press, Cambridge, Mass. 2004.

Lynch M., *Truth as One and Many*, Oxford University Press, Oxford 2009.

Lynch M., *Truth in Context: An Essay on Pluralism and Objectivity*, The MIT Press, Cambridge, Mass. 1998.

Malone T.W., *Superminds. The Surprising Power of People and Computers Thinking Together*, Little, Brown and Company, New York 2018.

Mann M., *The Sources of Social Power*, vols. 1–4, Cambridge University Press, Cambridge 1986–2012.

Mannoni S., Stazi G., *Is competition a click away? Sfida al monopolio nell'era digitale*, Editoriale Scientifica, Napoli 2018.

Mantelero A., The Future of Consumer Data Protection in the Eu Rethinking the "Notice and Consent" Paradigm in the New Era Of Predictive Analytics, in *"Computer Law & Security Review"*, vol. 30, issue 6, 2014, pp. 643–660.

Marcus A., *HCI and User-Experience Design: Fast-Forward to the Past, Present, and Future*, Springer, Dordrecht 2015.

Marr B., *Big Data. Using SMART Big Data, Analytics and Metrics to Take Better Decisions and Improve Performance*, John Wiley & Sons, Hoboken 2015.

Mayer-Schönberger V., *Delete. The Virtue of Forgetting in the Digital Age*, Princeton University Press, Princeton 2009.

Mayer-Schönberger V., Cukier K., *Big Data. A Revolution That Will Transform How We Live, Work, and Think*, Houghton Mifflin Harcourt 2013.

Mazur J., Right to Access Information as a Collective-Based Approach to the GDPR's Right to Explanation in European Law, in *"Erasmus Law Review"*, vol. 11, issue 3, 2018, pp. 178–189.

McEwan I., *Machines Like Me*, Penguin Random House, New York 2019.

McIntyre L., *Post-Truth*, The MIT Press, Cambridge, Mass. 2018.

Mckinlay S.T., Evidence, Explanation and Predictive Data Modelling, in *"Philosophy & Technology"*, vol. 30, issue 4, 2017, pp. 461–473.

McKinney J., Earl H., Yoos C.J., Information about Information: A Taxonomy of Views, in *"MIS quarterly"*, vol. 34, issue 2, 2010, pp. 329–344.

McLuhan M., Fiore Q., *The Medium is the Message: An Inventory of Effects*, Penguin Books, London 1967.

McLuhan M., *The Gutemberg Galaxy: The Making of the Typographic Man*, University of Toronto Press, Toronto 1962.

McLuhan M., *Understanding Media: The Extensions of Man*, McGraw Hill, New York 1964.

Mendoza I., Bygrave L.A., The right not to be subject to automated decisions based on profiling, in T. Synodinou, P. Jougleux, C. Markou, T. Prastitou (eds.), *EU Internet Law: Regulation and Enforcement*, Springer, Dordrecht 2017, pp. 77–98.

Miranda R., Chi è Dmitry Kaminskiy, la mente dietro il primo robot consigliere d'amministrazione, accessible online: https://www.formiche.net/2014/05/chi-che-dmitry-kaminskiy-la-mente-dietro-al-primo-robot-consigliere-damministrazione/.

Mittelstadt B.D., From Individual to Group Privacy in Big Data Analytics, in *"Philosophy & Technology"*, vol. 30, issue 4, 2017, pp. 475–494.

Mittelstadt B.D., Allo P., Taddeo M., Wachter S., Floridi L., The Ethics of Algorithms. Mapping the Debate, in *"Big Data & Society"*, vol. 3, issue 2, 2016, pp. 1–21.

Moore M., *Tech Giants and Civic Power*, Centre for the Study of Media, Communication and Power, King's College London, London 2016.

Mueller M., *Will the Internet Fragment? Sovereignty, Globalization and Cyberspace*, Polity Press, New York 2017.

Mumford L., *Technics and Civilization*, University of Chicago Press, Chicago 2010.

Narang R.K., *Inside the Black Box: A Simple Guide to Quantitative and High-Frequency Trading*, Wiley, Hoboken 2013.

Narang R.K., *The Truth About the High-Frequency Trading: What Is It, How Does It Work, and Why Is It a Problem?* Wiley, Hoboken 2014.

Nissenbaum H., Will security enhance trust online, or supplant it?, in R.-M. Kramer, K.-S. Cook (eds.), *Trust and Distrust in Organizations: Dilemmas and Approaches*, Sage, New York 2004, pp. 155–188.

Nissenbaum H., Brunton F., *Obfuscation: A User'S Guide for Privacy and Protest*, The MIT Press, Cambridge, Mass. 2015.

Noble S.U., *Algorithms of Oppression: How Search Engines Reinforce Racism*, NYU Press, New York 2018.

Nunziato D.C., Forget About it? Harmonizing European and American Protections for Privacy, Free Speech, and Due Process, "*GWU Law School Public Law Research Paper No. 2017*", vol. 52, 2017, pp. 1–20.

O'Neill C., *Weapons of Math Destruction. How Big Data Increases Inequality and Threatens Democracy*, Broadway Books, New York 2017.

Ohm P., Broken Promises of Privacy: Responding to the Surprising Failure of Anonymization, in "*UCLA Law Review*", vol. 57, 2010, pp. 1701–1777.

Paccagnella L., Vellar A., *Vivere online. Identità, relazioni, conoscenza*, Il Mulino, Bologna 2016.

Pagallo U., Algo-Rhythms and the Beat of the Legal Drum, in M. D'Agostino, M. Durante (eds.), *The Governance of Algorithms*, special issue of "*Philosophy & Technology*", vol. 31, issue 4, pp. 507–524.

Pagallo U., Good onlife governance: On law, spontaneous orders, and design, in L. Floridi (ed.), *The Onlife Manifesto: Being Human in a Hyperconnected Era*, Springer, Dordrecht 2015, pp. 161–177.

Pagallo U., *Il diritto nell'età dell'informazione: il riposizionamento tecnologico degli ordinamenti giuridici tra complessità sociale, lotta per il potere e tutela dei diritti*, Giappichelli Editore, Torino 2014.

Pagallo U., On the principle of privacy by design and its limits: Technology, ethics and the rule of law, in S. Gutwirth, et al. (eds.), *European Data Protection: In Good Health?*, Springer, Dordrecht 2012, pp. 331–346.

Pagallo U., Profili tecnico-informatici e filosofici, in A. Cadoppi, S. Canestrari, A. Manna, M. Papa (eds.), *Cybercrime*, Utet, Torino 2019, pp. 1–32.

Pagallo U., What robots want: Autonomous machines, codes and new frontiers of legal responsibility, in M. Hildebrandt, J. Gaakeer (eds.), *Human Law and Computer Law: Comparative Perspectives*, Springer, Dordrecht 2013, pp. 47–65.

Pagallo U., Durante M., Human rights and the Right to Be Forgotten, in M. Susi (ed.), *Human Rights, Digital Society and the Law. A Research Companion*, Routledge, London 2019, pp. 197–208.

Pagallo U., Durante M., Legal memories and the right to be forgotten, in L. Floridi (ed.), *Protection of Information and the Right to Privacy. A New Equilibrium?* Springer, Dordrecht 2014, pp. 17–30.

Pagallo U., Durante M., The Pros and Cons of Legal Automation and its Governance, in "*European Journal of Risk Regulation*", vol. 7, issue 2, 2016, pp. 323–334.

Parens E., *Shaping Our Selves. On Technology, Flourishing, and a Habit of Thinking*, Oxford University Press, New York 2014.

Pariser E., *The Filter Bubble: What the Internet Is Hiding From You*, Penguin, London 2012.

Paseri L., Riflessioni su La quarta rivoluzione. Come l'infosfera sta trasformando il mondo in "*Diritto, Mercato, Tecnologia*", 14 marzo 2018, accessible online: https://www.dimt. it/index. php/it/segnalazionieditoriali/16752-riflessioni-sul-la-quarta-rivoluzione-come-l-infosfera-sta-trasformando-il-mondo.

Pasquale F., *The Black Box Society: The Secret Algorithms That Control Money and Information*, Harvard University Press, Cambridge, Mass. 2015.

Pasquale F., Toward a Fourth Law of Robotics: Preserving Attribution, Responsibility, and Explainability in an Algorithmic Society, in "*Ohio State Law Journal*", vol. 78, issue 5, 2017, pp. 1243–1255.

Patterson S., *Dark Pools: The Rise of the Machine Traders and the Rigging of the US Stock market*, Crown Business, New York 2013.

Pearl J., Mackenzie D., *The Book of Why: The New Science of Cause and Effect*, Basic Books, New York 2018.

Pino G., Conflitto e bilanciamento tra diritti fondamentali. Una mappa dei problemi, in "*Etica & Politica*", issue 1, 2006, pp. 1–57.

Pitruzzella G., Pollicino O., Quintarelli S., *Parole e potere: libertà di espressione, hate speech e fake news*, Egea, Milano 2017.

Pizzetti F. (ed.), *Il caso del diritto all'oblio*, Giappichelli Editore, Torino 2013.

Pizzetti F., Il prisma del diritto all'oblio, in F. Pizzetti (ed.), *Il caso del diritto all'oblio*, Giappichelli, Torino 2013, pp. 21–63.

Popitz H., *Phenomena of Power: Authority, Domination, and Violence*, Columbia University Press, New York 2017.

Post R., Data Privacy and Dignitary Privacy: Google Spain, the Right to be Forgotten, and the Construction of the Public Sphere, in "*Duke Law Review*", vol. 67, 2018, pp. 981–1072.

Prince A., Schwarcz D.B., Proxy Discrimination in the Age of Artificial Intelligence and Big Data, in "*Iowa Law Review*", March 2019, accessible online: https://ssrn.com/abstract=3347959.

Quattrocolo S., Intelligenza artificiale e giustizia: nella cornice della Carta Etica Europea. Gli spunti per una urgente discussione tra scienze penali e informatiche, in "*La Legislazione penale*", 18 December 2018, accessible online: http://www.lalegislazionepenale.eu/intelli genza-artificiale-e-giustizia-nella-cornice-della-carta-etica-europea-gli-spunti-per-unurgente-discussione-tra-scienze-penali-e-informatiche-serena-quattrocolo/.

Quattrocolo S., New Questions and Ancient Solutions? Consolidated Regulatory Paradigms vs Risks and Fears of "Predictive" Justice, in "*Criminal Cassation*", vol. 4, issue LIX, 2019, pp. 1748–1765.

Rachovitsa A., Engineering and Lawyering Privacy by Design: Understanding Online Privacy Both as a Technical and an International Human Rights Issue, in "*International Journal of Law and Information Technology*", vol. 24, issue 4, 2016, pp. 374–399.

Radu R., *Negotiating Internet Governance*, Oxford University Press, Oxford 2019.

Rehm G.M., Just Judicial Activism? Privacy and Informational Self-Determination in U.S. and German Constitutional Law, in "*University of West Los Angeles Law Revue*", vol. 32, 2001.

Rifkin J., *The Zero Marginal Cost Society. The Internet of Things, the Collaborative Commons, and the Eclipse of Capitalism*, Griffin, New York 2015.

Riva G., *Fake news. Vivere e sopravviver in un mondo di post-verità*, Il Mulino, Bologna 2018.

Rodotà S., *Il mondo nella rete. Quali i diritti, quali i vincoli*, Laterza, Roma-Bari 2014.

Rodotà S., *Tecnologie e diritti*, Il Mulino, Bologna 1995.

Rojas R., *Neural Networks: A Systematic Introduction*, Springer Science & Business Media, Heidelberg 2013.

Rossi A., Palmirani M., A Visualization Approach for Adaptive Consent in the European Data Protection Framework, in "*2017 Conference for E-Democracy and Open Government (CeDEM)IEEE*", 2017, pp. 159–170.

Rossi P., *Il passato, la memoria, l'oblio. Otto saggi di storia delle idee*, Il Mulino, Bologna 2013.

Rubinstein I., Lee R.D., Schwartz P.M., Data Mining and Internet Profiling: Emerging Regulatory and Technological Approaches, UC Berkeley Public Law Research Paper No. 1116728, in "*University of Chicago Law Review*", vol. 75, 2008, pp. 261–285.

Said A., Torra V. (eds.), *Data Science in Practice*, Springer, Dordrecht 2019.

Sandel M.J., *The Case Against Perfection. Ethics in the Age of Genetic Engineering*, Harvard University Press, Cambridge, Mass. 2007.

Sartor G., Privacy, Reputation, and Trust: Some Implications for Data Protection, in "*Trust Management*" (conference proceedings: The Fourth International Conference on Trust Management, Pisa, 16–19 May 2006) Springer, Berlin, 2006, pp. 354–366.

Savulescu J., ter Meulen R., Kahane G. (eds.), *Enhancing Human Capacities*, Wiley-Blackwell, Hoboken 2011.

Schmitt C., *Dialogues on Power and Spaces*, Polity Press, New York 2015.

Schwartz M.H., Teaching Law by Design: How Learning Theory and Instructional Design Can Inform and Reform Law Teaching, in "*San Diego L. Rev.*", vol. 38, 2001, pp. 347–451.

Searle J., *The Construction of Social Reality*, Free Press, New York 1996.

Sears A., Jacko J.A. (eds.), *Human–Computer Interaction. Fundamentals*, CRC Press, Boca Raton 2009.

Selbst A.D., Powles J., Meaningful Information and the Right to Explanation, in "*International Data Privacy Law*" vol. 7, issue 4, 2017, pp. 233–242.

Serres M., *Times of Crisis. What the Financial Crisis Revealed and How to Reinvest Our Lives and Future*, Bloomsbury, New York 2015.

Shanahan M., *The Technological Singularity*, The MIT Press, Cambridge, Mass. 2015.

Shaw M., et al. (eds.), *Handbook on Electronic Commerce*, Springer Science & Business Media, Heidelberg 2012.

Shirky C., *Cognitive Surplus: Creativity and Generosity in a Connected Age*, Penguin, London 2008.

Shirky C., *Here Comes Everybody: The Power of Organizing Without Organizations*, Penguin, London 2008.

Siegel L., *Against The Machine: Being Human in the Era of the Electronic Mob*, Serpent's Tale Publishing, London 2008.

Sloan R.H., Warner R., Beyond Notice and Choice: Privacy, Norms, and Consent, in "*J. High Tech. L.*", vol. 14, 2014, pp. 370–414.

Striphas T., Algorithmic Culture, in "*European Journal of Cultural Studies*", vol. 18, issue 4–5, 2015, pp. 395–412.

Sunstein C.R., *#Republic: Divided Democracy in the Age of Social Media*, Princeton University Press, Princeton 2017.

Sunstein C.R., *Republic.com*, Princeton University Press, Princeton 2002.

Susi M., The Internet balancing formula, in M. Susi (ed.), *Human Rights, Digital Society and the Law. A Research Companion*, Routledge, London 2019, pp. 178–194.

Taddeo M., Defining Trust and E-trust: From Old Theories to New Problems, in "*International Journal of Technology and Human Interaction*", vol. 5, issue 2, 2009, pp. 23–35.

Taddeo M., Modelling Trust in Artificial Agents. A First Step Toward the Analysis of E-Trust, in "*Minds and Machines*", vol. 20, issue 2, 2010, pp. 243–257.

Taddeo M., Trusting Digital Technologies Correctly, in "*Mind and Machines*", vol. 27, issue 4, 2017, pp. 565–568.

Tagliapietra A., *Filosofia della bugia. Figure della menzogna nella storia del pensiero occidentale*, Mondadori, Milano 2008.

Tapscott D., Williams A., *Wikinomics. How Mass Collaboration Changes Everything*, Portfolio, New York 2006.

Tavani H., Levels of Trust in the Context of Machine Ethics, in *"Philosophy & Technology"*, vol. 28, issue 1, 2015, pp. 75–90.

Taylor L., Floridi L., van der Sloot B. (eds.), *Group Privacy: New Challenges of Data Technologies*, Philosophical Studies, Springer, New York 2017.

Tegmark M., *Life 3.0: Being Human in the Age of Artificial Intelligence*, Alfred Knopf, New York 2017.

Teti A., Intelligenza artificiale: la meta finale, in A. Teti, *PsychoTech – Il punto di non ritorno*, Springer, Milano 2011, pp. 27–59.

Thaler R.H., Sunstein C.R., *Nudge: Improving Decisions about Health, Wealth, and Happiness*, Penguin, London 2009.

Thouvenin F., et al., *Remembering and Forgetting in the Digital Age*, Springer, Dordrecht 2019.

Turilli M., Floridi L., The Ethics of Information Transparency, in *"Ethics and Information Technology"*, vol. 11, issue 2, 2009, pp. 105–112.

Tzanou M., The unexpected consequences of the EU Right to Be Forgotten: Internet search engines as fundamental rights adjudicators, in M. Tzanou (ed.), *Personal Data Protection and Legal Developments in the European Union*, IGI Global, Hershey, PA 2020.

Vayena E., Tasioulas J., The Dynamics of Big Data and Human Rights. The Case of Scientific Research, in *"Philosophical Transactions of the Royal Society A: Mathematical, Physical and Engineering Sciences"*, vol. 374, issue 2083, 2016, pp. 2–14.

Wachter S., Normative Challenges of Identification in the Internet of Things: Privacy, Profiling, Discrimination, and the GDPR, in *"Computer Law & Security Review"*, vol. 34, issue 3, 2018, pp. 436–449.

Wachter S., Mittelstadt B.D., Floridi L., Why a Right to Explanation of Automated Decision-making does not Exist in the General Data Protection Regulation, in *"International Data Privacy Law"*, vol. 7, issue 2, 2017, pp. 76–99.

Wachter S., Mittelstadt B.D., Russel C., Counterfactual Explanations Without Opening the Black Box: Automated Decisions and the GDPR, in *"Harvard Journal of Law & Technology"*, vol. 31, issue 2, 2018, pp. 841–887.

Webb A., *The Big Nine: How the Tech Titans and Their Thinking Machines Could Warp Humanity*, PublicAffairs, New York 2019.

Weber M., *Economy and Society*, vols. 1–2, University of California Press, Oakland 2013.

Weinberger D., *Too Big to Know. Rethinking Knowledge Now That Facts Aren't the Facts, Experts Are Everywhere, and the Smartest Person in the Room is the Room*, Basic Books, New York 2011.

Werro F. (ed.), *The Right To Be Forgotten: A Comparative Study of the Emergent Right's Evolution and Application in Europe, the Americas, and Asia*, Springer, Dordrecht 2020.

Wiener N., *Cybernetics: Or Control and Communication in the Animal and the Machine*, The MIT Press, Cambridge, Mass. 1953.

Wiener N., *The Human Use of Human Beings. Cybernetics and Society*, Houghton Mifflin, Boston 1954.

Woodward J., Scientific Explanation, in *"Stanford Encyclopedia of Philosophy"*, accessible online: https://plato.stanford.edu/entries/scientific-explanation/.

Yeung K., Towards an understanding of regulation by design, in R. Brownsword, K. Yeung (eds.), *Regulating Technologies: Legal Futures, Regulatory Frames and Technological Fixes*, Hart, London 2007, pp. 79–108.

Zarsky T., The Trouble with Algorithmic Decisions: An Analytic Road Map to Examine Efficiency and Fairness in Automated and Opaque Decision Making, in *"Science, Technology & Human Values"*, vol. 41, issue 1, 2016, pp. 118–132.

Zittrain J., Perfect enforcement on tomorrow's Internet, in R. Brownsword, K. Yeung (eds.), *Regulating Technologies: Legal Futures, Regulatory Frames and Technological Fixes*, Hart, London 2007, pp. 125–156.

Žliobaitė I., Measuring Discrimination in Algorithmic Decision Making, in *"Data Mining & Knowledge Discovery"*, vol. 31, 2017, pp. 1060–1089.

Zook M., Barocas S., Boyd D. et al., Ten Simple Rules for Responsible Big Data Research, in *"PLoS Computational Biology"*, vol. 13, issue 3, 2017, pp. 1–10.

Zuboff S., *The Age of Surveillance Capitalism. The Fight for a Human Future at the New Frontier of Power*, PublicAffairs, New York 2019.